LOCAL DEMOCRACY, JOURNALISM AND PUBLIC RELATIONS

This is a critical examination of the impact of sustained large-scale austerity cuts on local government communications in the UK. Budget constraints have left public sector media teams without the resources for robust citizen-facing communications. The "nose for news" has been downgraded and local journalists, once the champions of public interest coverage, are a force much diminished. The book asks, what is lost to local democracy as a result? And what does it mean when no one is holding the country's public spenders to account?

The authors present extensive interviews with communications professionals working across different council authorities. These offer important insights into the challenges currently being faced by communicators within local public services. The book also includes in-depth case studies on the Grenfell Tower disaster, the Rotherham child-grooming scandal and the Sheffield tree-felling controversy. These events all raise serious questions about the scrutiny and accountability of local authorities and the important role the media can and does play.

Local Democracy, Journalism and Public Relations provides new empirical data on, and the real-world views of, working communications teams in local government today. For students and researchers interested in local journalism and public relations, the book illuminates the current relationship between these professions, local democracy and political accountability.

Carmel O'Toole has worked in journalism and public relations for public and private sector organisations, including local government and Channel 4, since 1979. She is a Senior Lecturer in Public Relations at Sheffield Hallam University, UK. Her research interests include local media and crisis communications management.

Adrian Roxan is a journalist and public relations practitioner. He has worked as a journalist and in the field of public relations for more than 40 years in local government, the NHS and central government. He is currently a Senior Lecturer in Public Relations at Sheffield Hallam University, UK. His research interests include the media and its role in politics.

LOCAL DEMOCRACY, JOURNALISM AND PUBLIC RELATIONS

The changing dynamics in local media and public sector communications

Carmel O'Toole and Adrian Roxan

LONDON AND NEW YORK

First published 2019
by Routledge
2 Park Square, Milton Park, Abingdon, Oxon OX14 4RN

and by Routledge
52 Vanderbilt Avenue, New York, NY 10017

Routledge is an imprint of the Taylor & Francis Group, an informa business

© 2019 Carmel O'Toole and Adrian Roxan

The right of Carmel O'Toole and Adrian Roxan to be identified as authors of this work has been asserted by them in accordance with sections 77 and 78 of the Copyright, Designs and Patents Act 1988.

All rights reserved. No part of this book may be reprinted or reproduced or utilised in any form or by any electronic, mechanical, or other means, now known or hereafter invented, including photocopying and recording, or in any information storage or retrieval system, without permission in writing from the publishers.

Trademark notice: Product or corporate names may be trademarks or registered trademarks, and are used only for identification and explanation without intent to infringe.

British Library Cataloguing in Publication Data
A catalogue record for this book is available from the British Library

Library of Congress Cataloging-in-Publication Data
A catalog record has been requested for this book

ISBN: 978-1-138-04462-3 (hbk)
ISBN: 978-1-138-04464-7 (pbk)
ISBN: 978-1-315-17225-5 (ebk)

Typeset in Bembo
by Taylor & Francis Books

CONTENTS

List of figures vii
Preface ix
Acknowledgements xvi

1 Introduction to local government accountability: The role of public relations and the media 1
   Adrian Roxan

2 The history and evolution of local government and local democracy 13
   Adrian Roxan

3 The rise of public relations and the impact of the austerity years 25
   Adrian Roxan

4 Local media decline: A "sector in crisis"? 79
   Carmel O'Toole

5 Views from the foothills 104
   Carmel O'Toole

6 Today's newsroom: Adapting to digital 137
   Carmel O'Toole

| 7 | Case studies: Grenfell, child sexual exploitation and Sheffield tree-felling | 151 |
| 8 | Summary and conclusions
Carmel O'Toole and Adrian Roxan | 183 |

Index 199

FIGURES

5.1	Andrew Norfolk receiving his *Private Eye* Paul Foot Award from Editor Ian Hislop. The award recognised his investigative work on the child grooming scandal	105
5.2	Tim Minogue, Editor, "Rotten Boroughs", *Private Eye*, by Dara Minogue	110
5.3	Eileen Brooks by John Bates Photography	115
5.4a, b	Front pages of the *Whitby Gazette, Scarborough News* and the *Burnley Express* series newspapers are reproduced with kind permission of the publishers, Johnston Press (now JPI Media). Photography by Carmel O'Toole	121
5.5	Andrew Mosley, Editor, the *Rotherham Advertiser*	122
6.1	Ged Fitzgerald, former Chief Executive of Liverpool City Council. Picture courtesy of Liverpool City Council	140
6.2	Former *Sheffield Star* offices for sale in 2017. Photography by Carmel O'Toole	143
7.1	Grenfell Tower community memorial: 24 hearts representing each of the 24 floors of the building. Photography by Mark Gordon	152
7.2	Grenfell Tower, February 2018. Photography by Mark Gordon	153
7.3a, b	Community murals at Grenfell, February 2018. Photography by Mark Gordon	154
7.4	Community child mural at Grenfell, February 2018. Photography by Mark Gordon	155

7.5	"Feared no more", *Rotherham Advertiser* front page story, Friday February 26, 2016, coverage of trial linked to Rotherham's Child sexual exploitation issue, 2016. Reproduced with kind permission of Andrew Mosley, *Rotherham Advertiser* Editor	162
7.6	Rotherham Borough Council offices. Photography by Carmel O'Toole	163
7.7	The Vernon Oak is one of the celebrated trees of Sheffield earmarked for possible felling – protestors have placed a value on each tree marked for felling. Photography by Adrian Roxan	173
7.8	Sheffield Town Hall. Photography by Adrian Roxan	174

PREFACE

Adrian Roxan – where I started...

I started my first job as a journalist in 1978, working for a small, weekly local newspaper – one of three in the area covered by the local council in Haringey, north London. I began as the most junior reporter – fresh out of college – in a newsroom containing an editor, deputy editor, chief reporter, arts correspondent and five other reporters.

The *Hornsey Journal* covered a varied area, including the wealthy suburbs of Highgate and Muswell Hill, through the less salubrious but up-and-coming communities of Finsbury Park and Wood Green.

Our main competitors were the *Tottenham Weekly Herald*, which overlapped our target area in Wood Green – this was latterly joined as a rival by a freebie, the *Haringey Independent*. There was also the long established paid-for paper the *Ham & High*, which overlapped in the western area of our readership. Each reporter on the *Journal* was given a "patch" or area to cover with a brief to find out what was going on and provide a regular flow of localized news relevant to each "patch".

As part of my role, I visited the local police station every week to find out what, if any, newsworthy crime had been committed and soon, once I had shown that I could write a reasonable news story, became interested in covering the local council's role in the wider community of the paper's readership.

This was a febrile and frenetic time for local government, with the main news agenda being dominated by the "winter of discontent" in the last 12 months of the Labour government under Jim Callaghan. Margaret Thatcher's election brought a wealth of local government stories as central government embarked on a cost-cutting exercise for local authorities.

This would eventually lead to the showdown between Haringey Council along with around 20 other councils with central government over the Rates Act – commonly known as ratecapping – in 1984/5, but I left the paper in 1982.

But my time in reporting the local authority saw a plethora of stories come my way in the form of "cuts to services" undertaken by the Council in a not too dissimilar nature to those sought under the austerity period from 2010.

These stories didn't just present themselves. I got them by regularly attending council meetings – both full council meetings and many sub-committees. I spent many hours talking to councillors, council officers, local community groups and assembling a list of contacts willing to share what was going on.

I was not alone in doing this in a newsroom with six reporters, so it is fair to say that Haringey council found it difficult to act without the scrutiny of the local press – through three reasonably resourced local papers – and so was made fully accountable to its electors.

The picture today could not be more different, with shoestring budgets reducing local papers to a shadow of what I experienced in my first role in journalism.

The key is advertising, which paid for these reasonably resourced papers. Now advertising has migrated online and reduced in value so the model of a commercially owned local newspaper is fast receding from reality.

It goes without saying that, as the commercially viable model of local newspapers is fading, so its role as a guardian making sure that elected representatives – such as local councillors – are held to account for their decisions and actions is also a fast disappearing concept.

Carmel O'Toole – where I started…

I started on the *Belper News* in 1979 as a trainee reporter. The newspaper office was based then in the middle of the high street, in the heart of the little Derbyshire town. Local people would walk in with their obituary reports, racing pigeon and rugby match results, summer fayres and fund-raising events. They would also bring their stories about anti-social behaviour, crime, potholes and UFOs.

A central character in their collective and individual comments and concerns would be the local town and parish councils, publicly funded bodies.

People saw their local paper as an honest broker through which they could challenge the elected and their officials about controversial plans, failures to act upon issues of concern and unpopular decisions taken; in short, issues that affected their own lives and their local community. The news coverage and circulation area were crisply defined and as such known and relevant to a local Belper readership. The content was devised to resonate with local people and you did not stray from those defined coverage boundaries because another local paper would be picking up the torch for its own patch, be that Ripley (four miles away) or Heanor, Matlock, Chesterfield, Long Eaton or Derby. Each of those areas had their own distinct and dedicated coverage, with reporters who really knew the issues, people and character of their coverage area. In those days the *Belper News* ran to between 24 and 26 pages each week.

Colleagues and I would take local issues and explore the background, routinely trawling through council committee reports for proposals, recommendations and decisions. We knew when such reports were made publicly available and our right to access them. I would attend numerous local parish council meetings, enduring endless hours of discussions about dog fouling and cemetery maintenance and unruly grass verges for more meaty disputes about planning developments, financial irregularities and elected councillor misconduct. Occasionally councillors would seek to exclude me and other media from meetings to discuss items "in camera". I knew they had to invoke the "Public Bodies Admissions to Meeting Act" in order to legally do so and would insist they did before sending me out. This was an irritant for them but a dance to be done, to make them feel held to account. It was how it was meant to work. My job was to make them feel watched.

In turn, councillors acknowledged me as an adversary to be befriended and at other times kept at arms-length. I would also be lobbied to cover positive council stories. I developed good local contacts who would then volunteer stories and tip-offs and at times alert me to important issues otherwise going under the radar.

As a local reporter, I was accountable to the community I lived and worked within. I trekked out on my Honda 90 to the wilds of Horsley Woodhouse, Kilburn and Coxbench. I walked blocked footpaths with campaigning local ramblers, called on local vicars for stories about fund-raising for the church roof and went "undercover" with local CB radio enthusiasts, improbably called King Pin and Lady Fox at a time when it was all a bit cloak and dagger.

Down the pub on a weekend I'd know if I'd got it wrong and that someone would be more than happy to challenge me about letting them down or to offer some fresh and often unsubstantiated insight. Colleagues and I were a core part of the community and felt a responsibility to do the right thing. If I didn't, contacts would become elusive or wouldn't trust me or talk to me again. There was a self-interest imperative in there as well.

The pay was terrible, mostly still is, and the working hours long, with weekend and night meetings to cover as well as the day-to-day fixtures. But there is no other job like it.

My boss at the *Belper News* was an amply-sized local businessman called Arthur Chapman. He ran carpet and freezer-food shops. Hence my Christmas bonus was either a frozen turkey or discount on Axminster. He knew little about newspapers but was very proud of his proprietorship. To his credit he funded my National Council for the Training of Journalists training.

From *Belper News* to the *Worksop Guardian* (*WG*) for me and into the state versus NUM warfare of the 1984–85 miners' strike. I would drive to work through police roadblocks, there to catch car-loads of flying pickets. It was a time when my responsibility to my local readership was sorely challenged. As an independent and impartial voice, my reporting instincts were constantly pulled in conflicting directions.

In striking mining communities, national media were largely perceived as enemies of the miners, champions of the Government and the hated PM Margaret Thatcher. As a local reporter, I had a greater chance of being trusted. More than ever, the need to be the honest broker on the spot was crucial to my daily working life and trust in local media.

One of my regular tasks at *WG* was to call local constituency MPs and ask about any issues coming through their public surgeries that might make strong news stories. My reporting patch included that of Bolsover MP Dennis Skinner. He was known for his fierce mistrust of media generally. I'd brace myself for making that call. Mostly the conversational preamble would be minutes of his angry recriminations about media conduct, before getting to the meat and bones of constituent issues that might benefit from some local publicity. But that was how it worked, an adversarial love–hate relationship that ensured some balance and held a spotlight up to tough events in people's lives. Very often it was the conduct of public services, the elected councillors and their officials, which was called into question.

30 years on…

Almost 30 years on I returned to Belper in August 2017 and picked up a copy of the *Belper News*. At 110 pages it was a swollen beast of a thing compared to the publication I knew.

Invasion of the Body Snatchers suggested itself. The paper appeared to be the same but really wasn't.

The *Belper News* is now owned by JPI Media (formerly Johnston Press), a media group whose name you will become more familiar with as we progress through this book. It is one of the "Big Four" media owners in the UK.

Sure enough, the front page and up to page five were still Belper news-focused. But beyond that it carried news and features and advertising from places its predecessor would have been apologetic to touch upon. Unheard of towns like Renishaw (25 miles away) and Bolsover (20 miles) are featured alongside news features from Chesterfield (23 miles away) and wider Derbyshire. From a truly local paper it has morphed into something else, something diminished. It is reduced to being an edition of a paper with a much wider geographical remit, the *Derbyshire Times*.

You might consider there to be nothing wrong with that. Time moves on and businesses change. Financial pressures have to take account of more than nostalgia trips about how things used to be. What is not immediately apparent from this modern incarnation, is what is lost. It is a loss being replicated in newsrooms across the UK as a similar picture emerges. Smaller titles, swallowed into larger media groups; journalists' jobs lost and those that remain covering a wider area, doing more and more work for print and online. What is lost is the depth of knowledge, continuity of contact, and crucially that skilled interrogation of the issues important to our very local communities.

I asked the *Belper News* head office, now in Chesterfield, almost 23 miles away, for more information about local reporters and their emphasis on local councils and courts coverage. I received no response.

As a local reporter, I didn't always get it right, but like so many of my fellow local journalists I knew the territory and the role we were meant to play. Local councillors and officials knew we were on their case, knew how it worked and were looking over the shoulder of the decision-makers to spot potential wrongdoing and misconduct. There was an understood order and balance to the relationship.

This book's focus

This book emerged from common ground between the two authors. We both started our careers on local newspapers and ended up in public relations roles, both of us for some years within the public sector and local government in particular.

Public sector communications has always been a political football. You rightly have to justify spending money on citizen communications against frontline services funding. The counter-arguments are well-established, chiefly that as well as providing services to people, you have to communicate with local citizens about those services, take their views and consult with them about changes and developing needs.

Post-2010 and the Conservative/Lib. Dem. Coalition, the rhetoric against communications spending was intensified up by the then Secretary of State for Communities and Local Government Eric Pickles. He talked of "town hall Pravdas" and slated citizen newspapers for posing unfair competition to an already struggling local media.

> Localism needs robust and independent scrutiny by the press and public, and municipal state-produced newspapers suppress that. Town hall Pravdas not only waste taxpayers' money unnecessarily, they undermine free speech.
> *(Holehouse, 2014)*

Hand in hand with his assault on local government communications, were the unprecedented cutbacks to local government spending heralding the start of a prolonged and continuing "austerity" period. Inevitably this led to cuts to council communications budgets as councils sought to protect statutory services such as child protection and education. We look at this in Chapters 1 and 2 on local government.

We decided to explore how council communications leaders responded and what impact that might have on effective citizen information. The results of our research are set out in more detail in Chapter 3 on changing local government communications.

As we developed our research with heads of communications it became clear that we could not do this in isolation from what was happening within local and regional media. By 2010, this sector had already dramatically changed from the model within which we both started our working lives. With print advertising continuing to migrate online and the increasing thirst for and free offering of online content, local journalism jobs were being slashed. Media owners struggled to shut the stable door and establish a new and sustainable financial model. We explore this topic in more detail in Chapter 4, on the decline and change in UK local and regional media.

We also look at the impact of digital and social media on public sector communications and local media in Chapters 5 and 6 and suggest some conclusions to take this debate further forward.

This book came about because there is mounting evidence and concern that the vitally important scrutiny by local media of public services is in terminal decline. The role of local newspapers has been eroded by funding cutbacks, closures, job losses and a redefining of what makes and drives local news – all profit-driven and ruled by the mantra of online content as king. We explore this in Chapter 7, which features Trinity Mirror and the *Sheffield Star*.

What we found makes sobering and depressing reading for anyone who has ever been involved in local media. It raises questions about the public scrutiny of local services and spending and the arguments for the need for public investment in local media to protect local democracy. It also raises concerns about whether the loss of a highly skilled and well-resourced local media makes our country a less safe and transparent place to live. We look at this in our case studies in Chapter 7.

The overriding theme which emerges from this book is the question of local democracy and, in particular, accountability, with the role of both the communicator and the reporter under our scrutiny.

At the time of writing, political truisms are being torn up as the UK prepares to leave the European Union and political leaders across the world seek to reassert sovereignty over global co-operation. Behind these chaotic times is a sense that democracy is struggling to survive as people lose faith in their political leaders and their media, while the emergence of 'fake news' undermines long cherished 'realities'.

If democracy is to continue then some serious debate will be needed as to which models of accountability are relevant in these challenging times and we hope that this book can contribute to an understanding of some of the key questions facing local democracy.

For the purposes of this book we look mostly at local government and print media rather than the wider group of public services such as police, fire, ambulance and health services. There is further scope for research into the impact of the same issues on these public-sector organisations.

We hope to have offered some fresh insight that proves useful as the debate continues. We believe that the key issues can be summarised as:

- UK central government austerity cuts have impacted upon local councils. Funding for services has been dramatically reduced and one specific casualty has been councils' resourcing and capacity for communicating with local citizens.
- If councils are financially limited in their pro-active communications and local media is not training its sights so acutely upon local government business then who is, and what are the consequences? Is a perfect storm or rather perfect vacuum brewing?
- If local media isn't holding that spotlight up to public services, then decision makers are free to proceed without fear of challenge? Proposals, spending and mis-spending will go unnoticed and unchallenged. Local people who fund these services will be at best short changed but at worst defrauded.

This book sets out to explore these issues, examining the players, the commentators and the professional communicators who play their part.

References

Holehouse, Matthew (2014), 'Pickles at war with town hall Pravdas', *Daily Telegraph*, April 17, 2014, http://www.telegraph.co.uk/news/politics/council-spending/10772862/Pickles-at-war-with-town-hall-Pravdas.html (accessedAugust 8, 2017).

ACKNOWLEDGEMENTS

Our thanks go to all those who have given freely of their time, experience and skills to make this work possible. Credit must also go to those already involved in research on both topics and our thanks for the use of their own material, which has proved vital to our writing.

In particular, from Sheffield Hallam University, we would like to thank Dr Kerry McSweeny for her sterling assistance with the research, Dr Kathy Doherty for her kind advice and Professor Dave Waddington for his support.

1

INTRODUCTION TO LOCAL GOVERNMENT ACCOUNTABILITY

The role of public relations and the media

Adrian Roxan

> "We are witnessing the transformation of the structure of government beyond Westminster and Whitehall from a system of local government into a system of local governance, involving complex sets of organisations drawn from the public, private and voluntary sectors." (Stoker, 1996, p. 1)

This picture painted by political scientist Professor Gerry Stoker, while it summarises a moment in time towards the end of the Thatcher years, is just as apt today. It recognized that local democracy is no longer a simple equation of local representation governing local matters on behalf of the local population.

While this book will set out a complicated portrait of the current state of local democracy – and a tortured history of contention between central and local government to explain it – the events of the last 30 years have precipitated a new crisis in the UK's local democratic system.

Politicians and protestors of all parties and persuasions bandy around the importance of local accountability but there is little consensus as to what the concept of "local accountability" means and how it might work.

The starting point for any examination of the wider theme of the role of local government communications, the local media and their role in local democracy is to capture some definitions of local democracy and the accountability these theories contain.

Defining local democracy

Author and social theorist David Beetham defines democracy by saying it is "not confined to the area of government alone, but can be realized wherever there are common rules and policies to be made, and disagreement about these rules to be resolved, whatever the collectivity or association happens to be, from the family outwards". He adds

> What makes collective decision-making at the level of government especially important is that its association (the state) embraces everyone within a given territory, that membership and tax contributions are compulsory, that disagreement about its rules and policies is correspondingly intense, and that the institutions for deciding and enforcing these rules and policies are highly developed.
> (Beetham, 1996, cited in King & Stoker, 1996, p. 29)

Central to the most legitimate – and idealized – models of democracy is the principle that citizens need to be active and educated and that those elected to represent them should hear their voices.

How "active" and "educated" are defined and realized are at the core of any debate as to whether any model of democracy has ever truly succeeded in reaching such ideals. It is often argued that democracies should aim as high as possible in attempting to achieve these principles with the knowledge that these ideals will never be reached. Beetham expands on the practicalities of democracy:

> [P]opular control and political equality are the key democratic principles. They are most fully realized in small groups . . . in larger associations, and especially at the level of a whole society, practical considerations of time and space necessitate that collective decisions be taken by designated agents or representatives acting on behalf of the rest.

He argues

> democracy is realized . . . not as direct popular control over decision-making, but as control over the decision-makers who act in their stead. How effective that control is, and how equally distributed it is between individual citizens, and between different groups of citizens, according to their numbers, are key criteria for how democratic is a system of representative government.
> (Beetham, 1996, cited in King & Stoker, 1996, p. 30)

For such "control" to be exercised, Beetham suggests that authorisation and accountability are the key planks for the achievement of some sort of effective concept of democracy.

"Authorisation" is achieved through universal, equal suffrage and the use of this to hold regular elections to appoint key decision makers. In local government's case, this is achieved through the cycle of election of local councillors.

Such public representatives are then "accountable" to the people for the policies and actions undertaken in office with "the credible threat of being turned out of office in the event of 'failure' or abuse of trust central to the authorisation granted to them." Beetham concludes that,

To be effective, such a threat requires not only that the public have access to independent information about government activities, but also that the electoral process is not tilted to the advantage of the incumbents.

(Beetham, 1996, cited in King & Stoker, 1996, p. 31)

So the threat of being "turned out of office" is only a realistic prospect when those who have elected those representatives have "access to independent information about government activities", which begs certain questions:

- Where should electors seek such "independent" information?
- Who is best placed to provide such information in an impartial manner?
- Should a truly democratic society see provision of such information as a core principle?
- What does "access" truly mean in this context?
- Assuming that electors have access to this information, what constitutes a credible threat of being turned out of office?

Professor Lawrence Pratchett, an expert in business, government and law from Canberra University, contends that any attempt to renew local democracy – as illustrated by the attempts of the Labour administration 1997–2010 – is "symptomatic of wider failings in democratic culture and practice" (Pratchett, 2000, p. 6). He argues that moves to improve local democracy are central to attempts to fix the wider failings in society: 'It is more about renewing democratic understanding within communities, encouraging political awareness and enhancing opportunities for political participation.' He adds that "[t]he problem being addressed.... is not a failing in the formal institutions of democracy but a more deep-rooted failing in the relationship of citizens with the institutions of government" (Pratchett, 2000, p. 6). In essence, he argues that one central defect of the current democratic system is a lack of accountability.

Defining Accountability

"Political accountability begins when individuals are given responsibility for carrying out tasks on behalf of their fellow citizens. The division of civic labour, the delegation of particular roles to individual citizens, creates the demand for political as distinct from personal accountability." (Day & Klein, 1987, p. 6)

Using the Athenian state as a model, Patricia Day, senior research fellow from Bath University and Rudolph Klein, visiting professor at the London School of Economics, describe this early iteration of democracy as rooted in the concept of accountability.

It is a tradition of political thought which sees the defining characteristic of democracy as stemming not merely from the election of those who are given delegate powers to run society's affairs but from their continuing obligation to explain and justify their conduct in public.

(Day & Klein, 1987, pp. 6–7)

They add, pointedly, "From this perspective, it is precisely day-to-day accountability, in which rulers explain and justify their actions directly to the ruled, which distinguishes a democratic society from an elective tyranny" (Day & Klein, 1987, p. 7).

Critics would argue that attempts to apply the Athenian model of democracy to modern day societies would be simplistic in the extreme. Today's complex and multi-layered societies are the consequence of centuries of history and evolution and are on a scale that dwarfs the challenges facing the good burghers of Athens. Chapter three explores this history and progress in an attempt to explain how we have reached the models of democracy we have today.

Notions of equality – of status and expertise – are also central to any critique of modern democracy and so accountability becomes a more challenging mission when, as Beetham alludes to, incumbent representatives have an in-built advantage over those who might challenge them.

Day and Klein argue that accountability must include recognition that it is not just "political" decisions that must be accounted for but the quality of the way any democratic state performs on behalf of those it serves.

So the mechanisms for providing "checks and balances" on those in power must be developed. Essential to these will be the simple task of making sure that public resources are being spent appropriately and the monitors of this are fully independent of those being scrutinized.

The electorate pays its taxes and expects those it elects to use those resources for the purpose and in the interests of those being represented. One natural consequence of a democratic system is not all the electorate vote for those elected. But all citizens would expect a professional approach to the use of funds that would be monitored and accounted for through regular audit and inspection.

But Day and Klein further argue that there are "dimensions of accountability" with an initial distinction drawn between political and managerial accountability.

> Political accountability is about those with delegated authority being answerable for their actions to the people, whether directly in simple societies or indirectly in complex societies. Here the criteria of judgment are, themselves, contestable and reasons, justification, and explanation have to be provided.
>
> *(Day & Klein, 1987, p. 26)*

Importantly they emphasize the context of this accountability being the availability of information:

> The main issue in complex societies is whether the linkages between action and explanation are in place and, in if in place, adequate to the task in hand:

whether the channels of communication are operating and whether the sanctions are sufficient to compel a justification if needed.

(Day & Klein, 1987, p. 27)

They go on to argue that a secondary question is whether there is openness in the process and "the existence and availability of the information needed to assess actions". Day and Klein conclude in their discussion on political accountability that the quality of the information flowing within the system of government is a central priority and "the extent to which public actions are consequently open to scrutiny by individual citizens" (Day & Klein, 1987, p. 29).

It has to be acknowledged that different solutions to these questions would need to be found dependent on the system of government in operation. For example, local government is characterized by the election of representatives – councillors – to oversee the policies and take responsibility for political accountability at the ballot box.

The National Health Service is not run by locally elected representatives and has, in recent years, been put at arm's length by the 2012 Health and Social Care Act. Clinicians have always been principally accountable to their professional bodies for the care they provide, while hospitals, for example, are accountable to a complex structure which allows national politicians to intercede but not take responsibility – or accountability – for the outcomes.

Many schools have also been extracted from the local democratic structures where they have opted to become academies, with regional school commissioners, appointed by central government, seemingly all-powerful in directing the actions of academy trusts.

Indeed as the Conservative Government implemented changes to the school funding formula in 2018, it became increasingly evident that, while central government was responsible for the overall level of funding through this formula, how that funding was spent, on who, by whom, was not clear or accountable to any elected body.

A picture thus emerges of two of the biggest areas of public expenditure – health and education – where direct, or indirect, accountability to elected representatives has largely disappeared into an opaque structure where central government controls the purse strings but there is no obvious accountability for how that money is spent.

Such reforms in both the NHS and education have been justified by the Government under the accountability challenges defined by Day and Klein as "managerial accountability" – that the public is most concerned about the performance of our doctors and teachers.

Instead, initiatives such as free schools – supposedly accountable to parents but in reality often only accountable to those that run them – have led to some schools being removed from the accountability picture completely.

It is evident that no priority has been given in any of these shifts in governance of schools, hospitals and indeed some areas of local government as to who should provide information to whom and how.

As if this increasing complexity was not confusing enough, the drive by central government to introduce a further layer of "elected accountability" through the introduction of city or regional mayors runs the risk of just adding to the public's already stretched understanding as to who they should seek answers from when their local services fail them.

Information – the lifeblood of accountability?

"If many people feel that they have no real opportunity to alter what is done then there is little point in listening to what governors have to say. Participation and communication are thus twin aspects of democratic life." (Hill, 1974, p. 18)

For democracy to be a reality, Dilys Hill, an author on democracy and local government, suggests that the key ingredients that need to be created, nurtured and protected are participation and communication. Jim Chandler, Professor of Local Government and Governance at Sheffield Hallam University, amplifies this with a significant caveat:

> The attitude of British political elites to open government reflects a dilemma between the desirability of allowing citizens to participate in making policy and the problem that the majority of citizens are not seen to be sufficiently competent in the social sciences, or in ethical and moral values, to understand the complexities of governing.
> *(Chandler, 2010, cited in Chapman & Hunt, 2010, p. 103)*

The phrase "knowledge is power" is attributed to Sir Francis Bacon at the end of the 16th century, although some trace it back to Imam Ali in the tenth century. Whatever its origin, the idea that the person who has knowledge also has a degree of power is axiomatic within any society.

In a modern democratic context, this is open to analysis not only as a question of better information being provided to citizens but also as governments of all persuasions seek to gather and store information on their own citizens – dubbed by many as the "surveillance society".

The Freedom of Information Act 2000 marked an important staging post in a long and contentious history in the battle between those in power and those who sought more information – and therefore accountability – from those wielding power.

The era of mass communication – it is now over two hundred years since the arrival of the steam powered printing press – has been punctuated by a continuing tug of war over government information and the rights of citizens to have access to it.

In local government, that struggle for access has been a gradual process and Chapter 3 explores the history of local government's constant battle with central government politicians for hegemony. As social scientists Richard Chapman and Michael Chapman from Sheffield Hallam University commented: "It was not until 1908 that the press were permitted to attend meetings of the full council and it was not until 1960 that they were allowed to attend committee meetings" (Chapman & Hunt, 2010, p. 2).

Such a recent acknowledgement of the need for public scrutiny is put down to a range of factors. The process of opening up government to such scrutiny was addressed incrementally through the reform acts of the nineteenth century but the absence of a fully franchised electorate until 1929, when women were finally granted the vote, did little to encourage openness in government. The established executive saw little reason to share information in any detailed way with their electorates – and it appears a degree of "we know best" continues to prevail in some quarters to this day.

The desire for central government to exert control and the increasing professionalisation of local government administration were contributory factors in promoting a patriarchal approach to sharing information. Central government continues to attack local councils for expenditure on publicity, with Eric Pickles, Local Government minister under the 2010–15 Coalition Government famously looking to crack down on expenditure on "town hall Pravdas" as he called local council news sheets. He said little on central government's expenditure on putting its case to the electorate (Department for Communities and Local Government, 2010).

Meanwhile many local government officers were only too happy to protect information in their possession unless instructed by the politicians to share this with "less knowledgeable" electors. Their argument that electors would not understand the complexities they were dealing with goes to the heart of the question of education and participation in a democracy.

However, not all local government advocates were opposed to sharing information. Former council leader and Conservative MP Robin Squire introduced a bill into Parliament that eventually formed the Local Government (Access to Information) Act 1985, which was designed to end "unnecessary" secrecy in local government. Squire claimed his bill would aim to increase public accountability between elections and so strengthen the relationship between elected representatives and their electorate.

So the picture for local government is, as always, a chequered one, where some councils – and leading figures – show a more enlightened attitude to "open government", while others strive to keep accountability out of any collective vocabulary. The fact that there is such inconsistency in approach from local council to local council is a commentary in itself on levels of commitment within society as a whole towards openness and accountability.

A report published by the Constitution Unit at University College London reflects a worrying picture of the progress of the Freedom of Information (FOI) Act 2000 in local government. Among its findings were these words on accountability:

> FOI has increased accountability at local level but in ways officials and politicians don't always see, either as part of building up a "bigger picture" (e.g. a jigsaw effect) or alongside other mechanisms, especially the local media, consultations, and campaigns by NGOs.
>
> *(Worthy et al., 2011, p. 5)*

This marks a significant recognition that the local media, along with active citizens through organisations such as NGOs, are a crucial "check & balance" in the battle to make councils accountable.

The report also commented on the openness of decision-making: "FOI has not improved the quality of decision-making but a chilling effect can be seen in a few politically sensitive cases." The report ends its executive summary with this warning: "However, spending cuts will have a severe impact on FOI, which is likely to suffer. Increased use of contracting out could also increase problems of information sharing with private organisations working on behalf of local authorities" (Worthy et al., 2011, p. 7).

It is the last comment about "information sharing with private organisations working on behalf of local authorities" which betrays the increasingly complicated nub of the issue.

Until the introduction of the widespread use of private sector companies in the delivery of local services, the battle to increase accountability could be captured in a straightforward contest between those elected to represent and their constituents. With the arrival of the Private Finance Initiative (PFI) and the obligation put upon local authorities to put many services out to competitive tender, the muddied waters of this fundamental question of accountability became even murkier.

The UCL report raised concerns that private companies are likely to cite "commercial confidentiality" as a reason to withhold information and, in one case, a threat to sue if information is released. Jim Chandler (2010), while examining the impact of the FOI Act on participation in local politics, summed up the situation as follows:

> The government cuts across the capacity to secure more accessible local government by, in the name of efficiency, constructing ever larger local authorities led by increasingly smaller local elites of cabinet bound councillors, reducing local financial autonomy, setting targets that the authorities must achieve, and dividing responsibility for specific areas of social improvement into a numerous arms length partnerships.
> *(Chandler, 2010, cited in Chapman & Hunt, 2010, p. 118)*

It would be easy to conclude that the "political accountability" defined by Day and Klein has now transformed to the sole responsibility for local government being one of "managerial accountability", with the politicians and officers judged by their professional competence to deliver against centrally set policies. Chandler adds that "Individual citizens may have greater powers to find out how these issues are affecting them as individuals but are increasingly remote from any capacity to participate with others in determining what decisions are made for them" (Chandler, 2010, cited in Chapman & Hunt, 2010, p. 118).

Local democracy and accountability – the role of the local media

Any consideration of democracy needs to acknowledge the many varied models and the role that, as the UCL report acknowledges, the media plays, or it is assumed it should play. Deliberative, liberal and direct are the three most often cited models, but as Richard Perloff, author and Professor of Communication at Cleveland State University observes: "Theorists of all three approaches would agree that you cannot have a vibrant democracy without thriving communication." He goes on to cite James Madison as saying that "a democracy that fails to provide critical information to its citizens . . . 'is but a prologue to a farce, or a tragedy; or, perhaps both'" (Perloff, 2018, p. 45).

John Street, Professor of Politics at the University of East Anglia, identifies that the media's role may vary – in a liberal democracy it is the ideal of a free, but responsible press while direct democracies seek a more regulated press with popular control and deliberative democracies require regulated pluralism.

The United Kingdom adheres, like most Western countries, to the liberal model where a key characteristic is the rights and freedoms of the individual. Street goes on to suggest that the media has a range of functions in such a model: "First to enable citizens to choose between those who wish to stand for office and to judge those who currently are in office" (Street, 2011, p. 306). This would seem to present a key role for the media in providing an element of the function of accountability both when electors come to choose who represents them and also in maintaining scrutiny on them while in office.

Street also stresses that the media's function is "to provide a platform for interest groups to publicize their concerns and claims". He summarises these two key functions as "informing citizens about their (prospective) representatives' plans and achievements; it also means reflecting the range of ideas and views that circulate within society, subjecting those who act in the name of the people to scrutiny, to make them accountable" (Street, 2011, p. 306).

> "The core purpose of journalism is and should be about producing and distributing serious information and debate on central social, political and cultural matters. Journalists regulate much of what the public gets to know about the world they inhabit, and this activity is vital to a functioning democracy." (Gripsrud, 2000 cited by Gavin, 2007, p. 3)

Martin Conboy (Professor of Journalism History at Sheffield University) also cites Jostein Gripsrud (Professor of Media at Bergen University), who refers to journalism's role in reporting central government in the UK, but this description applies just as pertinently to that of local democracy and the role of the local media. Conboy goes on to cite Tom Baistow, journalist and lecturer at City University, London:

> [W]ith its unlimited capacity for comprehensive investigation of a situation and the detailed unravelling of complex issues beyond the scope of the oral bulletin, its unrivalled quality as a forum in which ideas can be exchanged and

pros and cons set out and argued – [the newspaper] must be the most important safeguard of the democratic process.

(Baistow, 1985 cited by Conboy, 2011, p. 179)

This view predates the arrival of the Internet but its description of the ability of the media to provide both information and debate in a digestible format bears some scrutiny today.

Denis McQuail, Emeritus Professor of Communication at University of Amsterdam, set out what society expects from journalism, arguing that "freedom of the press" lays no formal obligations beyond "doing no harm and obey[ing] the law". He added that "the news media generally resent and resist attempts to prescribe any role for them in society, except as self-chosen" (McQuail, 2013, p. 20).

However, McQuail acknowledged that there are many unwritten "and ultimately unenforceable" obligations to society, alongside external pressures. He accepted that the "strongest and clearest" of these pressures is the presumed role of the media in a democracy, "as a carrier of news and former of opinion and as a communicative link between citizen and government". He went on to say that "The relationship of journalism to politics is a central feature of the case, since the claim to press freedom rests in part on the needs of democratic institutions" (McQuail, 2013, p. 20). In other words, for freedom of the press to be maintained, democracies need to be effective in their operation.

The challenge to this supposition is the thorny question of media ownership, where accusations of self-interest and collusion between owners of the media and politicians have damaged the image of journalism as a 'free press'. It is not trite simply to examine the names that newspapers use – *Guardian, Herald, Messenger, Telegraph, Courier, Bugle, Clarion* – that speak directly to an assumed role as communicators of news and therefore that communicative link between citizen and government. Further, the media plays a role in reflecting public opinion. Justin Lewis and Karin Wahl-Jorgensen, both Professors of Journalism at Cardiff University, debate the formation and definitions of public opinion but acknowledge the important role of the media:

> Ever since their emergence, newspapers have been important social institutions precisely because they have provided a forum for citizens (albeit sometimes a fairly limited group of people) to discuss the issues that concerned them and thereby articulate a public (rather than individual) opinion and hold government accountable for its actions.
>
> *(Lewis & Wahl-Jorgenson, 2005, cited in Allen, 2005, p. 99)*

Whether the media then reflects a true picture of "public opinion" is open to considerable debate, with many, including Lewis and Wahl-Jorgensen, arguing that the news agenda is not driven by public opinion – whatever that may be construed to be – but "by politicians and other elites" (ibid.). Indeed, their own research suggests that many journalists assume "public opinion" without backing up such assumptions with any factual evidence or research.

Summary

There can be no doubt that the relationship between the media and democracy is a complicated and at times contradictory one. Many assume the media has an implicit role in informing and educating citizens in a democracy, but this is not a monologue. John Street identifies the role of the media in providing a platform for active citizenship to be heard and this he argues plays an important role in democracy.

At the core of all these varying views on how government and citizens interact is the need both for platforms for information and the information itself. The mechanisms for democracy – an effective model of representation, proper political accountability, the media as a channel for dialogue – must also be supported by a level of understanding as to how to ensure democracy is real rather than artificial. As leading PR academics such as Jacquie L'Etang have said, at a time of change, PR is needed more than ever.

Since this book examines a period of economic austerity since 2010, the question that has to be asked is whether, as the Government's programme of public service cuts in budgets for local councils has seen the scaling back or disappearance of public services, it has also seen a scaling back or disappearance of many aspects of any genuine democracy at a local level. Pratchett argues that moves to improve local democracy are central to attempts to fix the wider failings in society. By the same token, if local democracy were being damaged or even destroyed, it would not be unreasonable to question whether this is adding to the wider failings in society.

References

Allan, Stuart (2005). *Journalism, Critical Issues*. Berkshire, OUP.
Baistow, Tom (1985). *Fourth Rate Estate*, London, Comedia.
Beetham, David (1996). *Theorising Democracy and Local Government*. Basingstoke, Palgrave Macmillan.
Chandler, Jim (2010). *A Rationale for Local Government*. Abingdon, Taylor Francis.
Chapman, Richard & Hunt, Michael (2010). *Freedom of Information – Local Government and Accountability*. Farnham, Ashgate.
Conboy, Martin (2011). *Journalism in Britain – a historical introduction*. London, Sage.
Day, Patricia & Klein, Rudolf (1987). *Accountabilities: Five Public Services*. Abingdon, Routledge.
Department for Communities and Local Government (2010) https://www.gov.uk/governm ent/news/eric-pickles-to-stop-propaganda-on-the-rates-killing-off-local-newspapers (June 28) (accessed 1 February 2019).
Gavin, Neil T. (2007). *Press & Television in British Politics*. Basingstoke, Palgrave Macmillan.
Gripsrud, Jostein (2000). *Tabloid Tales – Global Debates over Media Standards*, Maryland, Rowman & Littlefield.
Hill, Dilys M. (1974). *Democratic Theory and Local Government*. London, Allen & Unwin.
King, Desmond & Stoker, Gerry (1996). *Rethinking Local Democracy*. Basingstoke, Palgrave Macmillan.
Lewis, Justin & Wahl-Jorgensen, Karin (2005). *Journalism & Critical Issues*. Maidenhead, OUP.
Mcquail, Denis (2013). *Journalism & Society*. London, Sage.

Perloff, Richard (2018). *The Dynamics of Political Communication*, 2nd edition. New York and Abingdon, Routledge.
Pratchett, Laurence (2000). *Renewing Local Democracy*. London, Frank Cass.
Stoker, Gerry (1996). *Local Government in the 1990s*. Basingstoke, Palgrave Macmillan.
Street, John (2011). *Mass Media, Politics & Democracy*. Basingstoke, Palgrave Macmillan.
Worthy, Ben, Amos, Jim, Hazell, Robert & Bourke, Gabrielle (2011). *Town Hall Transparency? The Impact of the Freedom of Information Act 2000 on Local Government in England*. London: The Constitution Unit, Department of Political Science, University College, London.

2

THE HISTORY AND EVOLUTION OF LOCAL GOVERNMENT AND LOCAL DEMOCRACY

Adrian Roxan

> **The origins of "modern" local government**
>
> "Not so long ago it was common for political commentators formally to acknowledge the existence of local government as vital evidence of the health of British democracy, before moving on (with a sigh of relief) to discuss more important matters, like the latest Cabinet reshuffle, the level of inflation, the state of the pound or public sector borrowing requirement. Matters are no longer quite so straightforward. Since the mid 1970s conflict over local government spending and services has filled the front pages of national newspapers." (Cochrane, 1993, p. 1)

Allan Cochrane, Emeritus Professor on Urban Policy at the Open University, points towards a difficult period for local government and provides an important commentary on the health – or otherwise – of modern local government. How did local government get to this point? What can the history and origins of the models of local democracy tell us about why such a battleground has developed? What questions can be asked about the accountability of our democracy – both at a local and national level?

Ron Fenney, author of *Essential Local Government* and a leading local government lawyer, traces the origins of modern local government to the period of the industrial revolution and suggests modern local government began in 1835 when municipal corporations were established (Fenney, 1996, p. 1).

The reality is that the labyrinth structures of modern local government are very much like the analogy of the onion with one exception. That analogy implies that peeling back the layers of the onion is the only way to establish the true core of the topic in question.

For local government, the onion has been constructed in reverse, with the core functions being covered over the last 180 years by layer after layer of complexity. This can be traced back to the Magna Carta, which celebrated its 800th anniversary in 2015. It was the starting point for the "onion" of local government that confronts us today. Its most famous clause gave free men the right to justice and a fair trial and so ensured that some form of local government was essential if this was to exist in a practical form.

The subsequent 800 years has seen the evolution of a system of local government which now presents us with a complex, intertwined set of authorities, laws and rights which cannot be summed up in a simple sentence. Or even in a paragraph – to understand what forms of local democracy and accountability exist, it is essential to appreciate and understand the competing voices and interests which have shaped and reformed the models of local government over the last 200 years.

The bare facts of the establishment of local authorities can be listed as follows:

- 1835 – municipal corporations established
- 1855 – the Metropolitan Boards of Works (forerunner to London County Council) created – this covered services such as sewers, drainage, lighting, paving, with the subsequent addition of the Metropolitan Fire Brigade.
- 1888 – County councils and county borough councils set up
- 1889 – London County Council (LCC) succeeded Metropolitan Board of Works
- 1894 – parish, urban and district councils established – these assumed the responsibilities of old urban authorities.

At this point, a model of local government, relevant to each locality was formed. How those who controlled them were elected and how accountable they were to those that elected them is a separate question but a seemingly coherent picture existed. The following 100 years of history is characterised by reorganisations and reviews inspired either by demographic changes – such as the rapidly expanding urban areas, particularly Greater London – or the changing functions and services being provided by local authorities.

It is no coincidence that the increasing need for local government can be traced to the period commonly known as the Industrial Revolution. John Kingdom, visiting fellow at Sheffield Hallam University and author of *Local Government Politics in Britain* marks this period as a key catalyst for the changes in local government that still have some resonance today. "It produced a new class of people (capitalists of bourgeoisie) made incredibly powerful by the fact that they personally owned the materials (factories and machines) which the rest of the community needed for its very survival" (Kingdom, 1991, p. 24).

He suggests that this new class were the drivers of a new state architecture. As new urban environments were created to supply a workforce for the burgeoning number of factories, so new state machinery was required to support these emerging communities.

A parallel can be drawn with the early philanthropists such as the Rowntree family and their support for the communities close to their factories through the provision of housing, schools and health services. Kingdom continues:

> Local government was directly affected through the process of urbanisation, which was central to the power of the bourgeoisie. As the new factories grew up to produce goods, so great new cities emerged to house and reproduce the labour force demanded by their gargantuan appetites.
>
> *(Kingdom, 1991, p. 24)*

In the early 1800s only one-fifth of the UK population lived in towns but 100 years later this had increased to four-fifths.

With this dramatic change came an increasing list of social demands that needed local government. New housing, health services, better transport, policing, health & safety at work, pollution and poverty all increased in priority on an agenda driven by the desire of the new industrialists to support their growing business empires.

Slums became commonplace in the big cities as basic housing was erected at breakneck speed to house the new class of workers. With poor housing conditions came disease, as inadequate drainage and sanitation accelerated the spread of deadly strains of cholera, tuberculosis and scarlet fever.

Transport became vital for both workers and business leaders looking to move raw materials and products as quickly and efficiently as possible. The world captured so vividly by authors such as Charles Dickens was one where vice and crime were commonplace, requiring an effective police force to prevent the development of social anarchy. Meanwhile the factories themselves became the focus for the health and safety of workers, the pollution being generated on a genuinely industrial scale, and low wages.

All of these issues have become regular agenda items for government in a modern society and so, driven, as much by the needs of the factory owners as the moral obligations of the problems their factories had created, a new form of local government was required.

As towns and cities had previously been defined by the monuments of religion through their identification with their local church or cathedral, so in this new industrial age the factories became the defining focus of the new hubs of local government.

At the same time, the workers were also getting organised. The Charter movement based around the People's Charter published in May 1838 was based around six key aims: manhood suffrage, the ballot, abolition of property qualifications for MPs, payment of MPs, equal electoral districts and annual elections.

So the challenge for the state, with such competing but in many ways converging demands, was a new form of municipal structure to reflect the new landscape being frantically created.

The early "piecemeal" models

In reality, the response was inadequate as the traditionalists resisting the "power grab" being inspired by the new industrial age clung to the existing mélange of government. And so began the creation of structures to address these many issues which in many respects, are still recognizable in the system of local government in place today.

Despite the lobbying of some reformers, there was no great master plan or strategic map but the establishment, on a piecemeal basis, of local boards and ad hoc bodies to address each of the issues as they reached crisis point. Bodies to oversee schools, hospitals, roads, prisons and slaughterhouses were put in place as the rapid urban expansions gathered pace. Pressures to address the wider societal issues such as public health were pursued on a more strategic level by those inspired by reformers such as Jeremy Bentham and the Philosophical Radicals.

Bentham believed that the greatest happiness of the greatest number is the only right and proper end of government and he is credited as an inspiration for a group called the Philosophical Radicals led by, among others, James Mill and John Stuart Mill (Kingdom, 1991, p. 15). Their theories of utilitarianism and the need for an ethical approach to government were influential in shaping thinking in this period as models of local government continued to evolve.

First shoots of accountability models emerge

As this new machinery of local government emerged, the first indicators can be seen of the need for such bodies to be accountable. Two pieces of legislation – the Poor Law Reform Act 1834 and the Municipal Corporations Act 1835 – highlight the dilemmas facing those attempting to shape local government.

The Poor Law Reform Act was a centralist reform designed to amalgamate existing parish councils into larger units controlled by central government. The Municipal Corporations Act, a year later, tackled the state of borough authorities and, with the exception of the City of London, which was exempted, attempted to install a locally led model of government based around financial probity and representative government (Kingdom, 1991).

These competing "movements" of centralism and localism came to a head more than 50 years later in the Local Government Act 1888. With Britain's fledgling democracy edging slowly towards full enfranchisement (which only came a further 50 years later with the vote being granted to women), the forces of reform – still driven by the new capitalists of the industrial age – sought a model to reflect the new priorities.

The outcome was, in typical democratic fashion, a fudge, but one that was created by the competing factions at play. The 1988 Act created the two-tier system that students of local government might recognise today. The blueprint set out a new set of counties divided into districts to allow for the new urban areas. The municipal corporations inevitably resisted and so boroughs with populations of more than 50,000 were exempted from being part of the new counties.

As a mirror image of the reality of the time, it made perfect sense to allow the existing, more rural units of government to continue but also to permit a new structure of urban boroughs to thrive to meet the demands of the urban age. The question of accountability of this new blueprint of local government was not fully addressed at the time. Instead, the control of these new "local councils" was often a power battle between the leading figures of local society. For many, the priority was that the local government matched the ambitions and priorities of the local factories and therefore those factory owners should naturally take the municipal leadership. For the more traditional parts of the country less affected by urban industrialisation, the old principle of those with land and property being in power remained the norm.

Indeed, it can be argued that the fate of poor people's lives was dictated with the emergence of these forms of local government with the simple question – does the landowner or the factory owner control your life?

The early accountability champions

Advocates such as Bentham and the Radical Philosophers were not alone in wanting to instil some structure and purpose into what remains the orthodoxy against which more recent reforms are judged today, but their thoughts continued to be influential.

John Stuart Mill argued in 1861 that local government needed to be established on two significant principles: that local government was an essential part of democracy and that localised government was essential (Kingdom, 1991, p. 232).

His arguments for the first principle were that local government allowed more people to participate and so spread the ideals of democracy through education and inspiration. His arguments for the second principle were simple – local delivery of government was more efficient because local knowledge and interest made it so.

To Mill's principles can be added a third strand which, while more a matter for debate, has come to dominate the ensuing decades right up to the modern day. The battle between the centralisers and localisers is evident throughout the period of modern local government. Those advocates see localism as an antidote or opposition to those who would see all government centralised in the hands of a core elite who claimed to know best.

This is summed up by Gerry Stoker when examining the evolution of the models of local government in this period:

> The vision of local government they offered was of a relatively autonomous, multi-purpose institution providing a range of services, with a tax-raising capacity and controlled through the election of representatives to oversee the work of full time officials.
>
> *(King & Stoker, 1996, pp. 6–7)*

Post-Second World War – the picture begins to emerge of today's local government?

The picture of local government recognisable today was further reformed in a number of reviews and initiatives undertaken after the Second World War. The post-war period saw a renewed manifesto for central government to rebuild – literally in many cases – parts of the country. The NHS was created, as was the welfare state following the 1942 Beveridge Report.

> "In retrospect it is tempting to view the years between 1945 and 1975 as a 'golden age' for British local government, before the advent of Thatcherism and all its works. It was time when spending appeared to rise almost inexorably and responsibilities were added incrementally in a way which seemed to make local government an increasingly important pillar of the British political system." (Cochrane, 1993, p. 7)

Allan Cochrane goes on to cite John Gyford (1985), an author writing on Labour politics, commenting on the performance of post-war local government: "Usually it did the right things for people; but sometimes it could do the wrong things to people; and only rarely had it previously discussed either of those things with people" (Cochrane 1993, p. 8).

This sense of unaccountable paternalism was a constant accusation levelled at local authorities and remains a feature of criticisms today. But it was also a period where local government in its widest sense saw many of its powers removed. Prior to the establishment of the NHS, health had been a local government responsibility.

For example, before the establishment of the National Health Service in 1948, local authorities such as the London County Council (LCC) were given responsibility for running local health services. In the LCC's case it managed 70 hospitals across the capital from 1929 to 1948, setting up what, at the time, was the largest combined health service in the world.

Around the same time, local authority powers to provide electricity (1947) and gas (1948) were removed and replaced by centrally governed authorities. This added to a list of responsibilities removed before the Second World War that included poor relief (1934), trunk roads (1936) and the management of supplementary benefits (1940). So the range of responsibilities which had been built up over the previous 100 years based around the requirements and aspirations of factory owners and landowners was being recast in the continuing battle between centralism and localism – with those at the centre seemingly winning the argument.

The focus of local government shifted from a significant emphasis on welfare to one where the main element of a local council's budget was spent on education and housing. By the 1950s, these two areas accounted for nearly two thirds of local government expenditure.

The expansion in housing activity can be directly related to the drive to build – and rebuild – following the devastating bombing in some areas during the war. The boom in education was cemented by the 1944 Education Act which stipulated that most children should attend a local authority school until the age of 15.

Overall, local authority expenditure began to rise as a fraction of overall Government spending with an increase "from 6.5% of GDP in 1955 to 8.8% in 1963" (McConnell, 1999, p. 24).

With these changes to the emphasis of local government came another important adjustment. Local councils fast became the most common "face-to-face" manifestation of government in people's lives. With this shift in perception came an increasing need for councils to improve their communications, although much of this need was not evident until the political upheavals that arrived in the 1980s.

> Councils increasingly had responsibility for the management of those aspects of the welfare state which required face-to-face "professional style" involvement with people variously defined as clients, parents or tenants even if the claims to professional status of many of the new professionals remained uncertain. . . . Local Government was to be the home of "street level bureaucrats" (Lipsky, 1979).
>
> *(Cochrane, 1993, pp. 14–15)*

Post-war local government reforms

Unsurprisingly, given the continuing expansion of the capital, London was the subject of a significant review in 1957, when a Royal Commission expanded the geographical reach of the London authority into surrounding counties including Middlesex, Essex, Surrey and Kent. By 1965 the Greater London Council had been formed – forerunner of the Greater London Authority today – with 32 London boroughs also established. Professor Tony Travers, local government expert from the London School of Economics, identifies one anomaly that remains in place today, with the recognition of the City of London Corporation as a separate body with a democratic source – a body that can trace its roots back to medieval times (Travers, 2015, p. 38).

In 1966, the Labour government of the day set up a review of local government outside London. It ushered in a period of review and counter-review as successive governments – Labour and Conservative – put their own imprint on how local government should be organised and structured.

At the core of these reviews was a constant battle as to which functions should be carried out by which authorities and who should be held responsible should any services be not up to standard – with accountability for quality becoming the increasingly dominant focus. Roads are a good example of this constant debate, with clarity as to whether central government or some iteration of local government was responsible for their upkeep being a typical issue of contention.

The picture was confusing to the public wherever they looked. London was its only special case, with disputes between the London-wide authority and London boroughs still evident today. Outside the capital, the parish, district and county responsibilities were just as complex, with each reorganisation or review putting a fresh layer of governance into the mix. In truth, the "onion" of local government was now a multi layered and impenetrable object.

The Thatcher years – the arrival of a third party and a key moment for local accountability

"Until the middle of the 1970s, local government in Britain was a political backwater. Local politics seemed to arouse little electoral interest. There was little open conflict between central and local government and the great debates about local government reorganisation failed to strike much of a chord outside the narrow confines of the academic and local government policy communities, except when they threatened the continued existence of traditional county names (such as Rutland and Yorkshire)."(Cochrane, 1993, p. 28)

But the reality of local government today cannot be explained without an examination of a seismic period of change that was sparked by the arrival of Margaret Thatcher's government in 1979. With her election came the wholesale shift towards the introduction of a third party or player into the central and local government equation, which led to another confusing facet for the accountability of local government.

It came under the auspices of the desire of the Conservative government to introduce the rigour and efficiency of the private sector into the delivery of public services.

It was also part of the increasing grip that the philosophy of neoliberalism was gaining on central government.

Neoliberalism put the role of the state into a new light. No longer was the state seen as a safety net – best characterised by the Welfare State established by the Beveridge Report in 1942. Instead the risks being taken were projected onto the individual and with this shift came the principle that citizens were freshly labelled as consumers.

The introduction of the poll tax can be seen as symptomatic of the continuing drive by the Conservative Party to bring local government to heel and into the control of central government. Conservative think tank and policy driver, the Adam Smith Institute, heralded the poll tax as a way of making councils more accountable to voters, forcing councillors to reduce expenditure in the pursuit of value for money (Adam Smith Institute, 1989).

However, these new consumers of local services were not going to be allowed to dictate how these should be delivered. As always, the key battleground in local government over the last 40 years has been how it is financed and who holds the purse strings.

The policy of austerity – introduced by the Coalition Government on its election in 2010 – was a natural progression from the policies of Thatcher and Major when the Conservatives had last held power from 1979–1997. The poll tax may be identified as the catalyst for the end of Thatcher's period in power but behind its botched inception was a desire to break the state's monopoly on the delivery of local services by creating a more direct relationship between its funding and delivery.

Two's company, three's a crowd?

The vehicle used to achieve this was the introduction of a third party into government. No longer was it a question of a wrestling match between central and local government – which central government always tended to win. Now the increasing role of the private sector became the emphasis with – initially – the door opened by the intended transformation of local councils from being deliverers of local services to a role more akin to an enabler or commissioner.

Phrases such as compulsory competitive tendering (CCT) and purchaser–provider split became commonplace. The suggested benefits of efficiency and effectiveness brought by the private sector were lauded as a challenge to the laxness and complacency of an alleged bloated public sector. While the idea of the private sector being involved in local services was not entirely new, the imposition of a requirement to put council services out to tender was:

> The government believed that where services are provided by a local authority directly, then wherever possible they should be subject to the competition of the market place and, if a local authority could not compete on price, the contract should be awarded to others.
>
> *(Fenney, 1996, p. 18)*

The Local Government Act of 1988 took this concept, first put in place in 1980 for a limited number of services, and extended it to a much wider list including refuse collection, street cleansing, school meals and care homes, among many others.

While in the early days of CCT, many contracts stayed with the "in-house" provider, the establishment of a foothold for the private sector has been accelerated over the subsequent decades. Local government has now, effectively, either lost direct responsibility for or out-sourced many services such as the management of schools, the maintenance of roads, the provision of housing – indeed many of the core functions of local authorities established by the reforms immediately after the Second World War.

Private sector companies now provide many core local government services, which has had an impact on how local councils and councillors are held accountable for these. Councillors – and council officers – need to be experts at drafting and monitoring contracts because, while the private company might empty residents' bins every week, the council is held accountable if any bins remain unemptied.

Yet, this shift towards greater involvement of the private sector in the delivery of public services, has not led to greater control for local government over decision-making or any subsequent improvement in local democracy:

> Thatcher's legacy to local governments was increased centralisation and the willingness of her successors to cap, limit and control local democracy in England. This country is one of the most centralised of western democracies, which is an odd legacy for a politician who so prized individualism and freedom.
>
> *(Travers, 2013)*

Such centralised control has been achieved by two particular blunt instruments – Whitehall's firm hand on the purse strings and the continued drive to see as much as possible of local services delivered by private sector partners. Councils such as Barnet in north London have become guinea pigs for the latter, with the majority of its services outsourced to one company – Capita:

> But what's fast changing in Barnet is how residents access their local services – everything from parking tickets to paying council tax to how their corpses are disposed of. In the past few years, the Tory-run council has taken almost every public service it can lay its hands on – and outsourced it.
>
> *(Chakrabortty, 2014)*

Reporting in the *Guardian*, Chakrabortty went on to say:

> [A] full council meeting will vote on whether to consider cuts and "alternative delivery models" for another tranche of services, including libraries, rubbish collection, street gritters and children's speech therapy, among others. Should they go the way of the rest and be outsourced, the local Unison branch calculates that Barnet council will shrink from having 3,200 staff in September 2012 to just 332.

But it is not just those councils with a Conservative majority that are facing up to the impact of the partnership with the private sector model being pushed from the centre.

In 2017, Labour-controlled Sheffield City Council faced a crisis in the media around its contract with a major contractor through a Private Finance Initiative (PFI). The contract, running over 25 years, involves the council paying its contractor to resurface all roads and pavements in the city. The full details of this crisis are detailed in Chapter 8. It is just one of many examples which further underline that the centralism versus localism battle in local government is still alive and kicking today.

So whither local accountability?

The implication this raises for local citizens is the question of accountability. If a service is not delivered, who should they complain to? If a tree is felled by a private contractor, who is ultimately responsible for that act? Does the council concerned have the resources or the expertise to manage the contracts it has let to the private sector?

These questions of accountability are at the centre of the dilemma facing local government going forward – and are at the centre of the nature of modern, local democracy. What had seemed, on the surface, a straightforward model of local democracy, albeit one that has been made more complicated by numerous reviews over time, has been turned into a Rubik's cube by the introduction of the third party.

The challenge for those professionals working in local government communication departments is how to manage the important job of dialogue with local citizens. Richard Perloff, Professor of communication at Cleveland State University, outlines the key aspects for communication within a democracy:

> Each of the three philosophical approaches to democracy assigns an important role to communication. To the ancient Greeks, vigorous debate and the formulation of cogent rhetorical arguments were core elements of direct democracy.
>
> In the view of liberal democracy advocates, free and open access to diverse media is the best way to guarantee truth and advocate different political ideas.
>
> For deliberative democrats, thoughtful reasoned dialogue builds the civic culture and "commitment to citizenship" that sustains democratic life.
>
> *(Perloff, 2018, p. 45)*

Perloff adds that "Theorists of all three approaches would agree that you cannot have a vibrant democracy without thriving communication."

References

Adam Smith Institute (1989). *Wiser Councils: The Reform of Local Government*. London, Adam Smith Institute.

Chakrabortty, Aditya (2014). 'Outsourced and unaccountable: This is the future of local government', *Guardian*, 15th December 2014, https://www.theguardian.com/commentisfree/2014/dec/15/local-services-barnet-council-town-hall (accessed 22nd October 2018).

Cochrane, Allan (1993). *Whatever Happened to Local Government?* Oxford, OUP.

Fenney, Ron (1996). *Essential Local Government* (7th ed.). London, LGC Communications.

King, Desmond & Stoker, Gerry (1996). *Rethinking Local Democracy*. Basingstoke, Palgrave Macmillan.

Kingdom, John (1991). *Local Government and Politics in Britain*. London, Philip Allen.

McConnell (1999) The Politics and policy of local taxation in Britain. *British Journal of Politics and International Relations*, 2 (1) 81–88.

Perloff, Richard (2018). *The Dynamics of Political Communication* (2nd ed.). New York and Abingdon, Routledge.

Travers, Tony(2013). 'Local government: Margaret Thatcher's 11-year war', *Guardian*, 9th April 2013, https://www.theguardian.com/local-government-network/2013/apr/09/local-government-margaret-thatcher-war-politics(accessed7th February 2019).

Travers, Tony (2015). *50 Years of the London Boroughs*. London, London Councils.

Further reading

Mill, John Stuart (1848). *Principles of Political Economy*. London, John W. Parker.

Stoker, Gerry & Wilson, David (2004). *British Local Government in the 21st Century*. Basingstoke, Palgrave Macmillan.

3

THE RISE OF PUBLIC RELATIONS AND THE IMPACT OF THE AUSTERITY YEARS

Adrian Roxan

> **Local government communication – history and challenges**
>
> "Nearly a century after the Reform Act had been passed, the main issues facing local government, which were fundamental to its credibility and legitimacy, can be summed up as professionalism, ethics, communication, and democratic accountability." (L'Etang, 2013, p. 21)

Jacquie L'Etang's excellent account of the history of public relations in Britain – titled *Public Relations in Britain* – sets out a clear picture of the emergence of the PR profession having its origins firmly rooted in the development of the need for communication within local government. L'Etang adds: "Local government in Britain developed key public relations concepts and contributed in an important way to public relations ideology, particularly in relation to concepts of professionalism and a public service ethos" (L'Etang 2013, p. 21).

L'Etang traces the main driver for this journey as being the shift towards a more professional workforce that saw local government trade union, NALGO (National and Local Government Officers Association) at its core. NALGO fought for better conditions for clerical staff – such as pension rights, salary scales and promotion by merit – in line with those conditions enjoyed by central government civil servants. Perhaps another example of the continuing comparisons and battles between local and central government?

As part of this campaign, the union recognised the need to promote the wider picture of the value of local government. As L'Etang observes: "[T]here was much public hostility to be overcome, a legacy of the 19th century form of local government under which officials such as the 'sanitary inspector, school attendance officer and health visitor were feared and loathed'" (L'Etang, 2013, p. 22). It is also significant that attempts to pursue this wider public education campaign only gained momentum when central government proposed cuts in local government expenditure in 1932 (L'Etang, 2013, p. 22).

The Second World War can again be seen as a key moment in the relationship between local government and the people it served and a shift towards a more direct form of local accountability. The war itself, as L'Etang charts, presented logistical challenges of communication as large parts of urban areas such as London suffered under bombing raids. L'Etang cites one volunteer:

> If there was a particularly big incident we would go up there and set up a table, just like the local citizens' advice really, advising people who were involved with the incident. . . . I also found myself picking up the press relations part of the organisation . . . that was my first experience of dealing with the press.
>
> (L'Etang, 2013, p. 26)

Once the war was over, the task of rebuilding began, with local government coming to the fore.

L'Etang cites a commentator from the period – Geoffrey Lewis, who finished his career as Director of PR for the London County Council – as saying:

> We had the re-planning of London after the war, lots of places were bombed out. . . . Local authorities found they were needing to tell people what was going on because things needed to be done. . . . We were going through a period when it was necessary to talk to people, simple as that.
>
> (L'Etang, 2013, p. 27)

So the post-war period, characterised as a period of huge renewal, saw the demand for communication by local councils grow inexorably. The new priorities of housing, education and health were accelerated by the birth of the National Health Service, the creation of the welfare state and the physical need to rebuild large parts of towns and cities.

The post-war era heralded a period where the British population – after the huge sacrifices made during the war – wanted a better society. Jacquie L'Etang identifies the challenges this created for local government communications.

> Post-war there were several opportunities for public relations to become an established part of the socio-economic framework: the large amount of new social legislation needed to be explained to citizens . . . the new administration's interventionist economic policies required some explanation and triggered opposition from business in ideologically rhetorical campaigns.
>
> (L'Etang, 2013, p. 62)

But as local government faced these challenges, so did a newly emerging private sector looking to be part of the post-war recovery that would lead, after a period of economic uncertainty, to a boom in consumerism in the 1960s and 70s.

And it was this consumerist boom that was to lead to the arrival in the UK of the more aggressive form of public relations now synonymous with the United States. Indeed, much of the transatlantic history of PR shows two very distinct origins of the profession on either side of the water. In the US, PR founders such as Edward Bernays were rooted in a desire to promote a new, thriving private sector looking to promote the "want rather than need" aspiration to the newly anointed "consumer".

The UK developed its own model from the roots of public administration, with local government the maternal bosom from which it emerged. But the 1960–1980 period saw the US version begin to materialise in the UK as private companies fought back against a central government looking to bring a number of industries into public ownership.

The 1945 Labour Government was elected with a mandate that enshrined the principle that public ownership was the way forward and embarked on a programme designed to bring the Bank of England, the coal industry, the railways, civil aviation, electricity and road haulage into public ownership. The gas, iron and steel industries were also earmarked for inclusion in this nationalisation programme and this sparked a reaction from the private sector that saw the establishment of a range of organisations designed to resist this trend.

In many respects, the history of PR in this period is very much a direct reflection of the economic and political context as the first shoots of neoliberalism as a philosophy began to be propagated. So local government communication, blissfully unaware of the impending changes under Margaret Thatcher's government, continued to nurse its concepts of public interest and public education being at the heart of its purpose.

1979 onwards – the local v. central conflict retakes centre stage

"The crisis in the relationship between central and local government continues. Since 1979 – as in previous governments – ministers have sought to increase their control over local authorities but the pace of centralisation has increased. . . . the message of central government was that it needed to control disobedient local authorities. Its measures and proposals were designed to increase centralisation and weaken local government." (Jones & Stewart, 1985, p. 3)

George Jones and John Stewart, who first met when they sat on the Layfield Committee in 1974, have been prolific authors on the case for local government. Tony Travers wrote in a tribute to them in 2013: "The Jones-Stewart combine has, since the 1970s, supported a traditionalist view of local government - in the sense that they have argued for proper, formal, local democracy." Jones and Stewart, commenting further on the Thatcher years, added: "The continuing crisis has destabilised central-local relationships and has undermined local accountability" (Jones & Stewart, 1985, p. 3).

Cochrane, writing in 1993, suggested that this dispute between central and local government was because "local government sometimes assumed a high political profile because it appeared to be an obstacle in the way of broader political change, rather than because it has always been a major focus of government attention in its own right (Cochrane, 1993, p. 48).

Political scientist Professor James Bulpitt argued that the conflicts of the Thatcher years were a consequence of the fudged reforms of the 1930s, confirmed after the war, that failed to set out a clear centre–local structure (Bulpitt, 1989).

Cochrane added: "This left local authorities to implement centrally agreed policies within a framework which also endorsed notions of local democracy, albeit on the (unspoken) assumption that there was little significant popular support for the institutions of local government" (Cochrane, 1993, p. 49).

Three particular policy issues – driven by Thatcher's government – were to characterise these continuing conflicts and precipitate a crisis that many believe was the nail in the coffin of Thatcher's period in power.

The first came in the form of what became known as ratecapping in 1984 Rates Act which saw central government decide the level of expenditure of individual councils and introduce penalties for any that looked to exceed their centrally determined level. 18 councils – 16 of them Labour – were identified in the first tranche of local authorities affected.

This led to high profile campaigns being launched by a number of Labour local authorities designed to engender community support for defying the Thatcher administration. A co-ordinated move was made by the Labour councils to refuse to set a rate which, following complex legal battles, ended in defeat with only Lambeth in south London and Liverpool refusing to set one.

The second policy issue was further reform of local government which saw the Greater London Council and six other metropolitan councils abolished in 1986 – all Labour controlled at the time. This move was justified on the grounds of cutting waste at a time of significant national focus on a struggling economy with high unemployment and a stuttering industrial performance.

But the party political nature of this decision did not escape many commentators, including Tony Byrne, author of a guide to local government: "As *The Times* (1 August 1985) commented, 'A convincing case for abolition has yet to be made with intellectual vigour and sufficient fact . . . ministers will seem to believe that in this matter assertion can substitute for argument'" (Byrne, 2000, p. 52). Indeed former Conservative Prime Minister Ted Heath went further in describing the reform as "the greatest act of gerrymandering in the last 100 years of British history" (Byrne, 2000, pp. 52–3).

The third, and perhaps most significant, issue was the Conservative government's move to introduce the community charge, quickly dubbed the poll tax: "The introduction of the poll tax in the late 1980s was part of the continuing campaign by central government to gain control over local decision-makers, at least in financial terms" (Cochrane, 1993, p. 61).

But opposition to a shift in local taxation from property to individual sparked a violent response and widespread opposition. Added to anger at a local level over ratecapping and the abolition of Labour controlled local authorities, it was to prove the death knell for Thatcher.

It was the "flagship" of the 1987 Conservative Government's programme but its unpopularity contributed substantially to the pressures which led to the replacement of Margaret Thatcher as Prime Minister and leader of the Conservative Party at the end of 1990.

(Cochrane, 1993, p. 67)

The impact of all these conflicts on Labour local authorities was to put them in almost permanent campaign mode throughout the 1980s and, with the Greater London Council as an exemplar, to invest in higher levels of communication expertise to state their case.

The old-fashioned public relations department with a Head and Deputy Head of PR was replaced by a Head of Communications with a much broader remit to take on the development of each council's corporate messaging.

Image and branding became important as councils – on a regular war footing with central government – looked to state their case and retain Labour's power base in local government. With such a large Conservative majority in the House of Commons, Labour had come to see its local power bases as important to protect – albeit the 1990s was characterised by a battle between Labour Party modernisers and the "left" who were often in control of Labour local authorities.

The period post-Thatcher, up until the election of Tony Blair's Labour Government in 1997, saw some retrenchment from the Conservatives as they clung on to power with a slender and ever-dwindling majority.

Janice Morphet, visiting professor at University College London, commented on the state of central/local government relations by 1997:

Local authorities considered that their right to govern had been undermined (Stoker, 2004) and had been taken over by both central government and a series of quangos. Additionally, there was a view that local government's role was increasingly being invaded by the private sector and that increasing pressure on delivery was being accompanied by reduced funding.

(Morphet, 2008, p. 11)

The arrival of a Labour Government under Tony Blair in 1997 did not see the significant shift in trust in local government that many local authority leaders – particularly Labour ones – were hoping for.

The New Labour administration was not hostile to the role of the private sector in local government and saw the continuing role of private companies as a catalyst for improvements in efficiency. Blair's government argued that local government needed stronger leadership, greater coherence and integration, and improved standards of services. But critics such as Arthur Midwinter from the University of Strathclyde were not convinced: "Modernisation became the label for the package of reforms on the New Labour agenda, although it is difficult to regard it as a coherent governing philosophy" (Midwinter, 2001, p. 311).

Far from returning some of the powers and responsibilities back to local authorities, the new Labour Government surprised many by introducing a new challenge to improve efficiency – called Best Value. Local councils had long been derided for being wasteful and inefficient in the media and by the Conservative government from 1979–1997. Tony Blair's new regime saw little to be gained from challenging this and instead, through its Best Value programme, embarked on a process to modernise local services.

Quangos such as the Audit Commission were given heightened status to bring forward research that was critical of the way local services were run. Much of this critical thinking was constructive in suggesting ways to improve the interaction between a range of local bodies such as the police, social services and the NHS.

But the die was cast, with little hope for local authority leaders that the continuing stand-off between central and local government was going to develop into a more co-operative relationship.

By the end of Labour's stint in power, moves such as the introduction of academy schools and a reliance on private finance initiatives to fund capital investment in local projects saw the entrenchment of the private sector in local authorities rather than the reassertion of public over private that some had hoped for.

By 2010 the economy was in trouble following the global financial crash in 2007/8 and for some local authorities the situation had worsened significantly. For example, Kent County Council had an estimated £50m held with Icelandic banks that collapsed during the crisis and the knock-on effect of the financial crisis was felt across the local government sector.

The programme of austerity introduced by the Coalition Government elected in 2010 produced an even greater financial squeeze for local councils. *The Economist* magazine, reporting in January 2017, set out the current picture facing local councils in stark terms:

> "Britain is in the middle of a painful fiscal squeeze. Since 2010 the budget deficit has been reduced from 10% to 4% of GDP; by 2020 it is forecast to be almost eliminated. To achieve this, the government has slashed spending. Hardest hit has been the Department for Communities and Local Government, which provides councils with most of their funding. And so local authorities have been forced to embark on an epic economy drive. Their spending on public services will be 22% lower this year than in 2010." (*The Economist*, 2017)

The current picture 2015 onwards

So some key questions come to the fore:

- What impact has the current financial crisis and the fractious relationship with central government had on local authorities and, in particular, what has happened to the vital relationship between councils and their citizens?

- What resources can councils devote to communications?
- What about the local media? How has the council/local media relationship fared during this period?
- What can councils do to maintain a dialogue with local residents?
- Are councils genuinely accountable to those who vote for them?

. . . and from the Communications perspective:

- If the austerity policy has been a difficult time for local authorities, how does the picture look for those in charge of their communications?
- How have the public relations departments – better known as communications – fared and what has austerity meant for them?
- What about the relationship with the local media – has that survived?
- What impact has the digital age had on local councils and their relationships with their citizens?
- Perhaps most important of all, what does this mean for local democracy?

Through a series of one-to-one interviews conducted over the 2016–17 period, the following sections include the thoughts and views of communications professionals in local government facing up to how to keep the channels of communication open. They were asked questions about seven key areas in relation to the impact of austerity on their jobs, their councils and the communities they serve.

These are captured under seven headings:

1. Resources and cuts
2. Digital media
3. Council publications
4. Local media
5. Consultation
6. Partnerships
7. Accountability

The councils included in these interviews cover different types of authorities – city councils, county councils, district councils and borough councils. The councils covered have different political parties as their majority group.

Their views are grouped into relevant sections:

1 Resources and cuts: What has been the impact of austerity on the resources of councils?

While resources are not always the answer to every question, there can be no doubt that local authorities in many parts of the country faced significant reductions in their budgets following the introduction of the austerity policies in 2010. These led councillors to reassess their priorities with the oft quoted "frontline services" – support for the more needy through social care or housing – being protected.

Each council is different – both in terms of size and responsibilities – so no two budget reduction programmes were the same but it was inevitable that communications would be seen as a service area ripe for budget cutbacks, partly because it was not seen as a "frontline service" and partly because the impact of the move to digital communications offered up the opportunity for real savings anyway.

The responses to questions on this first issue illustrate that each of the councils interviewed endorsed this perspective when making decisions about cutbacks. The emphasis is also clear on communication functions adopting strategies designed to raise money or, at a minimum, finance some of the existing activities.

Council F (based in the Midlands) sums this up:

> I think the reality now is that we just don't have enough people, we can only really do enough for this authority. I think if we were to do that it would need some pump priming in terms of additional capacity, and we're certainly not looking at that at the moment. It was being considered, but there is no slack – we are looking at opportunities but not as an agency, so we're looking at things like oh that old chestnut statutory notices, can we bring them into our own publication? We're looking at things like we recharge a lot of the statutory notices to utilities, so we might place an advert in the local paper or wherever, because we're the legal body that has to do that, but then we charge British Gas or whatever for that advert. But if we put that advert in our own publication can we recharge them so we're getting the money in. So we're looking at things like that, we do sell our design because we're in a quite a fortunate position I think that we are still able to use external designers, so I think we do have some very good campaign collateral and we do sell that. But honestly it's minor stuff compared to having to find £167,000 next year. It's worth doing, particularly if it doesn't take a lot of time for us. We do do other things, like we maintain websites for a couple of the district councils, so it's not like we don't generate any income at all, but in terms of going for that quite radical agency approach which one or two authorities I know have done successfully, I don't see that happening in the near future.

The significance of this comment comes in the changing focus on looking at ways that income can be generated. While partnerships between councils on activities such as the maintenance of websites would be welcomed by those focused on efficient use of public money, it begs the question as to whether as more and more time and resources is spent on raising money, this distracts from the core communications objective of keeping residents informed as to how their money is being spent.

One obvious solution saw many local authorities look to centralise their communications function and move to a more "commercial" model based on an external agency function – set up an internal agency to sell its services inside and outside the council.

Council E (based in the Home Counties) described this as:

> When I joined there were 18 full time equivalent communications roles in the council working in a central corporate team and then dotted around working directly for services. In 2010/11 the council undertook a value for money review of its services as we volunteered to be the first to take part. I was encouraged by the board to find a better model than the one in place. I came up with several and the one chosen was to centralise (move people and communications budgets into one council team) and adopt the account management model we have now, so that directors losing "their communications person" would still get the benefit of someone knowing their service inside out. We restructured at this point too, and each year since then due to budget pressure:
>
> 2011–18 FTE – v sorry, can't remember the £ staff/services budget but think it was close to £1m
>
> 2012 – 11 FTE – £600k staff and services
> 2013 – 9 FTE – £450k
> 2014 – 7 FTE – £380k

This paints a clear picture for this local authority of significant cuts in the resources available for communications with centralisation being one of the common solutions used to save money. This centralisation can lead to a loss of the "local" voice and "local" expertise in communication with service departments such as education and social care, where communication with schools and clients is crucial to the relationship necessary for service delivery.

Another vivid picture painted by these interviews was the incremental nature of the budget reductions over a number of years. These interviews reflected a five-year period (2010–2015) but many commentators on local government saw these as the "easy" years for cuts in expenditure as waste and inefficiencies were stripped out. As the period progressed, it becomes clear that these "easy" cuts were not enough and significant restructuring and redundancies were the only way for some councils. The following extract from **Council A (based in the North East)** also reflects the regional differences of the budget reductions. Much of the evidence collated on how councils have been affected by the austerity years indicates that areas such as the north east of England have suffered particularly high level of financial reductions:

Well I started here in 2010, and at that point we had around 30 people in the communications team, which was a stand-alone team of communication and marketing professionals with some discrete elements. So there was a web team, a marketing team, a press team, in a kind of traditional model. Since that time we've been through a series of budget reviews and at various stages we've done different things. The first step was we made a small number of redundancies, and if I can put this kindly, that was really taking out some of the dead wood of the team, of which there was some. And that may have been a change that the new head of comms might have done anyway.

We then went on to more substantial budget cuts, and at that point we centralised any outlying functions that may have been in the council, of which there were some, in the regeneration team we had marketing people, the children's services team had some people, and various things like that. So they were all brought under one central team, and we made some redundancies as a consequence of that centralising as well. And at that point we moved to a kind of account team model, we had teams working on behalf of service directorates. The next wave of cuts have been much much more deep, much deeper – we were challenged to go to a business critical only service. All four services in the council had the same challenge, and effectively the cuts at that point were a 50 per cent cut – a 50 per cent cut to a team which is predominantly staffing budget, with very little revenue spend, has a big impact. I talked that through with my colleague who was head of policy at the time, and we took the view that we were each facing the same level of cuts, and we didn't see that we could deliver a minimum credible business critical service if we each took that cut separately, there just wouldn't be enough bodies to provide a service.

So we took a, I think, a brave step at that time, that we would bring the two teams together. And in doing that we put ourselves on offer as part of a management review that was going on at the same time. As it turns out, I was successful in that, but [the head of policy] stayed with us as a senior specialist as well. So we got the two together, and initially we ran them as two distinct teams under one management, but in the last budget round we've actually merged job roles, so we now have policy and communication officers who multi-skill across that. And the idea of that, the old idea of having single discipline communication officers went a long time ago, we'd already moved towards a sort of generic communication officer role, so we no longer had a marketing team, or a press team, or … we expected people to be multi-skilled. And we'd already put that direction of travel in. But now we're looking at a much broader integration of people thinking about communication and policy in a single job role as well, and that's even more challenging. We've got a learning and development programme in place to support people through that, and all my team are now members of the CIPR, they're all moving towards accredited practitioner status through the CIPR CPD scheme. And it has been really challenging, there's not just a professional difference in terms of discipline, there's a cultural difference from two teams with very different outlooks – the communication team which is much more used to working at a fast pace, deadline driven, and the policy team which is usually more reflective, and taking a bit more time to think through things in more depth. And that's a difference in culture, but that's not a bad thing, I think bringing those two things together can be a positive. The rationale we've given to that is that the team now, policy and communications, our role now is to help [the council] understand and communicate its place in the world. It's to help us understand the policy landscape, it's to help us understand where we want to be as an organisation, and how we influence the world around us. So it's all about positioning, how do we position [the council] locally, regionally, nationally, internationally, because we've got an international dimension to our team as well.

And it's all about positioning, I think bringing together policy and comms is helpful for that, and it has had some benefits, but it has had some challenges in terms of getting there as well. In terms of scale, where we were in 2005, as I say a core team of 30, a policy team of the same, we now have a joint team, core team of about 16, so that's a massive reduction. So about 8 would have been previously comms specialists, and about 8 would have been previously policy specialists.

The dilution of the communication specialism is evident with this local authority – understandable given the significant level of budget cuts required. Some would argue that this is an improvement bringing, as the interviewee suggests, a broader understanding of the council's role and policy direction but the loss of the "bread and butter" functions of communication such as regular outputs of information, consultation and building relationships with service users cannot be understated for this council.

So if you were to put the communication and policy functions together as they were then, you've effectively gone down from around 60 to 16, is that right?

Right, yep. There are more people than that here, because we've also moved to an income generating team as well, so we've got lots of people on temporary contracts doing specific pieces of work, where we've found temporary funding. Some of that is wooden dollars moved around inside the organisation, where people are paying for something over and above the core minimum credible business critical service, and genuine external funding where we're working on behalf of another region, or we've accessed European grants, or whatever. So there's some work which is genuine income, and some which is a bit of a top up from the organisation itself. So overall, there are probably still around 23 I think it is in the team all together, once those temporary posts are taken into account.

The reference here to "European grants" is another factor that local authorities will be facing with the decision of the UK to leave the European Union. While the final Brexit outcome is still unclear at publication of this book, there can be little doubt that such income sources are likely to be less available with the UK leaving the EU.

Another aspect has been the pace of changes as the budget reductions bite. **Council B (based in the North West)** is a relatively small district council in a larger conurbation and the pressures on a smaller scale of operation where expertise may also be more limited was also a problem in making a shift to more efficient and cost effective methods of communication.

> ### In historical terms, do you know if that's a change in the direction of staffing the unit?
>
> The unusual thing about the communications team here is that it doesn't incorporate the digital side of things, although we're currently going through a review and it will do. So there's four people in the digital team which at the moment is separate but I think should be included in the figures. There's also four people in the print team which is separate. The core part of the communications team, it's 11 people, up to about 10 full time equivalents, there's 11 if you include the designer who is within the corporate comms team – I think one of the features I've noticed is that although the number of posts might not have been reduced, often it's people who are working shorter weeks, often young mums with children, and so they're reduced down to three days a week or four days a week, and we've got a lot of those. And we've also got a lot of people like myself who are on temporary contracts, filling in to fill gaps before a permanent structure is put in place, and there's a lot of that about.
>
> There was a head of communications, and my view looking at what's happened here and elsewhere is I think that some of the stability that perhaps existed within communications has been rocked through austerity. So for instance the head of communications post, particularly if it was a reasonably well-paid post, has often come in the firing line, whether it be for political reasons because they've seen it as spin or whatever, that is an area that has been vulnerable. What's happened here in [the council] is that there hasn't been a head of communications for some time, and they've been filling with people like myself to try and manage the way through. My contract will finish on 21st August, and they will be trying to recruit to a permanent post, I don't think it'll be at the salary that previous posts have been at, and I don't think that is untypical of the sector. I think the digital revolution has also had a huge impact, and a recognition that we need to be doing more around the website, social media, and we're doing that, and we're doing that with arrangements and linked arrangements with the digital team, but structurally that currently isn't reflected.

The challenge of embracing the opportunities of digital communication are significant for all local authorities but the task has been made that much harder due to the attack by central government on local authority communication. Eric Pickles, local government minister in the early days of the 2010–15 coalition government, was quick to condemn 'town hall pravdas' as he called them but with this condemnation comes a lack of understanding of the need for expertise in translating communication in local authorities from the old print based approach to an genuine online service.

The comments from **Council D (Based in the North)** highlight another factor that came through in many of the interviews – that some councils are more corporate and collegiate in their approach while others retain an element of autonomy for each service department. So centralising a function such as communications can lead to an exacerbation of the sense in some councils that not all departments pull in the same direction:

> The two immediate things I think are that there was an initial round of fairly deep cuts in local government which necessitated a change in the way that communications was resourced. So certainly the current authority and previous authority there was a centralising of staff, there was a reduction of staff, there was a centralising of budgets. And so my experience is that local government has moved from a situation where quite often there were professional communicators in individual departments each carrying budgets, relatively small budgets, but that round of cuts necessitated a kind of scooping up of those people and those budgets and initial chunks being taken out.
>
> So in my previous authority they centralised something like £1.5 million worth of budgets from across the organisation, often in small pots, and the first thing that happens is that someone takes £0.5 million off the top. And then there's a further reduction in the staffing costs, because all of a sudden there's a single team. And of course that had serious impacts for the way in which local government was structured to meet the demands of services, quite often it meant that services were finding it quite difficult to work with centralised comms departments because 'you took my staff' and 'you took my budget', and when they got over that they were making demands precisely because you got their staff and their budgets that you couldn't meet because the staff and the budgets were no longer in place to provide the kind of support they were used to, the budgets were not there to provide the kind of activity they were used to. And so of course one of the things that happened as part of that is that there were sometimes budget and sometimes government driven decisions.
>
> So lots of local authorities lost that kind of centralised publication that would arrive however often it arrived on the doormat of the resident. And certainly both here and in my previous roles that was a decision for budgetary reasons on both occasions, rather than because Eric Pickles had said so. But both authorities made the decision that they needed to stop trying to send some

> Pravda to residents, and from my point of view from a personal point of view I think that was the right thing to do, for reasons that I think will become clear when I talk about the second part of that.
>
> I think the other thing that happened over that three or four or five years of significant diminution of resources is that social media became a massive issue and a massive challenge to organisations and local government, by no means exclusively so. But when I first arrived in a comms role four and a half years ago I arrived to manage a newly constructed centralised comms department full of communications professionals, not one of whom was actually using a Twitter account. I think the authority probably had a Twitter account at that point and will have had something like 720 followers. That number five years later, four years later will be more than ten times that, it will now be thousands of followers, and actually would probably have multiplied five-fold in the first year, because the challenge that I brought was to make use of it.
>
> And so there was a challenge I think came from social media, but also a huge opportunity, because as those resources had diminished social media presented us with a set of tools and a set of behaviours which meant that we had to understand the way in which we could talk directly to customers. In and of itself that's not got us the whole way, because I've seen research previously that suggests that actually quite early on, and I think this is still true authorities were using social media simply as a means of still broadcasting the stuff that they used to put in the press release, or they used to put in the magazine that went to every home in the city. So the initial inclination I think was just to continue to use it as a platform to shout to people on a one size fits all basis.

This further emphasises the point that for a genuine transformation of local authority communications to take place with the use of social media as its platform, resources and expertise are necessary.

Council C (Based in the Midlands) reinforces the picture that no two councils have been either faced the same level of budget cuts or responded in the same way:

> **In terms of communication function over that period of 2010–15, have you had to make cuts and reduce any of what you've been doing?**
>
> On the whole metropolitan councils like ours haven't done well over the past five years. So by 2017 [the council] will have lost half its government grants compared to what it had in 2010, and that's £250 a head per man woman and child less to spend on services in [the council area]. So that's a big budget reduction, alongside that the changes around education with schools becoming academies, so contracting there. [The council] has managed well, it has very good finance people who have been very clever and good with money to avoid real swingeing

cuts until now in front line services, although there has been some impact on front line services, quite a lot of impact on front line services. We are now getting to the stage where we are looking at things like libraries, the real core services, the real heart and soul of the council. So probably 2016/17 but particularly 2017 and 2018 budgets is the precipice that we're looking at at the moment.

My last team review which actually removed posts was 2011–2012, but actually that was more about streamlining and refocusing. I've made substantial savings through centralising the communications budget, so in 2008/09 we were spending more than a million quid a year on comms all over the place, pens with labels on and things like that. Now we're spending £250,000 a year, no it was more than that, it was £1.3 million, because I've saved a million pounds a year. So, I've managed to on the whole, I've contracted, so when my deputy left on VR there was an organisational VR scheme last year and he took VR, so he's a hole that I haven't replaced. So when people leave we're not particularly filling them, but we're not, I haven't had to have wholesale cuts to the team, the refocusing was the right thing to do anyway.

Resources and cuts – a summary

- The scale of cutbacks in communication resources has been significant with 50% reductions commonplace.
- This has led to a centralisation of resources with the "local" voice of different council departments diminished or lost completely.
- Corporate publications in printed form are fast disappearing with their replacement online being a cost saving exercise as much as recognition of the advances in digital communication.
- This does raise the question of whether some residents – perhaps those of most need due to their low income – are being disenfranchised from communication by their local council.
- The digital age is recognised by all interviewees as something with real potential but the backdrop of significant budget reductions has made the adoption of positive – and expert – strategies much more difficult.
- The status and so the pay of local authority communicators has been downgraded under the twin pressures of budgets cuts and attacks by central government on local 'propaganda'.
- Mergers and partnerships have come about through necessity with some advantages gained in monetary terms but little evidence offered that such arrangements have improved the delivery of communication.
- The agency model – adopting the practices of the private sector – has been the direction for some, with the "selling" of communications to partners in the public sector mimicking the role of private communication consultancies.

2 The arrival of digital forms of communication and its impact on councils and their role

As the austerity policies of the Coalition Government came into force, local councils were also facing the impact of the ever-growing digital footprint leaving its mark on all aspects of communication and on many facets of service delivery.

The world external to local government was changing rapidly with the revolution in consumer behaviour towards an online economy rippling across the delivery of services. Service users, clients, consumers – whatever their title – expected their local council to provide a 24/7 response to their need for local services. Whether it was paying their council tax, registering to vote, paying their rent or simply accessing information about services – all the challenges of the digital era presented themselves.

But, at the same time, councils needed – and continue to need – to be aware that many of the poorest members of their communities who are often those most in need of a council's services, didn't necessarily have the same access to digital resources.

So the dilemma for many was how to embrace the digital changes being demanded while retaining their ability to reach those who can be described as the "hard to reach" citizens without daily access to the internet.

Add the opportunity – with the overwhelming budget pressures – to save money and it is clear that squaring this circle was, and remains, the biggest challenge.

So **Council F's** description of its response to this dilemma was not unusual:

What do the digital team tend to focus on?

They are a mixture of technical and non-technical – there's 10 of them, much of them is around maintaining our council website, and one or two other spin off websites as well. We do have two colleagues in there who do have a social media specialism as well, so they support us with day-to-day social media. But the majority of people in that team are on the technical side.

Would that include the Search Engine Optimisation (SEO) function for the council?

Yes, that includes that. I think in terms of our digital developments, because we've had such a huge reduction in staff a lot of what we're doing at the moment to be honest is treading water. So there is some of that going on, there are some developments in social media, but a lot of it is basically just maintaining the integrity of the large website portfolio.

While the resources for this council are not insignificant for the digital side of communication, the comment "at the moment to be honest is treading water" underlines further the pragmatic approach taken by councils where the priority is saving money rather than being able to adopt a forward looking strategy for improving communications using digital channels.

Council E's comments reflect the way in which some councils have used the opportunities presented to change the communications function:

> **What area of work has been most significantly affected – i.e. pro-active public information/communications campaigns, citizen communication, media relations or other?**
>
> We have become more targeted with our advertising and marketing campaigns; we've shifted from paper based to predominantly digital citizen comms alongside adopting a new transactional/"do it online" style website; we've stopped our city-wide resident newsletter (was 10x per year, then quarterly from 2012) and are about to stop our tenant newsletter.
>
> **What external pressures have also guided your choices around what and how to prioritise your management of the communications function?**
>
> The rise of social media; our local print media moving online (leading to a more effective 24/7 news operation – our two papers are weeklies in print); change of political administration ([the council] remains a no overall control council). I think regardless of budget pressures we would have changed the way we worked.

Council B's comments best capture the 24/7 culture being developed and facilitated by the digital world:

> **Where is the digital team?**
>
> The digital team is currently within the customer contact centre, so again that's not a particular problem because a lot of their queries may well just be straightforward customer contact queries. I think what's happened during the time that I've been here is that there's a greater understanding that we can do more digitally, and we're trying to get more of that contact digitally, but there are issues that come through the contact centre and the digital team that have huge reputation impact so working closely with the comms team and the reputation management side has become much more clear, the need to do that, and those relationship linkages are there, but structurally it's different.
>
> **How much has social media had an impact on staff in terms of working practices and the pressure on staff?**
>
> I think that is still a bit of a bone of contention. Thankfully when the [local nightclub] fire broke, I was the one who got called at three or four in the morning and got on and got sorted. And there's much more agile working, so

particularly the staff who work three days a week, they've got their RAPs and they can set up from home and they can do stuff from home, and that works really well. So the digital guy was on with stuff straight away, I got into the Town Hall and we got on with it. But I think that there is an issue around out of hours, because traditionally some councils would pay people additional payments, and that's no longer there. Now, wherever I've worked the police and people who might have to go out out of hours there were additional payments, but generally councils didn't, you just did it as goodwill. I don't know what'll happen when I've left, I think that they'll get somebody in, but I think it is a bone of contention, and people feel that if it's all landing on the press side that the comms side, senior members, that they should be involved as well. So that is something that has to be resolved.

How much of it is driven by public expectation that the local authority should be 24/7 now, rather than 9–5 Monday to Friday as it traditionally was?

I think that's difficult to know, I mean I would say that my experience is that certainly the local media here, in the past many years ago when I was working in the North East, there would be an expectation that they could get in touch with you out of hours, and we'd be inundated with press enquiries all the time, they loved to drop something on you last thing on a Friday afternoon [laughs]. I don't think that happens as much, and I think we've got fewer press enquiries, yes you might suddenly get a big national issue and everything goes pear shaped and you've just got to muck in basically, but my experience would be that we've basically got the [local paper], and after a Wednesday you don't really get an awful lot. We've also got the digital ones like [a local paper] and [another local paper] do have their digital side of things, so they do expect things to keep rolling through, and they will expect us to respond to enquiries within core hours really. And if there's stuff they need out of hours, particularly I think during the elections, we stayed up all night, it's manageable. But I do think, the big one for [the council] is the roads, because of where we are located next to the motorways if the roads clog up the public expect to know, and they expect to know that we're keeping them informed. Now, that was the reason why, basically the main task I had when the [local nightclub] fire took place was to let people know because there were roads closed. And it was let's let them know before the main commuter time. And the reason I acted so quickly and got here and got everything moving very fast was based on experience, because we'd had a Friday afternoon back in December where everything was clogged up, and we were criticised for not getting information out. Even if it's just on our social media, we're seen to have done something, so yes, I think there is an expectation, but we're not as aware of it because generally we've managed it.

The one aspect of the new digital communications culture that these comments emphasise is the arrival of 24/7 expectations that have emerged within all other walks of life. Local authorities are now expected to react to events at any time of day or night and, while it is true that this has always been the case with a major emergency such as flood or other such catastrophic incident, the expectation is now there for everyday delivery of services. The media is also a factor in that journalists are now working round the clock due to the 24/7 nature of news and this has an inevitable knock on effect for local authorities.

Council D's responses go further in questioning the long-term vision of where councils will be when the full implications of the digital world are embraced. It raises questions about who communicates and where communication takes place:

What are the challenges facing the council in projecting itself?

I think increasingly the challenge, particularly in a digital place, where 78–82% of people in [the local area] are now regular online users, part of the challenge actually is building not organisational websites, but building place-based approaches for partners because the customer doesn't care. They want to go into something that says "where I live" and they want to be able to report antisocial behaviour. The fact that that goes to the police, as opposed to I want to report graffiti which may go to [the council], as opposed to I want to report tipped waste which might go to [the council], none of it actually coming back to the local authority in itself. But I think you're absolutely right, and increasingly I think we need to consider that the one stop shop that you're describing is in fact likely to start being a one-stop shop online. I think the challenge for us then is going to be understanding how we fill the gaps for those people for whom online is not a serious or an acceptable option ... It's the transactional stuff – my mum'll use it to put pictures of her holiday on, or have a conversation with her grandkids, but would she go online and buy something from Argos? No, I think there's a confidence issue there, there's a trust issue there that needs to be overcome for some people. But it reminds me of something I said some years ago, because I like to try to be provocative about what I do for a living, and I remember sitting in a room full of comms professionals maybe four years ago and was on the panel during a debate, and the debate was is traditional comms dead? And the question was designed to determine were we now to stop issuing press releases, because of Twitter. And my response I think was not the one that the chair had expected, because I think he expected me to say yes, he expects me to be provocative enough to say yes, but actually I think it's a stupid question, I think the question comms people needed to ask themselves is why they've been wandering around for 30-odd years claiming they were marketing professionals, when actually all they were doing was issuing a newspaper, running a website with the same bloody awful vanity publishing on it, and talking to journalists. It wasn't about Twitter, the question for me was why had they not in those 30 years, as communications experts, used home helps to talk to vulnerable sections of the community, why had they not worked with their new one stop shop front of house services, why were they not using call centres?

Among the most important are people like receptionists?

As somebody much wiser than me said, "the brand is what the brand does", and I think that's a key thing, one of the things I hope I bring to my role is you do not gain and maintain reputation by issuing press releases, you gain and maintain reputation customer by customer, transaction by transaction, day after day. And you can lose them as simply. The big risk in that is that the customer now talks back, and you get one transaction with one customer wrong on one day, and there is a young woman right now sitting in [the local area] composing 140 characters that could ruin my organisation's reputation by teatime. That's a much bigger challenge than comms. I can help you recover that reputation as it goes viral, or as it starts to appear on Buzzfeed, or as it appears in the *Mirror*, but what I can't do is stop it happening. And the days in which the comms people and the PR people thought somehow they were in control has gone, they were never right actually in the first place, but you're absolutely right, what that comes to is an idea that is fundamentally about culture and behaviours, and no amount of 'spin' can stop that. And so, I don't know if you've read Robert Phillips' book, I shared a platform with Robert when he launched it three months ago, and that's essentially the core of Robert's argument, that type of PR, Robert doesn't believe that PR's dead any more than I do, he just believes that it is in fact the way you're describing, it's how does the big man talk to the member of the public, does the receptionist smile, did we get the process right, are we learning when we get it wrong, are we capable of being human on Twitter? And that idea that you can have some centralised broadcast function that reassures you everything is alright because we the council said so was never proper, it was never that safe. And actually, it's doomed, his view is that the debate we need to be having is not about trust, that people invest a lot in the single PR function which demands trust, but is actually about the whole organisation being trustworthy, and it's a small distinction but it's probably an important one. And I think that's the big challenge, and I think the social media stuff has absolutely opened us up in a way that means we've got to understand what you've just said, which is kind of almost end to end trustworthiness.

The responses from this communications head reveals the continuing debate among local councils about who should communicate, how and what platforms they should use? And this respondent raises the important question of trust and where that emanates from with the communication behaviours of the whole organisation being the focus for building a council's reputation.

So what does this all mean in practical terms? **Council C's** responses describe the day-to-day impact of shifting communications on to digital platforms and the pitfalls and opportunities this can present:

If you were to describe that particular period, what other changes have affected how you've restructured what you're doing?

I think massively digital and social media of course, and the decline of print media. One of the other things that strikes me is that there is a reputational impact about increasing communication functions or doing something fancy with communication functions in times of austerity, something that's not the austerity that means there's less money to spend on any function in a council, it's also that the perception of spending money, as I say to my finance director no one ever marches on the town hall saying 'save our press offices' and they never will. So I think as much as we are affected in the way that every support service are, probably it's more acute here because the perception is that we're overpaid spin doctors, that's how it is. And I think austerity has sharpened that focus, and I think it's made it more difficult just to spend money in the way that we used to because everything is questioned, probably rightly but you wouldn't ever get a pen with a label on it these days without expecting to end up with the local papers saying cash strapped council as it makes hundreds of people and cuts services are spending money on pens.

What about the change in terms of digital?

We'll get there I think. At the minute I don't want to scare the horses on that, there probably will always been the need for a leaflet or something like that if it's part of the rest of the mix. I'm really lucky like that, my web editor is [an individual] who is a very early adopter of all of these kind of things which is why we've got such a big Facebook following, because she set it up and we found a brilliant geek who gets it, so we've been lucky to have [this individual] that's allowed us to experiment on things, we've done online forums, we did a big thing called [project title], that was 2010 where we had a great public online debate over several days about the future of the city. I love the way that you can experiment and if it goes wrong, apart from the reputational issue it doesn't cost anything. So we've just set up an Instagram account and we've been Instagramming very beautiful photos of [the council area] and just seeing how that goes. That conversation with people, so having that conversation with angry people, when you stop it that's very interesting I think, we have an out of hours press office function, but that's mostly about if there's an emergency, but if my press officers are monitoring Twitter at night do you then get involved in discussions about car park penalty notices and things like that, all that feels like little details, but actually it does change the way you work, because you do become a 24/7 operation and you become very closely aligned to customer care then in comms, and we're still working that through, it's quite interesting.

How much have you been able to manage services?

We just ask people to put together a business case if they want to set up their own Twitter or Facebook, because we want to encourage people to do it, but the business case needs to say how they're going to manage it, who's going to do it, and then [this individual] will sit down and do a little training which is just about don't say anything stupid, make sure that they know what they're doing, and then keep an eye on it. And then after three months or six months if you've still only got five followers of this Twitter account then you'll bring them back in and say is it really worth it. Some of them, the library's Facebook account is lovely, [the council] park rangers, they haven't got a huge number of followers, but they do lovely countryside pictures and all that kind of stuff. Some of them are a bit random, but we encourage people, so we train them, teach them, show them how to do it, and ask them just to put together a sensible business case.

And has there been any kind of negative impact?

All the time, which is why we keep such a close eye on it and do It out of hours as well, the press officer will keep an eye out of hours, you can just get a feeling in your gut can't you?

And what impact has that had on the more conventional ways of working in PR?

It's made you much more cautious, you have to keep things much more under control and under wraps. And if you've got something, you can break stuff on social media as well if you wanted to go a certain way. So it's just that understanding exactly the impact of it. My Leader doesn't use Twitter, nor does my deputy Leader, although he lurks around watching it all the time, but I have a couple of cabinet members who are very feisty on Twitter and the deputy leader of the opposition is very accomplished and comfortable with using social media, so you can just keep an eye on those accounts and see what's boiling up.

What about bringing staff into the new era of multichannel communication?

They're good, some of them are better than others, some of them are more comfortable than others, but they all know they have to do it. If you're an out of hours press officer you get an allowance for that, but you have to do the social media too. Some of them aren't as comfortable, what we're trying to do is avoid people, so that [an individual] who's very good at doing the rebuttals on Twitter, media relations coordinator, so you end up saying [this individual], will you do that, and asking [the individual] to do anything

> tricky, and asking [the individual] to put pictures up on Instagram, and it's really easy isn't it to get your expert to do it, but really important that it's not doing that all the time, you're pushing them and saying you're going to do that, you set that up, you sort that out. So some are more comfortable than others, clearly my younger members of staff it's just how it is. My designers are a bit more of a challenge, my graphic designers, there's four of them, very used to traditional ways of working, so moving them online to much more web and electronic, that's been quite a challenge.

The digital challenges – a summary

- As budgets are cut, the imperative to save money on printed material switching to online communications is clear BUT staff are still needed to run online communications and there are concerns about both having enough resources but also having the skill base necessary
- The question of those residents not online is a continuing issue with many of these being the very residents in need of regular communication – whether they are elderly and so isolated in the community or on low incomes and so reliant on council services
- Where should digital communication be based within a local authority? In a centralised function? In customer care? Within individual services? The need for a clear strategy with these questions answered is facing communication professionals.
- The 24/7 culture places new expectations on councils that are even harder to meet in an economic framework of austerity. Local authorities are not isolated entities and reductions in budgets for other parts of the public sector – police, NHS, voluntary sector – places even further burdens on local authorities with their "statutory" role in focus.
- Loss of control of the 'brand' and reputation of the council – so many more council employees communicating online with the risks of reputational damage on the rise. Meanwhile local authorities are not immune from the 'spin doctors' accusation levelled at central government – particularly when it is central government making the accusation.
- Training staff to deal with the digital era comes across as a priority for all those interviewed.

3 Council publications and regular communication with the communities they serve

Austerity policies and the digital age have brought council publications into focus – partly because they can be expensive and so there are significant savings to be found by alternative methods but partly because the Coalition Government has made "town hall propaganda" one of its key criticisms of local authorities' activities in this area.

Again councils face a dilemma when considering this question. Money can be saved and the shift to online communication is inevitable but council publications have historically been one of the central forms of communication and their potential demise raises questions about how best to retain what they achieved through cheaper digital means.

Council F adopted an interesting approach by continuing to publish a written communication but using a commercial model to maintain it:

> **I've got a copy of your magazine and it is very much citizen focused isn't it?**
>
> It is, there was a complete change around, that paper is toilet paper, it's certainly not glossy, and the devil is in the detail, because I think we're at a time when people will pick up a tiny detail and it will blow up out of what we consider to be all proportion, but that's not the point is it? We have stopped doing a lot of ancillary magazines that we used to have, we used to have one for young people, we used to have one for over 60s – quite infrequent, but again that has gone. It didn't actually cost a lot, we only did it once a year, but again I think a lot of that was about the perception. [The] magazine, it was very well received, people still ask for it, which is good. But what we do still have, which I think a lot of authorities don't have any more, is a council newsletter four times a year which is the one you've got there.
>
> **And the government was quite prescriptive about the frequency of publications, so did that reduce?**
>
> It was six, but actually it had already reduced under the previous administration, it had already gone down to four. So I don't think there was any chance of it going up anyway, so I think this is probably unrelated to the code of local publicity. We call it Eric. So we have retained that, and as you say it's got a completely different focus to the previous newspaper which was much more council focused, very much about council services, quite hard hitting. The new style is softer community focussed, much more services in general not just council services. We don't have many pictures of councillors at all in that.
>
> **Which used to be quite a feature?**
>
> It was, but it became very unpopular, so we took a completely fresh look at that. But even then it's subtler and softer, it still needs to work hard for us, so I think we're very careful that each one has quite tight underpinning messages even though the delivery might be different. It goes door to door, we've reduced that slightly because of the cost of doing it around the borders of [the council area] it costs a lot more, but it reaches 90-odd per cent of people. And we get very few complaints about it, which is a blimmin' miracle actually. And

> we do try and include benefits, like the one you've got in your hand there has got lots of discount vouchers, so we know when we print discount vouchers we get a lot of people ringing up asking for another copy, which is practically unheard of. And certainly as things stand at the moment, we've already cut the [publication] budget last year and the year before in terms of reducing the cost of the actual publication and reducing the boundary distribution, so as far as I'm aware, but you never know in local government what's going to come next, but as far as I'm aware this is not under threat, so the newsletter is not under threat in the next couple of years – I would say certainly between now and the next local election.

While this was unusual to see a printed publication continuing, it was clear that this was only because it had changed emphasis, moving away from being about the council and councillors and more of a local newsletter with discount offers and wider news about what is happening locally. Does this shift, while economically viable, reduce the information given to local residents about the performance and activities of their local council and councillors?

In **Council E's** case, printed publications have gone completely:

> **What actions or measures have you taken to adjust or re-focus your use of resources to prioritise your communications activity?**
>
> We've stopped our city-wide resident newsletter (was 10x per year, then quarterly from 2012) and are about to stop our tenant newsletter.
>
> We introduced a new approach where all council printing had to go through the print room (cracking down on maverick behaviour) and worked with finance to block printing purchase orders being raised with other vendors (saving 750k that first year!); we introduced a message calendar which helps the team determine whether do take on a request from a service or not (i.e. "is it one of our priority messages?") – and this also helps comms planning and reporting with political colleagues; we increased our use of social media, working on a rota basis and are just about to buy an online tool to help us be more slick in this area.

Council A has cut back significantly but still clings on to a small amount of printed material:

> Things like publications, we used to produce, I think at one time they produced ten issues of [one publication], our residents' magazine, a year, when I started it was down to six, but we're now down to two a year, and we do them to fit in with the budget cycle. So we'll do one in November time when we're

consulting on a budget, and we'll do one in Spring once the budget's been settled, just really to communicate to residents what we're spending their money on. They tend to be, obviously there's much more content than that, we talk about all the council services and things that are going on, but the purpose of them is to help with that budget consultation. We actually cover our costs on that, because we do bring in some advertising, mainly for partners, not for commercial, things like health, the police.

Council B's comments reflect on the impact such cutbacks in printed material have had on the commercial sector with the very "competitors" – local newspapers – suffering as revenue from printing council publications diminished:

To go back to the core functions of the team, regarding publications, where was [the council] on that, was [the council] publishing a regular magazine?

Yes it was, and I think that probably when that was happening I'd seen that trend coming through even during the Labour times when I was at [the council] and there was this groundswell, and some of it was coming from the newspapers themselves around the idea that local authorities were competing with newspapers for advertising. Actually I think the experience has been that by councils cutting back on their publications it's actually had an impact on the printing revenue of some of those publishers, because they were being printed by the local papers.

So I could see that wind of change coming through, even before Eric Pickles came in, so I think there was that view that things could be done differently, people were seeing it as propaganda, which in my view I just could never see that, because there was the whole issue around local newspapers geographically their circulation areas never married with those of the local authorities, and I think there was some really good practice at that time where local authorities were publishing publications that had health, police and various partners, we were all working together pretty well to talk to people about their public services and it was a really important tool for the public to know what was going on and being able to access services.

So that's where it was at, I think when Eric Pickles came in that sort of trend became much stronger, it was down to four publications a year. We've stopped, this has been one of my concerns in coming into [the council], no residents survey, no council publication, a website which could be improved, and where are our eyeballs, how are people… and I think the saving grace is that we still have pretty strong media within this area, and focusing on media and social media, we had a major incident, we had a fire at [a local venue], and social media, Twitter, was absolutely critical for keeping people informed, and the media were feeding off that and we're finding new ways. But I still have a concern that by

The rise of public relations   51

> publishing our residents magazine electronically, which has got much reduced circulation, that some of that core business, some of that core information, that if we're going to persuade people to do things differently and manage expectations, and explain the difference between revenue and capital etcetera, that there's a whole area that we're not getting that communications and engagement, and we're missing a trick. But that is very much resource driven.

Finally **Council C**, while adopting a defiant tone, followed the trend of reducing its printed output:

> ### How much have you been affected by Eric Pickles?
>
> We still do a quarterly publication that goes to every household. I think this'll go next year, I think this will be my next budget cut, because it's a painless one I can make.
> Big fat Eric? I don't care anyway, I'd say it to his face [laughs]. It [the magazine] was six times a year in 2010, I think we went quarterly three years ago, as we were into it. And we don't get such a jolly magazine, and also we badge it as a partnership thing rather than a council thing, so it has all our partners in, and advertising, and it's so featurey, we've never had that even when it was six times a year, we never had an issue with it.

Council publications – a summary

- There can be no doubt that Eric Pickles' exhortations have worked in reducing the number of printed council publications based on this sample. The question that has to be asked is whether this is good for local democracy when a council effectively ceases all forms of written communication as one respondent states? The replacement with digital communication can offset this potential accountability deficit but, as previous responses indicated, progress on developing an effective digital set of platforms is at a very early stage for some councils with skills shortages being a significant issue.
- As one respondent put it: "no residents survey, no council publication, a website that could be improved" – where are local people getting their impressions of what local authorities are delivering – or not as the case may be? Could the answer be that, in line with the historical battle between central and local government, central government is quite happy to emasculate local government's ability to voice its case?
- There is some irony in the respondent who commented that the very people who want to see council publications cut back as they see them as a threat to their business – the local press – lose out due to the loss of the printing contract for the council's publications.

4 The relationship for councils with their local media

At the centre of the philosophy of local democracy is the need for politicians – national and local – to be accountable. A central plank to such accountability is that citizens should be informed on how their politicians are acting and be able to hold them to account for their policies and decisions.

For every local authority, this accountability has, in the past, been most often clearly evident in the local media – usually in a local newspaper. However, as this book explores in later chapters, this plank of accountability is under threat – from the budget cuts in communications for local councils and the increasing number of local newspapers that have either closed or dramatically reduced their ability to report local news.

So how has the relationship with the local media fared?

Council F's responses illustrate a wide held concern that cuts to budgets mean the ability of councils to seek to communicate has been diminished and that there is a danger that councils will purely provide reactions to questions. This, of course, begs its own response – who will be asking the questions that allow the electorate to be informed?

> ### How have the cuts been covered in the local media?
>
> It's generally been positive or neutral, amazingly, and I do think that does reflect a lot of the hard work and the lobbying we did with our own politicians in the early days when we could see this juggernaut coming, because it happened at pretty much the same time as we got a new completely different Labour administration, they pretty much copped for it. Because although the previous administration had been salami slicing basically, they had been tackling it, but the big stuff arrived when the new administration arrives, so we got in there pretty early and we gave our best advice which was to be open and honest and get it all out there, and work as much as you can with the media, get them in, and we've had several media conferences which have been well attended. We use that sparingly obviously, because of who we are and where we are we don't want to drag the media up in the hope of some massive announcement when there isn't, so we've got to be quite careful. But I think since the beginning of austerity we've probably had three well attended media conferences, and generally the coverage has been very balanced. We have quite a bit of TV because [the council] is a bit of a funny one in terms of media, we're a bit of a jigsaw puzzle, and the [local newspaper] has definitely been more critical of us over the last two or three years. But generally not about the cuts, which is interesting, other stuff, more trivial stuff if you like. But the other thing about the [local newspaper] is that they've pretty much crunched themselves down to [the local area] now, so for example you can't buy the [local newspaper] in [the local area], I think it goes about as far as [the local area boundary] now and that's it, there's a cut off. It's very city focused. It doesn't

mean they don't cover us, but they tend to prefer the negative stuff, I completely get it. [The council] has been in a mess for a couple of years, we keep thinking what's next? And I think from the beginning certainly in terms of austerity that's been one of our key messages, because it's true, because otherwise you wouldn't be saying it, is that actually [the council] is not in meltdown, we've got good financial management but we have to make these cuts, we have no choice. So that's always been one of the underpinning messages, it's not a crisis, but we've got a very hard job ahead of us. But I think certainly in terms of priorities inevitably our big priority has been around cuts to services, explaining that as best we can.

What broader impact do you think any budget cuts have had on external perceptions of the organisation – have you done any evidence gathering?

No, we don't have anything. We haven't done, apart from the citizens' panel, but that tends to be one-off questions about particular services usually, we haven't done any polling or any research at all.

What's your greatest concern about the ongoing impact of any budget cuts on the work of your team and their ability to keep local people informed?

I think my biggest concern is about becoming primarily reactive, and to me that's not communications, it's not what we should be doing. It's part of what we should be doing, but I think with a team of eight or nine for such a vast authority I think it's inevitable that we will be dealing with the main priority, which will be explaining the cuts. And I think much of the rest of the stuff will be reactive. It's almost going back to the press office model isn't it, I hope we won't get there, and we'll certainly fight against it as much as we can. And I think we are in a more fortunate position in that, fortunate or unfortunate depends on how you look at it, in that [the council] is not massively under the media spotlight, because most of the papers are weeklies, and most of them have got one editor running about four of them and three staff working on six of them, there isn't the level of in depth scrutiny that some places will be facing. But nonetheless we do have more than our fair share of trivial enquiries that can often take as long to deal with definitely. And because the other thing is that we also manage reactive and proactive social media, and obviously that side of things is increasing, which is a good thing because it costs us nothing, but on the other hand you need people, it doesn't run itself, and it does bite back. And that's been one of our points in arguing for a level of protection over the next year in terms of who's in staff, it will affect our social media as well. Surprise surprise, there's a real human behind it, it doesn't run itself! [laughs]

Council E spells out the concern that just as councils have cut back their resources, the media have been doing likewise:

> **What impact have any budget cuts had on your relationships with local, regional and sector media contacts and coverage?**
>
> The media's own budget cuts have made far more of a difference – with the exception of one new FM station for [the area] which has just started, the local/regional media now seem to have fewer reporters, a greater number of junior roles, and are managed more remotely. This means some of our broadcast features don't make the cut (BBC and ITV reporters cover such a large patch, we may be competing with places over 80 miles away) and local print journalists may have less time to focus on each piece.

Council A's comments reflect the increasing "oven ready" PR approach where councils know that, due to the reduction in reporters, they can place their material in their local media without too much journalistic scrutiny:

> **What kind of relationship have you got with your local media, and how has that changed over the last five-year period?**
>
> We have a very positive relationship with the local media, it's a healthy relationship, they hold us to account, they challenge us, but we can have constructive conversations with them and the editors are very responsive to that. They've changed enormously from when I started here, Trinity Mirror Group who have the [first local newspaper] and the [second local newspaper], when I started here there were effectively two newsrooms with two editors running two papers with distinct characters. That's all gone, they've now got a single editor across those titles and other titles in the group, [the area] as well. And there's a single newsroom, they've moved to a digital first editorial approach where everything goes online first rather than in the printed paper, which is effectively secondary to their website which has a massive following.
>
> To some extent, newspapers are a secondary by-product of their online operations, and that's how they're acting. What they haven't been able to do is quite figure out how to monetise that and make it work for them commercially. They're surviving rather than thriving I would say, we'd see them as a partner, we'd share concern about that, we see them as important in terms of plurality, it's an important part of holding local authorities to account. Their staffing is significantly down on what it was, they've got a lot of quite inexperienced journalists now as well. And if I'm being cynical and selfish it means I can get more or less anything in the paper unadulterated, I can get first person pieces in from members unadulterated, so from my cynical PR perspective it's a bit of an open goal, because they're desperate for content and we're very happy to give them content.

> I would say that they are still good at holding us to account and letting us know when things have gone wrong, journalistic integrity is still there, and we do have occasional stand-ups and that sort of thing, and it's a healthy debate. But I wouldn't say we fall out, if I think they've got something wrong I'll say "I think you've got something wrong", and by and large they'll listen. But it's far easier now to get your stuff in a paper than it ever was, there's not much selling involved in trying to do that. In terms of broadcast media there's [a local newspaper] and BBC in the city, seem to be reasonably healthy, and again they're on a skeleton staffing, and they struggle to get to things which we think are important. There's not a lot I can do about that, it's not lack of will, they just haven't got the people to get to things.
>
> Apart from the BBC always send three people out to anything, that's always been the case, I go a long way back in local government, the BBC have always been over staffed, they've always confused matters because you've never been sure which bit of the BBC you've been talking to, it's always been like that and I've always felt it's been profligate.

Council B reflects that the local media still has influence but warns that the commercial picture may erode that further over time:

> **In the five year period do you think there's been a shift away from the importance of local media?**
>
> My gut reaction is that they've still got huge influence. It's always said that they've got an influence beyond their readership, they all feed off each other don't they, so if something breaks in the [local newspaper] or [the local radio station] or even nationally, everything follows it. So I know when the [local nightclub] fire took place we were trending on Twitter, and that was because people were starting to have conversations digitally, so the digital side of it was important, but I think that possibly some of it started through the media. People were noticing it so the media feed off the media, it's quite difficult to know, I suppose you can track it through things like Hootsuite and things like that, but the influence side of it in terms of reputation I think members will still always be very precious about what's published in the media, and it's about what they feel about the council's reputation. And that's important because they're key stakeholders. Equally the employees, it's always said if you've got internal messages you shouldn't read about it first in the local media, but they are going to be reading the media and it will have an impact about how they feel about the council and the issues. So I do think they're still really really important, but I do think there is other power out there, I think where it is different in terms of relationship is that most councils have cut back on their advertising, there's interesting stuff going on with statutory notices in Scotland, and again that's a debate to be had. We were the whipping boy in terms of lost

> revenue, although it was probably actually estate agents and car dealers that were taking their advertising around, but if you think about, I know probably going back about 10 years ago now, how many recruitment adverts, at that time I was in [the council area] and the [local newspaper] the Thursday paper was packed with council and public sector recruitment adverts – a) we're recruiting fewer people, b) it's all gone digital, so I think that relationship, that money side of it, and then of course you've got to think about the residents' magazines and newspapers that were published through them, so they're doing pretty well to hang on in the current climate I think.

Council C's comments reveal that councillors are still very concerned with what appears in the local media and puts an emphasis on this. But the local media itself is an ever-changing beast with the agendas of individual journalists being important in how their publication or programme covers the council:

> **In terms of the local media, how has that relationship changed over the last five or six years?**
> We have a good and positive one with them on the whole, we have BBC [region] which is as shambolically run as every BBC local radio station in that the afternoon show rings up about stories that are on in the morning, they have a newsy [who] does the breakfast show, quite focused, newsy, bright, it's quite assertive, it's reached the stage where the local hospital won't go on breakfast in the morning, but it sometimes feels like we service that show entirely. So [this journalist] who runs the news desk up there will be on this afternoon, it'll have happened about an hour ago, when they've had their story planning at the BBC they'll be on the phone three or four reporters wanting stories for breakfast and planning. So we always try and do it, we always try and avoid no comment or empty chairing, usually we manage that, so they like us for that. When we have big things like [a communications project] we did loads of briefing, loads of stuff pre-embargo and all that kind of stuff.
>   Same with the [local newspaper] who we on the whole have a quite robust but good relationship with, quite an ambitious political editor who is now the chief reporter, so he's the chief reporter and the political editor so that's really easy for him to come out to cabinet meetings when he's chief reporter. He's quite sharp, has lots of contacts, gets regular leaks from members that are managed, but on the whole, you know we fall out and members get really pissed off, we still have to have conversations with members about not having rows with reporters on Twitter. And then we have a weekly paper as well that's a freesheet that has a journalist on it that dislikes the Leader and the Chief Executive and me as well, so he has a go when he can, but that's kind of a personal thing that he's got, but it's only a freesheet. Midlands Today and

Central, but Midlands Today maybe once or twice a week there's a [council] story on there so we have quite good relationships as well with our local reporters, and do off the record stuff. My members would say the [name of local newspaper] always gives us a kicking and they're unfair to us, but a lot of the time when you look at it it's because there's been a, y'know.

How much importance do elected members put on the local paper?

Too much, and probably less than the local radio, the Leader's very good and she listens to [the local radio station] every morning, I think the others for some reason or whatever reason take less notice of the [local newspaper], which was enormously powerful even when I came to work here it was selling 80,000 copies a day, so it has a big history of everyone used to take the [local newspaper], and members are very sensitive to it, always wanting rebuttal letters.

Do you have a view at the local level about the BBC and local newspapers, and the idea that they're sucking local media dry?

I can't see that, and I started my career as a local newspaper reporter. The BBC would just swan up and swan around saying "we're the BBC" which was intensely irritating when you work for a local newspaper, but the BBC local website is shit, the [local newspaper] is great, it's got every local story you want on there. BBC news website is never going to compete, so. . . . I don't know, the BBC are quite interesting, we're managing the Syrian refugees issue majorly here at the moment, we have had a third of all Syrian refugees over the past two years have come to [the area] because we've got this special Home Office scheme where people at particular risk are coming here. So for the past two weeks we've had probably twelve different parts of the BBC chasing us for interviews with refugees you have to manage very carefully, and at one stage we said to one of them please can you organise this all, "yeah, we'll organise it", and you do, I don't want to be miserable about the BBC, because I love it very much, but that kind of lax organisation, seventeen people chasing the same story, when I think actually can't I just give it to [name of BBC programme] and they can do everything else with it.

Relationship with local media – summary

- The question as to how local residents know what their local council is doing on their behalf is also an issue for the local media
- The period of austerity has coincided with a dramatic period of challenge for local papers – and in some cases – local broadcast media as well

- The relationship with local papers is patchy with some being on good terms with their local council and others being hostile – in some cases in comes down to the attitude on one journalist as local papers cut back on staffing as well
- As councils cut back on consultation mechanisms such as citizens' panels with these becoming one-offs on particular, strategic issues such as the overall budget, are local residents getting a view from the local media as to what individual services are doing on their behalf?
- Local media is stretched itself by loss of advertising putting a squeeze on resources. This has undoubtedly led to less scrutiny being focused on local authorities.
- With the exception, in some councils, of the regional BBC network, the media is "surviving rather than thriving . . . we see them as important in terms of plurality. It's an important part of holding authorities to account" as one respondent put it.
- With cutbacks in evidence in the local media, less experienced journalists are being employed with less knowledge and so a diminished ability to root out the stories that hold councils to account.
- This leads to a PR-isation of local media "we can get more or less anything in the paper unadulterated". Council communicators do not welcome this but councillors and council staff continue to see local papers as important and so there is no agenda for the local press to be ignored.

5 The impact of austerity on effective consultation with local communities?

Consultation is at the heart of the local democracy conundrum. If the day-to-day coverage of the local media is diminishing and a council's communications function is being cut back, what is happening to the important area of consulting local citizens? Regular elections provide the fulcrum of local democracy but how do citizens know what their elected representatives are doing on their behalf and are they consulted when major changes or decisions are made?

Council F demonstrates a continuing commitment to the principle of consultation but raises the question as to what should be consulted on and how within the changing communication landscape.

Do you evaluate people's perceptions, or how effective your publication has been?

Yeah, it's a little hit and miss, we use everything we can get our hands on, but no sort of paid… so we use citizens' panel, and we use other sort of metrics like number of visits to the website and when we use a QR code, so for each one we have a list. And the citizens' panel works quite well for us, in terms of perceptions – it's about 800 so it's quite extensive, it's shared with the districts so we put fairly regular questions in there. I mean they are people who've self-selected, but it's run by our policy team so they try and make it as representative as possible. They tend to be a bit more interested than your average person, but they're a fairly good barometer. They're also as likely to be critical I think as anybody else [laughs].

Have you been able to consult local people and the media on the impact of any budget cuts?

We have put a lot of thought and effort into the budget cuts, that's been our priority for the last two years, trying to get that right. So we, all the budget cuts have been branded The [publication] with a strapline of 'Making difficult decisions together', trying to make it as engaging and consultative as we possibly can, when you are basically taking people's services away from them. So we've worked across the board really, we've worked very closely with services. Each cut is completely different, and has a completely different audience, there have been hardly any cuts to universal services. So you're looking at for example some very niche services for perhaps a couple of hundred families with severely disabled children, who are going to get a 50 per cent reduction in the short breaks budget. There's only 200 of them but to them it's a massive impact on their lives. So for example for something like that we will do it very closely with the team that knows them best, they know that audience, we would never presume to know so we would work closely with them to develop material, still under the [council] theme so that there's consistency there, develop materials for them, for the young people themselves, whilst we'd still do the media stuff around that so we're not trying to bury it, but really our main audience would be those 200 families, and looking at their needs so that they can meaningfully take part in the consultation. And as a result, the plans change, the cut didn't change, and we didn't claim it ever would, the amount of money that was going, but the way that we did things, so that particular example we've gone out three times for consultation to those roughly 200 people because things have changed every time.

But then for example we've had other ones around more mass market things like school crossing patrols, we've done a lot of work around that, but each one has a different audience, so we've looked very much from who is the audience for this consultation and how can they access it. For example we're doing one at the moment around community transport, well the majority of the people who use community transport funnily enough are on a bus [laughs], and whilst that consultation will be online, of course it will, because there will be lots of other interested stakeholders, but the main stakeholders are the people sat on the bus so we've done a paper copy and put some pens on the buses, and encouraged the drivers to collect them up. So each one has been different but with common messaging all the way through, so all our comms team who've been involved with it, all the consultation to start with, a common set of messaging, there's a microsite around it which explains the background to the cuts.

The complexity of consultation is an important issue with cuts to some services being about a small but vulnerable group of residents. The danger of assuming that consultation is just about a big survey or getting views from the local media is one that is highlighted.

On the specific issues of cuts to services **Council E's** response indicates that consultation has not been as effective as it would have liked:

> **Have you been able to consult local people and media on the impact of any budget cuts? If so how and when and what were the results?**
>
> The changes to communications were included as part of the general budget consultation in that year – didn't set the world alight. We do have citizen user groups including a group that checks our communications annually for accessibility. They've been supportive of a greater use of online material in general.

Council A has clearly fought hard to maintain a level of consultation:

> **You mentioned the council publication which is two times a year around publication, what about the broader consultation that the council has participated in in the past? How much has the relationship with your key stakeholders been affected in terms of consultation?**
>
> Moving to a business critical level we've included consultation within that, I personally feel very strongly that, whilst we've got diminishing resources it's never been more important for us to communicate. There's that much change going on in terms of the services people experience, the relationship that the public will have with their council, the decisions that we're making, there's a huge amount of change. And we have to have sufficient capacity to be able to tell people about that engage people in that, let people have their say about that, so that's still a very important part of what we do. And obviously the kind of democratisation that happens with more digital channels is helping us with that, and some of the more traditional, we've got an approach here called [a project], which was developed, which was all about trying to engage people in the way in which they want to be engaged with, rather than imposing some strange council bureaucratic approach.
>
> So we have a [project] that we've got an online forum that's doing consultation, we do a lot of public events, community events, which are not sort of town halls where somebody gets up and shouts, and the person who shouts loudest gets what they want. It's more about facilitating engagement, and helping everybody in a room get to have their say and make their contribution. So we've got a very active approach to consultation and

engagement, the budget consultation we did three years ago, we did our first big austerity budget for three years, a long term, medium term view, three years' worth of cuts effectively. We had 50,000 responses to that consultation exercise, and normally a budget consultation you're lucky if you get over 1000 normally. So that was a big, big exercise, and it got a lot of people angry, and I think a lot of people exercised about things they were going to lose, but that was exactly what they wanted to do. We wanted to make people aware that these things were at risk, and that they should have a say, and that they should get angry, and they should voice their concerns. Similarly, our local plan, we did our local plan and we had 25,000 responses to that consultation, it's because these things are contentious but you've got to explain them, and be honest about them for people to be able to have their say. So the local plan, we were starting to eat into the green belt to accommodate our future housing need, and that provoked a lot of interest as well. But it's enabling that to happen, and capturing the feedback, and responding to it which is really, really important. And we can't let that go, when we talk about business critical, these are the business critical things that a comms team for the council has to be able to facilitate.

And elected members, they've been supportive of that? Do they recognise the need to keep communication, that during a time of huge change you've got to consult, got to communicate?

It's because effectively we had a 50 per cent cut, members kind of nodded that through without really thinking through the consequences initially, and subsequently I've had a bizarre situation to be in – I'm implementing the cut they're asking me to make, and then I was being challenged about why I was doing it, and why we were cutting back communications. . . . so, because you told me to [laughs]. So it's been of a bit of a strange situation, and yes they are supportive, they kind of realise that they need this stuff, and they are supportive. I think I wouldn't get away scot free, but I've got an understanding for the next three years that we are at rock bottom, and minimum credible means minimum credible. As I say, I won't get away scot free, but I won't get another 50 per cent taken away. I'm touching wood as I say that, but . . .

There's no low hanging fruit, I mean where we're looking at now is care services, and the worry that we've got when we're getting to that kind of sector is that when you stop cutting the grass, or you stop picking up the litter, lots of people make a lot of noise about it. But when you start having an impact on care, these are people who don't normally complain or they're kind of unheard, so we have a concern about that as well I think. You don't get the same kind of outcry as if we threatened to close the City Hall or the city pool, there'd be petitions from around the country. [People in care] are relatively small in number, but the consequences are enormous.

While **Council B** reflects that consultation has suffered as part of the austerity cut backs:

> **And in your experience, how effective are councils being in communicating with communities about the impact of cuts and in consultation?**
>
> I think there's been some really good practice and I think in some areas those things are working really well.
>
> **This responsibility for consultation falls on the communications team so is this an additional workload?**
>
> I think that's an interesting one, and there was a survey recently by the Local Government Association, and one of the things they noted was, and this has happened here in [the council], is that residents surveys that used to be part of the bread and butter really, again that's one of the areas that has had the chop. And I think the big issue for us in communications is knowing where the eyeballs are in terms of where should we be putting our communication resources, and what are the key priorities for the public. Now, we can pick some of that now through website digital customer contact, members contact etc., but we no longer have a residents survey, again that's a cutback. And the consultation side of things, certainly here, is done through a different area, but my experience is that there isn't as much consultation going on – we support the things that we need to, so we've got a boundary review commission going on at the moment, so the things that are statutorily required etc. but I think there are so many changes, and so many big things happening that the consultation side of it perhaps isn't supported as much as it might have been in previous years.

Consultation is one of the casualties of cuts with digital changes expected to pick up in this area without the necessary expertise being in place

Council C's comments reflect that councillors themselves are learning as they go along about the new political imperative of trying to consult on the major changes they are having to make.

> **What about things like public consultation exercises, have they suffered in terms of numbers?**
>
> Yes, the amount of money, but we just had a big engagement programme on the combined authority, because it was so controversial here members got a bit anxious about it, and suddenly said you can have up to £250,000, I ended up spending 60 I think on engagement [laughs]. So we had drop in sessions, we had

online forums, we had citizens' panel, that was expensive, that was 30,000, we had press releases, we had social media, we reached half a million people through Twitter, we did some ward forums which are our traditional evening ward sessions with councillors and leaflets, we produced some posters to advertise the drop in sessions and so on, because the subject matter was so dry we didn't get great reactions. But we did that whole range of things, that included social media.

One of the things we've discovered, the live online forums are quite powerful, but the software we have doesn't really allow for live chat because you can't follow threads, as the web editor says it's like being at a party where you're trying to follow everyone's conversations in the room. So we need to refine all of that, but actually that engagement programme, it was probably on the wrong subject, it was only done because the councillors were anxious about people calling for a referendum, was quite helpful for us to understand what engagement works best with local people these days.

In the context of what you said earlier on about cuts, how important do you think members will see the kind of engagement and consultation that you're talking about?

I think they're just beginning to see how important that is, so this community engagement piece we want to do in the Autumn I think will be really important we get that right, then members can start to see that actually communities have brilliant ideas about doing it, and actually are sensible and get it. But you need that two-way conversation dialogue, it isn't about broadcast any more, it's about conversation.

Do you think that message about two-way conversations has finally got across?

Yeah, I think it's also about us, members are very swayed by what the local paper says, so we had an example where we cut a service that supports disabled people back into work, hugely expensive because of the bespoke service, and the decision was taken to cut the service rather than to think about better ways of delivering it, and it was flawed all the way along. But there was such a furore in the local paper that the Leader has now said that service is not going, we're here to protect the most vulnerable, we're a Labour council, I'm not going to let that service be cut. In fact there was probably another better way to deliver it, and it was officers' fault that we didn't work that through, but by having those conversations with communities hopefully then members understand that actually it's not hugely helpful to do whoever shouts the loudest will change the decision about, and I think because traditionally the media has been so important that has been their default position. So it's about changing the relationship I think.

Consultation – a summary

- Increasingly councils are consulting more narrowly on specific issues – particularly budget cuts – and less on council wide consultations to measure progress on priorities
- Where consultation on wider programmes of cuts has taken place, there needs to be more community engagement and understanding of the nature and impact of these cuts
- Question of who shouts loudest raised – the example given of when litter is not picked up or grass not cut, general outcry ensued but cuts to more sensitive areas such as social care don't get the same level of noise as they affect a smaller group of people who often struggle to have their voice heard
- This raises the difficult question as to who is listened to the most and which channels or platforms of communication produce the most democratic results in terms of capturing a true picture of local residents' views – as one respondent put it, "it isn't about broadcast anymore, it's about conversation" but conversation with who and how is the challenge
- These questions go directly to the core of the issue of accountability – who to consult, when and how on which issues and at which times? As one respondent suggested, when huge changes/cuts are being made, consultation is more important than ever

6 Partnerships and the private sector and ways of sharing and saving resources?

One approach which has been adopted by many local authorities has been to move towards a partnership model with other public bodies such as the police and NHS – and through regional devolution with other local authorities. Such partnerships can yield shared resources with the inevitable budgetary savings that follow. But has such an approach diluted the ability of councils to communicate and consult when such complex arrangements lead to a whole new set of accountabilities? It is also clear from some of the responses that rather than better communications and accountability being the impetus, the driver for these changes has been the need to save money.

The experiences of **Council F** demonstrate that while this may improve working between different councils, it is neither easy to explain or simple to deliver.

What impact have any budget cuts had on your relationships with local regional and sector media contacts and coverage?

I'm not sure it's had a massive impact, because I think when we can we do prioritise media, so they generally will get their answer. I'd be surprised if they had seen much difference, I think generally we have had good feedback from having a static news desk, when we first started off we were rotating all the

> time, now we've got two permanent members of staff, so I'd be interested to know, but I don't think it has had a massive impact, and actually in some ways it might even be positive because we've actually got real news now, because for many years we weren't really interesting, we just got on with stuff and there were very few negative stories until about three or four years ago. The cuts are hard news, and we're getting them in, and also quite a lot of the issues that we've got at the moment are quite complex, we've got combined authority and devolution and they're big and they're coming but they're actually really boring for most people, and complex. And obviously there's a lot of public affairs involved in that as well. So certainly with the larger media players we have been spending quite a lot of time with them trying to get them to understand, briefings and off the record things, just to help them to understand the impact, what it is and what it isn't, what devolution could mean.
>
> At the moment we're looking at a combined [area] devolution deal, which when it was first announced was really interesting, but now because of the internal machinations of ministers coming up and talking to council leaders, and it's really really boring for most normal people, but it is a very significant thing for the council. And likewise a combined authority which would be working with all the districts in [the area] which are part of the devolution deal, see even I can't explain it very well, but the local media need to understand it because it is going to be quite significant. So I think in terms of that we've actually had closer relationships with some of the key players, because they've actually needed a level of explanation that perhaps they've not needed in the past. So I would say probably no major impact, but in some ways perhaps even positive, but we've had to talk to them more, you can't just assume you can put out a press release about some lovely thing we're doing and they'll just print it, so it's perhaps a bit more complex.

And **Council E** shows that the complexities of these partnerships cannot always be overcome but they tend to be driven by efficiency and budget savings with the implications for accountability rarely mentioned.

> **Have you been encouraged to restructure as an income generating team and if so how and towards what kind of model? Have you been encouraged to consider or act to merge communications resources with other organisations and public sector agencies? If so how, when and what new model is emerging?**
>
> These were models I looked into when proposing the centralisation of the team in 2010/11. All teams going through the value for money exercise had to do so. We explored what it would be to become a social enterprise (rejected as we felt the new model meant we had little time spare to pick up other people's

> work, and council work may suffer as a result). We asked other public sector comms teams within [the area] whether they would be keen to merge, specifically police, fire and health. The police were mid-way through their own exercise which led to their comms team being regionalised (they work for the whole Thames valley region and not just [the area] these days) which didn't work for us – fire were too small to make a difference – and health were about to split into clinical commissioning group and other teams, and it felt the wrong time for them. We also lightly explored options with two other nearby councils, but it struck me that unless the councils were merging, there wouldn't be much of a saving as the same amount of work would still need to be done.

So partnerships and mergers may seem an attractive option in saving money but "the work would still need to be done" brings into question whether worthwhile savings can be achieved while still maintaining the quality of the communications.

For **Council A** a similar story with efficiency and savings the catalyst but some recognition of the need for any such move to be controlled locally rather than imposed by central government diktat.

> ### How important have partners become?
>
> We have good working relationships with all our partners, I wouldn't say we've got anything closer than that though. We do do some joint projects and that sort of thing, but there isn't any integration as such between different organisations. I can't think of anywhere where we've moved to a point where we're sharing teams or sharing people, and personally I think that's probably, if I was asked "what will you do next for more efficiency?" I would probably struggle to think of anything else other than we'd have to move towards greater integration with partners.
>
> ### Is devolution on the agenda for you?
>
> We've got an active live, very live negotiation going on with the Treasury at the moment, and we're probably days away from a devolution deal, hopefully, fingers crossed. What that will mean, the way that works at the moment, we've got seven authorities as part of that combined authority, we work together on that, we lead on our portfolio is transport, so we lead on all transport communication. [The council] coordinate the corporate combined authority communication, and the other portfolios [the council] lead on inward investment, [the council] lead on skills, so there's that kind of division of work, and we talk to each other and have protocols for how we work like that. That works ok, I mean whether the devolution deal wasn't there we'd change that, we'd move toward greater integration, we'd have to see.

> **How much of that do you think has been driven by issues around democracy and Northern Powerhouse initiatives from the government, and how much of that has been driven by just the need to actually recognise that local government can no longer continue in its current model, it has to start getting into more integrated partnerships of this nature?**
>
> I think that's right, the partnership itself isn't the solution, it's what you're actually doing with that partnership, and what functions, what's the substance of the deal rather than what's the governance of the deal is what's important to us. So I think taking ownership for things, and taking local responsibility for things, it's going to come with a cut, it's almost inevitable, these things are going to come with less money. But at least we've got control over that, and we can come up with local solutions rather than feel that we've got them imposed on us. And that's the opportunity I guess, nobody's going into this thinking we're just going to get all the cash from Whitehall and be immune from any further... y'know, that's just not going to happen.

There is some irony in seeing devolution being pressed by central government yet so much of what local authorities deliver is being centralised as part of cost cutting measures. For partnerships to work – whether in one specific area or as part of devolution, the evidence suggests that this may create more work rather than less which will present a challenge with already reduced resources.

There is also little or no focus on retaining or improving accountability – the NHS, the Police and, indeed, each local authority can and will have very different approaches and cultures around accountability. The key questions about how the public who are the recipients of services experience these changes and benefit from them is not at the top of the agenda.

Council B's experience further bears out the dilemma of how to raise money or cut costs and still retain an element of control and accountability.

> **Has [the council] had a significant shift towards income generation?**
>
> Yes, basically we have areas of the team that are funded, for instance public health, that side of it, we've got a member of the communications team who is employed by [the body], which is the regeneration arm, and although he's working within the team he's actually funded elsewhere. And I think there's all sorts of appetite for collaborative arrangements and funding coming in. For me the dilemma is we could take on additional work but if we take on additional work there has to be people and funding to support that.
>
> So collaborative working with other local authorities, or with the health sector is a great idea as long as there are the staff there to do it. And I think

> that's where the challenge lies, because everybody can see it as a potential saving and that's where the income generation would come in, we're also looking at say, advertising on roundabouts and signage, that sort of thing. But I think those sort of things traditionally the issue is how much does it cost to support a member of staff to do that work, equally advertising on the websites is another area we're looking at at the moment that traditionally we've avoided because we've not wanted people to be distracted by commercial advertising, but there's now a public sector local authority focused organisation out there that's managing that, that we may well decide to go along with.
>
> **Have any of the core posts here been funded by generating income by selling the services they offer?**
>
> No, it might be an idea, but I think to do that you've got to have the right skills in place, and my concern would be you'd have to have capacity there and if you were going to sell to other organisations you'd have to know the council itself wasn't going to be suffering because it didn't have the support it needed. And because of the capacity issues at the moment I wouldn't be comfortable with that. I would say that it has been looked at, it's there that's something that's an aspiration, but in my time that I've been here it hasn't been a priority. Posts have been funded through other ways, there's the police and crime panel as well, and we provide support, and that's manageable. To take it beyond that I think would take it to breaking point I think if I'm honest.

Income generation is being prioritised but, as the respondent states, this in itself has to be resourced properly if the benefits of income generation are going to be realised.

For **Council D** the question is not whether but how this will progress with a significant question about how individual, discrete client groups can be reached by different council departments and different partners and still achieve a seamless and coherent approach.

> **Which takes me onto partnership working, how much have you seen a change in the last 5–10 years in partnership working?**
>
> Just as an example, we have 42,000 tenants, and we provide a regular newsletter which we're slowly replacing with an email version to 42,000 tenants. The crossover for that group of customers with some of the public health messaging ought to be fairly obvious, and I suspect if I were to ask colleagues in public health where are your key audiences they will tell you quite often it's people with tenancies.

You mentioned you work with schools?

Yeah, we have Service Level Agreements with a bunch of them, largely around crisis comms. One of the things we've been doing as a tactical thing rather than anything very important, as I arrived the authority was about to get rid of its contract with a thing called Gov Delivery which allows for emails, and the reason I like it, to go back to the beginning of our conversation is that it allows customers to sign up for information on topics they're interested in. When we brought it in there were about 370 different topics, which tells its own story, because that's actually about an organisation that's building things in because they think it's interesting for them, because nobody gives a toss about that sort of stuff. So it was a rebuild, and we did some research through customer services, we did a test with the existing users, we got that down to about 14, but we've left in place an account for each of the local schools and they're increasingly using that, and that's just a neat thing. So the school newsletter can be sent by way of an email to parents if parents have signed up for it. We found it very useful in the winter, because we did all the joining up stuff so schools who use it can put the name of the school 'closed because of severe weather' in the header, and explanation in the body of the email, send that to parents but automatically that will update the council's Twitter feed. So if you see on Twitter you'll get the same headline and you'll know, so joining up that kind of comms. And I think there is something about the way that schools, so we've attempted to make that proactive comms, and we've certainly offered schools support around the more proactive communications planning. Not very many of them have taken us up on that, it's the crisis comms where we tend to secure the contracts because they feel vulnerable, and it doesn't take much and schools are in the news, so we provide support to those, but we have made that offer around more proactive comms planning and around the use of social media and electronic stuff to communicate.

So back to the partnership, there's obviously partnership internally and partners outside?

Increasingly so, I suspect that is what it looks like in the future. We're currently looking as an authority at the rebuild of the website, and alongside that the intranet site, I don't believe in websites, I tend very much to the Government Digital Services view of this, that we need to be building online services and not websites. And I think if you take that approach, when you start to think that the customers don't really care who provides things, you end up you need your customers to be served on the basis that we have an understanding who they are as individuals and families, that we understand as an individual or as a family they might have very different requirements to people who live half a mile away, but actually have different availability of resources because of where they live. So I think you can take a more personal and place based approach to

> the presentation of online services, and once you do that, reporting racist graffiti doesn't come to the council, reporting antisocial behaviour doesn't come to the council, but it can be a presentation of those services in a place based way. And getting those partners into that place based approach is going to be critical, and we're seeing that now in there's almost a public service reform.

The compartmentalised nature of local government means that there may be different communication solutions for different groups of residents who are receiving services. The point about similar audience for tenants and public health issues may be well made but can the silo nature of public services ever be broken down to allow this kind of joined up communication to take place?

Council C's responses indicate an even wider set of potential relationships and the challenging agenda this creates if partners are at odds on any aspect of activity.

> **Who are the main partners you see as being not just stakeholders, but partners you want to work with?**
>
> There's reshaping going on about the partnership at the moment which I think is quite interesting. So Clinical Commissioning Group, the Partnership Trust and the Acute Trust for Hospitals, they're three branches of health. [The local] Police, to a lesser extent the fire and ambulance, they're less on the ball than the police and health. And our two universities are really important to us. And [name] housing, which is the [name] because we sold off the housing before I came here. So those are the key partners.
>
> **[The local] police have been very vocal about how they're suffering under the cuts, is that something that you see as partnership territory if you like?**
>
> At the moment we're just talking about going out and doing a big engagement exercise this Autumn and we'll have people like the police with us when we go and talk to communities and do some quite interesting things, we're talking to Demsoc at the moment about some citizens panels at the moment where we say what if we all just disappeared tomorrow, what would you do in your area? So there's been quite a lot of media locally about police station closures in [the area] which are difficult to manage, and the local BBC station has got a thing about the police not turning up to crimes any more, all that kind of narrative that you'll have seen all over the place. So they're very focused on doing something positive around that.

Partnerships and devolution – summary

- Devolution through working in conjunction with a number of councils and increased working with partner public sector bodies such as police, NHS and fire services are on the agenda but there is no great shift towards this on a grand scale – more a piecemeal approach where either central government dictates or local relationships make it possible.
- Revenue through income generation such as advertising is on the list of possible ways to offset the impact of budget reductions but the most important consideration appears to be savings not accountability.
- There is some potential for greater joined up thinking – and delivery – of communications/consultation when dealing with the same groups of residents but from different service departments.
- Meanwhile the conversion of many schools to academies has moved them outside the remit of some councils' communications and they are being treated as potential clients to buy in services such as crisis communications.
- This raises a wholly separate question, not specifically addressed in this research, as to how this informal internal market operates. Public money being shifted from one organisation to another along with resources or, in the case of schools, from the public sector into a quasi private sector where academy chains are established to secure a profit.
- The accountability for this public money and how it is spent is not addressed here but raises many questions about what has happened to accountability for one of the largest areas of activity for local authorities – education – and its disappearance from the accountability map.

Which introduces the final area of questioning of local government communication professionals – local democracy and accountability.

7 The impact of austerity on local democracy and local accountability

Council A's response yields a highly practical and pragmatic approach but also raises the important issue of exclusion.

Are there elements of the population that you serve that you think are being disenfranchised by a race towards digital?

I think there's always that risk, and I wouldn't pretend that risk doesn't exist, but I think for too long we've used that as an excuse for not being digital, and it's become a reason not to do it, rather than concentrating on the 90 per cent of people who are online. The problem with digital exclusion is that if we don't get our service offer right digitally, we're excluding 90 per cent of the population, and that would be a criminal thing. And we shouldn't use the other side of

> digital exclusion as an excuse for not doing it. What we need to do then is make sure that we're not excluding people, we find other ways of helping people.
>
> Our approach to that where it's possible, and it's not always possible, is to help people become digital themselves, because if we're doing that we're improving their own abilities to connect with the world, because that's the way the world operates now. Our approach shouldn't be 'oh don't worry about that, here's another way of doing it', to most people the approach should be 'let's help you get online'. That's where we're putting a lot of our effort as a council, I wouldn't say that's my area of responsibility, but as a council that's where we're putting a lot of effort.
>
> There will always be people who are excluded, but when you start getting down to it people who would access it in different ways, we're in touch with them in many other ways anyway, we're probably caring for them, or have some contact with them in other more direct ways. There's different ways of engaging with those people because they're part of our direct clients if you like, that we're talking to in lots of ways.

This offers an interesting idea around how councils might help those who are not online to do so. If a council wants a common approach to communication and consultation, it may, as this respondent suggest, need to invest in helping people with their digital capacity. At a time of budget reductions, this will be a challenge.

For **Council B** the issue of electoral registration and electoral engagement are raised with the inevitable question of the engagement of different age groups with democracy being aired. The move to digital should, logically, increase engagement with the under 35s but there is the much wider question as to whether local councils, and what they deliver, is relevant and of interest to anyone in that age demographic. And so the wider issue of democratic engagement is central to this question.

> When we talk about local media, the profile of audience tends to be older, but young people are not engaging politically with the democratic process. In a sense there's an imbalance there.
>
> I think I'm more hopeful of that, I know in the run-up to the last election because we had... I forget the title of it but you had to be on the register as an individual, that's coming up. And we also wanted to get the register up, so we did a lot of outreach work in the colleges trying to get young people engaged, and I think the stats were pretty good on that. But I do think there is that issue about persuading young people that it's worth voting, and I think people probably, one of the exciting things about the digital revolution is that people are probably a bit less respectful [laughs]. I mean I think there's a negative side of that, but that deference, I think people are far more likely to go and have a rant on the council website or Twitter or Facebook or even the media than to

> say well I'll go and vote and make a difference. So I think it's probably something to do with the power shift, so if you're a young person, I've got a daughter who's 22 now and she'll go and vote because she's been brought up on that, but it's quite an archaic thing to do in the current context isn't it. I think it is a challenge, it's like all of the other challenges isn't it really, about how do you persuade people that it can make a difference.
>
> Local council elections struggle to achieve a reasonable turnout among the general population with 31% being the average in 2012 when no other elections were held at the same time. This is not just an issue of persuading young people to engage and vote but one of encouraging all local residents to see their local councils as important.

Council D's response shows a much more strategic view as to where the changes inspired by austerity and the digital age are pushing local authorities as entities and what that means for local democracy. Such a radical restructuring of local government as suggested in these answers would herald yet another new era for local councils and local accountability.

> **Do you see challenges in how the Government's policies are changing the way local authorities work and what does that mean for making sure councils are accountable and accessible to everyone?**
>
> I think it depends on the Government's arrangements, and I said we'd get to this, but for me one of the things I will write down when I'm finished – I think it's increasingly accepted in my industry that we no longer need to rely upon the local newspaper to arrive on the doormat of 240,000 households so that our customers know what the council is doing. The newspaper in its physical form is dead. And it's being replaced with the same brands and the same challenges, but it's arriving in your pocket on your phone, whether that comes from my Twitter account, or the [council] Twitter account, Government's Twitter, however it's getting there, we can now have a digital individual relationship with customers that mean that they know what is going on.
>
> When I first started saying that five years ago that was controversial, and I've had lots of former journalists who are in PR in local government shout at me, I've been heckled 'rubbish, rubbish', because the idea that the physical copy of the newspaper is dead is difficult for some people to come to terms with. Now, that's much more acceptable now than it was when I started saying it four years ago, here's the bit that gets difficult – those same tools that let me talk to customers let customers talk to me, and there is I would argue an equivalent out-dated mechanism by which we currently let the council talk to the council, and I think those are elected members.

That's not me suggesting for a single moment that we need to dismantle democracy, far from it, but I do think that we will find ourselves over the next five years as devolution kicks in, and at the minute the devolution deal for Manchester demands that they have an elected mayor, nobody has started talking about how that elected mayor starts to replace three hundred and something, god knows how many elected councillors across the Greater Manchester area. Los Angeles has 15 elected city councillors, [name of council] has 84 – at some point, as we genuinely start to build that conversation, as we take a genuinely place based approach, I think we're going to have to start asking ourselves how we build modern governance structures which reflect the change in behaviours and the change in tools and the organisational humility that we've been talking about, that's a massive, and of course there's not a cat in hell's chance that the major political parties are going to start having that conversation any time soon because they would effectively be putting their rank and file out of jobs. These are the rewards that you get for being a time served active party member of any stripe.

But sooner or later I think we do have to accept that there are ways of enabling the customer to be heard in the town hall, there are ways of enabling the customer to be heard in whatever the headquarters are of that new place based public services approach, which can be much more inclusive, much more digital, much more real time than relying on Victorian structures around elected members. And as I say, when I leave local government I will write that down more carefully and make that case because right now it'd probably get me fired.

But nonetheless I think it is an inevitability, and I think that what we're seeing now is we're seeing the beginnings of that debate, I don't think that the Conservative government is any more keen to say that out loud than perhaps I am, but I think it is starting an inevitable movement towards it. You cannot sustain hundreds of elected members in Greater Manchester just for local government services alone with a police and crime commissioner and an elected mayor and all that stuff, and at some point I think we will see a fairly radical restructuring of the governance structures.

That in turn will lead to a fairly radical restructuring of the kind of support services that we'll see alongside the governance. So at the minute [the council] has its comms department, the elected mayor for [the area] having replaced a lot of that stuff, the Greater London Assembly is a good example, so Boris has a comms function, and the Greater London Assembly which is what, 15, 20 people for the entirety of London is the thing that holds him to account. It's absolutely not inconceivable that that kind of two tier structure could replace every single councillor in [the council], and that you would then stack up your communications function, your HR functions, your finance functions inside that structure, and then broaden that structure to take account of health provision, fire and rescue and so on. I suspect it's quite exciting, I think there's probably a massive debate and a huge amount of change to be had, and there's a fight to be had over it, because I think for a lot of people that would be difficult. And not just politicians. In 2015, what are there, 320 local authorities – how do we justify, with all of this tech, how do we justify 320 executives, 320 finance departments, HR departments, legal departments, comms departments. That innovation has often been provoked by the reduction in resources, I think it will now follow a conversation about government change.

Possibility of local government restructures?

And you're absolutely right, because once they open that can of worms around structure, the debate about what can be decided and determined about them is already on. Manchester has been essentially told that they can manage the NHS budgets for Greater Manchester. So what they can do is already up for grabs, and then the question is what are the structures that then enable that, and I think that's an inevitability, I do.

[re Northern Powerhouse] There is a school of thought. I think at least one Labour leadership candidate has described as outsourcing cuts to local government. I'm not certain that's right, and... you may see deals soon where the emphasis on the money is different. Because the underlying issue is the extent to which major cities ... are capable of making the money work to hit the kind of levels of productivity you would expect from European cities of the same size. And we're a long way short, at the moment all of those cities are a net drain on the British economy. And the argument goes if you let us get on with it, if you let us keep the business rates, if you let us make decisions about infrastructure and inward investment, we will become a net contributor to the economy and the people that we serve will be better off as a result. That's the real test, and... the Manchester thing is interesting. But I think you'll see different solutions in different places.

Impact of austerity on local democracy and accountability – summary

- Engagement with local councils is a major challenge and some of the immediate solutions put forward revolve around using the transformation towards digital communication as an opportunity to change the way the dialogue is pursued
- Low turnouts at local elections are the norm – how can electors be encouraged to believe their vote counts but consultation and communication between elections is also a challenge with some residents excluded either through their lack of digital capacity or their isolation
- There are a number of new models emerging – devolution, mayors and other regional frameworks – but these have yet to prove they have the answer to the lack of accountability.

- But the one aspect of the shift to digital communication is the ability for a conversation to develop more readily between those who serve and those being served – or between those who rule and those being ruled.
- The greatest challenge of all will be how to create a new model of accountability for local government which harnesses all the benefits of the new platforms of communication but which retains the key principles of a genuinely democratic system.

Summary conclusions

So, in summary, austerity and the changing digital landscape are having a mixed impact on councils across the country with all communication functions being affected by cuts in some way, but the way in which councils have responded has varied.

Responses have been based on the initial position councils found themselves in when the Coalition Government's "austerity" measures began in 2010. The relative financial 'health' of each council, how the cuts on budgets have fallen and the political response from elected members are amongst the key factors.

Some obvious trends emerge:

- One multi-award-winning local council with a strong reputation for proactive campaigning predicts further budget cuts will force them to slice back to a reactive media response service. In another authority the communication team has been cut from 18 FTE roles to just seven over the past three years
- Across the board there's a general picture of stretched resources, cuts in communication tools such as public polling, and the scrapping altogether or changed focus and reduced production quality for citizen publications
- The sector recognises the challenge to better understand and exploit changes brought by social media [and is taking steps to address this?]
- There is an overall sense of austerity cuts being a "kick up the backside" for local government forcing radical communications overhauls, with more emphasis on social media and customer care as the way forward
- Many of those interviewed made the connection between cuts in their own budgets and cuts in local and regional media. One outcome was that journalists were becoming ever more reliant upon "oven-ready" PR supplied content.
- With fewer journalists on the ground, public sector teams were much less likely to see active and experienced journalists scrutinising their organisations.
- This uneven picture is further complicated by the status of communication as a function and a strategic role in each authority. Where councils had already put "communications at the top table", the reductions in resources where these occurred were less radical. In councils where communications was not at the centre of the council's function, the impacts of any cuts in resources were more keenly felt.

The Local Government Association, which represents councils across England, conducted its annual survey of heads of communication in 2015 which produced some interesting findings:

- 71 per cent of councils were planning measures to make savings or generate income in 2015/16 with the picture significantly varied among different types of local authorities;
- 18 per cent of councils currently shared or pooled staff with other organisations

So the challenge being thrown down to communicators within local public services is not a consistent one. Some face larger spending reductions, some face different priorities depending on the size and nature of the authority while almost all communicators face the challenge of bringing their organisations into a more modern communication landscape with social media, online communication and an ever changing local media presenting an agenda for radical change.

Professor Tony Travers, writing in 2013, commented:

> Local government in Britain has had to face centralisation, more or less consistently since 1945. As a result, it has become increasingly easy to see weak local democracy as the norm. The proliferation of quangos, micro-quangos and a chaotic sprawl of public-private bodies generated in the past 20 years does not equate to a form of localism that can be viewed as democratic. With trust in national politicians at a low ebb, elected local government offers a solution to a number of British democracy's current problems.
>
> *(Travers, 2013)*

(The identities of the interviewees have been kept anonymous so each council is listed without identifying either the interviewee or the council concerned. This confidentiality was agreed with each interviewee. Other local information has also been redacted as part of this agreement around confidentiality.)

References

Bulpitt, Jim (1989). *Walking Back to Happiness? Conservative Party Governments and Elected Authorities in the 1980s*. Oxford, Blackwell.

Byrne, Tony (2000). *Local Government in Britain: Everyone's Guide to How It All Works*. London, Penguin.

Cochrane, Allan (1993). *Whatever Happened to Local Government?* Buckingham, Milton Keynes, Open University Press.

The Economist, https://www.economist.com/britain/2017/01/28/britains-local-councils-face-financial-crisis, 28th January 2017 (accessed October 22, 2018).

Jones, George & Stewart, John (1985). *The Case for Local Government* (2nd ed.). London, George Allen & Unwin.

L'Etang, Jacqui (2013). *Public Relations in Britain*. Abingdon, Routledge.
Midwinter, Arthur (2001). 'New Labour and the modernization of British local government – a critique', *Financial Accountability & Management*, 17 (4), 311–320.
Morphet, Janice (2008). *Modern Local Government*. London, SAGE.
Travers, Tony (2013). *50 Years of the London Boroughs*. London, London Boroughs.

4

LOCAL MEDIA DECLINE

A "sector in crisis"?

Carmel O'Toole

> "...the media's ability to hold to account those who wield power in local communities may be starting to decay. And this, just at the point when greater localism and more devolution is being demanded by the public and enabled by central government." (Rona Fairhead, Chair of BBC Trust (Fairhead, 2015))

Concerns about a decline in local media, the fate of printed titles in particular, loss of thousands of journalists' jobs and a move to online content, have been increasing since about 2001. So too have concerns about the concentration of media ownership within a small number of companies. Debates about a "loss of plurality", where declining media print titles leave local areas covered by just one newspaper, or less, have by some accounts been around since the 1940s.

What is attempted here is a clear account of the current narrative from different perspectives and a collation of some of the most pertinent recent analysis. We take a closer look at the diversity of views. This is not the first publication to attempt a narrative on this issue. It borrows from some excellent independent research.

As well as a clear lineup of players with active interest, there is also an emerging and increasingly clear list of issues which are central to the discussion.

- Media ownership and the "Big Four"
- Journalist and production staff job losses, newspaper closures
- Revenue from advertising lost to online
- Loss of media plurality
- NUJ "Local News Matters" campaign
- Hyperlocalism
- Impact on local democracy – the "democratic deficit"
- BBC local journalism fund and the Bureau Local

Media ownership and the power of the "Big Four"

Today in the UK, just four publishers account for 73 per cent, almost three quarters of local newspaper titles. They are Reach (formerly known as Trinity Mirror), JPI Media (formerly Johnston Press), Newsquest and Tindle. More of these later in this chapter (Moore, 2014).

With the emergence of the internet and free online media content from the early 2000s onwards, advertising, the valuable financial lifeblood of local newspapers swiftly began to migrate online. The biggest revenue earners of property, motoring, recruitment and classified advertising deserted the print option for the cheaper and global reach of the internet. Digital advertising revenue in turn has failed to meet the gap left by the loss to print.

Successive media owners failed to keep pace with the implications of these momentous changes. Keen to meet the new public appetite for online content, they raced to provide free and unfettered online news content whilst failing to plan for the financial fallout. This failure to plan did indeed become a wholesale plan to fail. The casualties were newsroom and production jobs and the consolidation and closure of titles.

Dominic Ponsford is Editor of the *Press Gazette* (formerly *UK Press Gazette* (*UKPG*)), now wholly online, the country's leading media commentary and analysis site. He considers the regional print media to be in "fairly desperate times" and facing a year on year 10 per cent decline in print presence (Ponsford, 2017).

The issue inevitably divides opinion, with some upbeat about the radical changes and what they offer. Media owners appear to skirt past the casualties and signpost to the benefits their jobs and profits bring to the wider UK economy. Those on the receiving end of change, the journalists and media commentators, are more pessimistic.

There are clearly polarised protagonists in this debate: the news makers or journalists, as broadly represented by the National Union of Journalists, and the media owners. Next are the wider commentators and stakeholders such as MPs, central government, the BBC, the successor to the Newspaper Society, the News Media Association, and of course independent journalists themselves.

The News Media Association

The News Media Association (NMA) was created by the merger of the Newspaper Society and the Newspaper Publishers Association in November 2014. Its executive committee represents some of the biggest groups in UK media, including Johnston Press, Archant, News UK, DMG and Guardian Media Group.

The NMA website (www.newsmediauk.org.uk) highlights some fine examples of campaigning national and local journalism, many of which illustrate the power of holding public services to account, from school dinner staff seeking the Living Wage to the chronicling of child sex abuse scandals.

It is this capacity to champion the public interest and hold the spotlight up to the use of public funding that many commentators also consider is threatened by changes to local and national media. We will look in this chapter at the specific change and factors contributing to them. Later in the book we look in more detail at the impact of social and digital media, and at examples of continuing best practice where investigative journalism is still being invested in, supported and is having an impact. And there's room too for the independent beacons of optimism, where investors such as Iliffe and Tindle groups are bucking the trend of cutbacks and re-investing in local print media.

By July 2017 the vast majority of local newspapers in the UK were owned by just 10 companies, down from 12 in 2015 when the "Local World" group was bought out by Trinity Mirror (now Reach) for a reported £220m (HoldtheFrontPage, 2017). Then, in April 2017, Iliffe Media group bought KM Media group, acquiring the *Kent Messenger* and associated titles (Iliffe Media, 2017).

Current leading media groups are: Archant, CN Group, DC Thomson, JPI Media (formerly Johnston Press), Iliffe, MNA Media, Newsquest, Press Association, Tindle Newspapers and Reach (formerly known as Trinity Mirror).

In February 2018, Trinity Mirror bought the UK publishing assets of Northern and Shell, which included the *Daily Express* and *Daily Star*. A month later Trinity Mirror changed its name to Reach (BBC News, 2018a). In July 2018, Reach reported a £113m half-year trading loss, with Chief Executive Simon Fox citing a "difficult trading environment" (BBC News, 2018b).

Media Groups

Archant – founded in 1845 with the launch of its first local weekly newspaper the *Norfolk News*. It now employs 1500 staff and owns regional newspapers with titles in East Anglia, London, Kent and the South West. Archant *"news brands"* include the *Eastern Daily Press* in Norfolk, the *East Anglian Daily Times* in Suffolk and the *Ham & High* in London (Archant, 2017).

CN Group – a media company based across Cumbria, North Lancashire, Dumfries & Galloway and Northumberland. The Group operates with three Divisions, publishing, radio and print. Daily and weekly print titles include: the *Cumberland News*, the *Hexham Courant* and the *North West Evening Mail*. It also owns the Bay and Lakeland radio stations (CN Group, 2017).

DC Thomson – Dundee-based DC Thomson media group began publishing newspapers in 1886. It owns regional daily Dundee titles *The Courier* and *Evening Telegraph* and Aberdeen titles, *The Press and Journal, Evening Express* and *Aberdeen Citizen*. It also publishes national weekly titles the *Sunday Post* and *The Weekly News* and online title, *Energy Voice* (DC Thomson, 2017).

Iliffe Media – a family-run, independent media group, led by Edward Iliffe which is publisher of the *Cambridge Independent*. Iliffe bought 13 newspapers and their website from Johnston Press in December 2016 (Iliffe Media, 2016) and in April 2017 acquired the KM Media group portfolio (Iliffe Media, 2017).

JPI Media (formerly known as Johnston Press) – founded in Falkirk in 1767, JP was formerly one of the UK's largest local and regional media organisations in the UK. It owns 13 daily newspapers (including the hugely successful 'i' daily news digest), 154 weekly paid-for newspapers, and 37 weekly free newspapers, plus a number of glossy monthly lifestyle magazines and smaller specialist local publications. In November 2018, Johnston Press, reportedly in debt to the tune of £220m, was forced to put itself into voluntary liquidation. JPI Media, a new company formed from the group's creditors, then re-financed JP. In a statement, JPI Media said the deal would secure "jobs and the [future] of its brands and titles" (Giordano, 2018).

MNA Media (www.mnamedia.co.uk) – Based in Wolverhampton, it runs daily newspapers the *Express & Star* and *Shropshire Star* plus 16 weekly newspapers including the *Shrewsbury Chronicle* and *Telford Journal* plus four magazines

Newsquest – headquarters are in London and its "news brand portfolio" includes 19 daily newspapers, 150 weekly newspapers, and a wide range of regional magazines, published online and in print. Local print titles include the *Northern Echo*, the *Watford Observer* and *Berrow's Worcester Journal*, said to be the world's oldest newspaper, established in 1690.

Press Association – national news agency covering the UK and Ireland. As well as being the home of the UK's national newswire, PA supplies words, images, video, graphics, live data, social media content, editorial services, to media outlets, digital brands, businesses, and public sector organisations in the UK and overseas (PA 2017).

Tindle Newspapers – Surrey-based and famously founded by Sir Ray Tindle with his £300 soldiers' demob money at the end of the WWII. Sir Ray was knighted in 1994 for his services to the newspaper industry. He stood down from running the group in 2017 at the age of 90. He started his first newspaper in Tooting. He is credited, by Peter Preston of the *Observer*, with rescuing dozens of local newspapers, including the *Tenby Observer*, when it was threatened with closure (Preston, 2017a).

Reach (formerly known as Trinity Mirror) – proclaims itself to be the "*largest news publisher in the UK and Ireland*", with over 200 titles in its portfolio. London-based, it owns daily and weekly print titles including the daily *Birmingham Mail* and *Derby Telegraph*, and the weekly titles *Gwent Gazette* and *Wirral News*. In 2015 it acquired "Local World", the print newspaper group set up by David Montgomery, a former senior executive at Trinity Mirror (HoldtheFrontPage, 2017)

Media ownership

According to the 2016 Deloitte "UK News Media" report, this sector contributes £5.3 billion to the UK economy and supports 87,500 jobs. Produced for the News Media Association, which represents the interests of industry proprietors, the report goes on to say: "Newsbrands act as the public's watchdog. By scrutinising and holding the powerful to account on behalf of their readers, newspapers underpin the democratic process" (News Media Association, 2016).

Here's one opinion unlikely to find favour in under-resourced newsrooms:

> News providers are in the extraordinary position of providing a service that has infinite demand, in an era where consumers are being conditioned to expect ever-cheaper prices for products. As in every other competitive industry, consumers will weed out poor quality media and pay for what they value. It will be a long and unpredictable process for many media proprietors, and distinctly uncomfortable for journalists who never before had to compete for readership. But one thing is certain. Those who equate the decline of print media with the end of journalism may just suffer from a lack of imagination and a fear of creative destruction.
>
> *(Kissell, 2013)*

What makes local news authentic and vital is that it is produced within the communities it covers. It is locally accountable, familiar with local insight, and nurtures local contacts and relationships. It builds continuity of contact and knowledge that in turn earns it a consensual licence to operate and the respect of local people. This traditional model is under threat, if not already fatally wounded. More and more news offices are leaving the high street for out- of-town bases. The days of popping in to talk to your local reporter are fast diminishing. Reporters are now more commonly known as multi-media reporters. Many write for the media titles' online hub first and then print version second. They have to know how to produce filmed content and use key social media feeds to source and propagate news and to respond to reader feedback.

Regional sub-editing hubs are replacing local specialists, as is regional content production. We see the off-loading of community coverage to the creatively christened "community content curators" – what used to be called local village correspondents. These are not journalists but enthusiastic local amateur writers. They used to get paid by lineage, a print measure reflecting the quantity of copy published. They are now being elevated to something more akin to untrained junior reporters, replacing very local coverage that would have been picked up by trainee reporters. More of this in our chapter on the impact of digital and social, where we take a look at the *Sheffield Star* and Reach newsroom models.

The more remote the news production process becomes the less media organisations are entitled to claim to be truly local. For local media reporters, their community patch is also the place where they learn their craft. Some of the UK's most distinguished journalists, whose work today chronicles some of our most complex societal issues, started their working lives on local papers. Andrew Norfolk, now Chief Investigative Reporter for *The Times*, is proud to reflect that he started his career on the *Scarborough Evening News*. Tim Minogue, who edits *Private Eye*'s "Rotten Boroughs" column on local government misconduct, began as a trainee on Mirror group titles in Plymouth, Tavistock and Truro. Both testify to the importance of their early training to their future careers and skills base. More of both later in this chapter.

Newspaper closures and job losses "Monopolising Local News"

One of the most incisive research reports so far into this issue is "Monopolising Local News", by a research team from Centre for the study of Media Communications and Power at King's College London (Moore & Ramsay, 2016). It looks at media ownership, seeks to map media plurality across the UK, including identifying coverage gaps and to critically review the notion of a "democratic deficit".

The research focuses upon local authority districts (LADs) and examines key themes around the role of journalism in democracy; the term "democratic deficit", media monopolies and the failure of public policy to address concerns.

Study key findings show

- the number of local newspapers is declining, though not as fast as predicted. Local weekly newspapers still cover most of the country, but local daily coverage is absent in large parts of the UK
- 1,112 distinct daily and weekly local newspapers were identified as circulating in the UK, as of November 2015
- Over two-thirds of LADs in the UK (271 of 406) are not served by a dedicated local daily newspaper that either reaches a significant number of households or circulates a significant number of copies in the area. These LADs contain over 56 per cent of the UK's population.
- Local daily newspapers are almost always located in urban or metropolitan areas, leaving many rural areas (and smaller towns) with weekly print news coverage, or – where local weekly news websites publish throughout the day – the journalistic capacity of a weekly, rather than a daily, newspaper.
- Over half of Parliamentary constituencies – 330 out of 650 – are not covered by a dedicated daily local newspaper. Of those that are not covered, 206 were only reported on five times or fewer during the official 2015 general election campaign across all major UK national news outlets, meaning that these constituents are likely to have received limited independent news and information about their local candidates immediately prior to the election.
- The study shows that there are high levels of dominance by single owners, including many monopoly areas:
- Four publishers – Trinity Mirror, JPI Media (formerly Johnston Press), Newsquest and Tindle – account for 73 per cent of these local newspaper titles across the four nations of the UK. Archant accounts for a further 7 per cent, while the remaining 58 publishers of one or more local newspapers account for just one-fifth of titles.
- 43 per cent of the 380 LADs in Scotland, England and Wales are served by a single publisher providing one or more titles: 165 local newspaper monopolies.
- 96 per cent of LADs in Scotland, England and Wales have a dominant publisher (accounting for over 50 per cent the circulation of local papers publishing in that area); only 17 LADs do not. In 262 LADs (69 per cent), a publisher accounts for over 70 per cent of circulation figures.

- Following the October 2015 deal transferring ownership of the majority of Local World titles to Trinity Mirror, the latter company now dominates the local news market in 90 LADs across the country.
- An analysis of local newspaper website audiences in a sample of LADs shows that monopoly coverage or dominance of a single provider is often not reduced by the availability of online content. Of 20 sampled LADs with monopoly print coverage, 16 had monopolies in online local news provision. Of 20 sampled LADs with a dominant print publisher (but not a monopoly), all continue to have a dominant publisher online, and four receive monopoly provision of local online news.
- Three of the four main local news groups have reported significant reductions in staff, including editorial staff, over the last five years.
- The issues raised by the decline in the number of local newspapers and their plurality, and the decline in the number of journalists at a local level, do not appear to be addressed by the rise in digital readership of local newspaper content.
- There is currently not enough information by which to judge the full extent or effects of this decline on the provision of local news about public affairs across the UK.
- On the basis of its actions, the government does not currently appear to share the concerns raised by journalists, academics, the National Union of Journalists, parts of the trade press, the BBC and civil society groups about the decline of local newspapers and its implications for democracy. This study does not assess the content of local newspapers. Its examination of a potential democratic deficit does not, therefore, represent any criticism of the work of individual local journalists.

Four main policy implications emerge from this study:

1. The existing plurality framework is not ensuring "sufficient plurality" of news media ownership in multiple local areas across the UK. In 165 LADs in England, Scotland and Wales, a single commercial news publisher has a monopoly. The government should, as the House of Lords Communications Committee recommended in 2014, consider a major upheaval of the existing media plurality framework.
2. While there is evidence to support intervention, there is not yet enough detailed and local evidence to target specific interventions, such as the BBC's proposal to employ 100 new local reporters.
3. Subsidies currently given to local media – which run into the hundreds of millions of pounds – are not targeted at promoting innovation, entrepreneurialism, plurality or at addressing a potential democratic deficit.
4. There is an urgent need for further research to establish the nature and extent of local news provision and inform potential policy interventions.
(Moore & Ramsay, 2016)

The National Union of Journalists (NUJ)

The NUJ was founded in 1907 and describes itself as the "voice of journalists and journalism"(www.nuj.org.uk/about/). Its members, based in union branches, or "chapels" across the UK, work to promote and protect the pay and conditions of its members and media freedom, professionalism and ethical standards.

As concerns about changes in the media landscape have increased so too has the trades union's efforts to raise the profile of this issue in wider society.

"Local News Matters"

In January 2017 the National Union of Journalists renewed its "Local News Matters" campaign to again highlight the importance and plight of local newspapers. Events and rallies were held across the country to focus the spotlight on the work of local journalists.

As part of the NUJ campaign a report was commissioned from the Media Reform Coalition, "Mapping Changes in Local News 2015–17" (Media Reform Coalition, 2017). This sought to build upon the findings of the earlier King's College report.

In her foreword, the then NUJ President Michelle Stanistreet wrote of a "sector in crisis". She continued that "since 2005 there has been a net loss of almost 200 newspapers in the UK: During this period the number of journalists has halved. Numerous daily titles have gone to weekly publication and many weekly titles no longer have dedicated editorial teams."

> The revenue of the vast majority of media organisations (81%) continues to come from print readership, with 12% coming from digital, a News Media Association survey found. However, the industry is closing its newspapers and pursuing digital-only strategies without a business model which will replace and enhance print revenue.
>
> *(Stanistreet, 2017)*

The NUJ called for a parliamentary inquiry into the state of local news. It wanted local newspapers to become recognised community assets, to prevent newspaper titles closing overnight and to give potential new owners, including local co-operatives, the time to put together bid to run local papers.

In a UK parliamentary debate on local and regional news, Helen Goodman, Labour MP for Bishop Auckland and former Chair of the NUJ's parliamentary group said:

> [L]ocal news is essential for our democracy. It is through local news that people like us get our messages across to our communities, but more importantly, it is the way that communities hold us to account. However, local news is not only about democracy and boring council meetings or boring court reporting,

important though those are; it is about the way that communities are bound together. It is through local newspapers and radio stations that people know what is going on and identify with their local communities.

(Hansard, 2017)

Some of the UK's most respected commentators are now increasingly setting out their views on this issue

> I think, we have to face up to the prospect that for first time since the enlightenment, you are going to have major cities in the UK and western democracies without any kind of verifiable source of news. That hasn't happened for 200–300 years and I think, it is going to have very profound implications.
>
> *(Rusbridger, 2014)*

During campaign week local NUJ branches across the UK organise events to celebrate the impact and history of local news, involving thousands of union members, reps, chapels and branches from across different sectors of the media. A key focus is seeking to put pressure upon media owners to halt job cuts and increase investment in local journalism.

Specific campaign demands include:

- A short, sharp, national, parliamentary inquiry into the state of local news*
- Local papers should be treated as community assets
- New rules to prevent local media outlets from closing overnight – they should be offered to potential new owners, including local co-operatives, with the time available to submit a bid for alternative media ownership in advance of any closure
- Action by government and employers to stem the relentless job cuts
- Increasing investment, from a range of sources, for quality local journalism.

(UK Parliament, 2017)

*In March 2018, the government announced the commission of the Cairncross Review into the future of sustainable journalism. It reported back in February 2019 (Cairncross, 2019).

As part of the 2017 campaign the NUJ also commissioned research from the Media Reform Coalition into local media. Called "Mapping Changes in Local News: More Bad News for Democracy?", it was published by the Centre for the Study of Journalism, Culture and Community at Bournemouth University.

The report reflects a general trend of newspapers closures and its key findings are:

- UK regional newspapers saw a net loss of 9 titles between November 2015 and March 2017, with 22 titles closing and 13 launching.
- Two daily news sources were lost – the Nuneaton News and MK Web, the online output of OneMK.
- The number of Local Authority Districts (LADs) in the UK with no daily local newspaper coverage rose to 273 (of 406 across the whole UK).
- Five local authority districts suffered a loss of plurality through closures, and were reduced to single-publisher monopolies, increasing the number of local monopolies to 170 out of 380 in England, Wales and Scotland.
- In combination with previous research, this identifies 1,103 local newspaper titles in the UK as of March 2017. The effect of closures and new title launches on plurality has been small. Although three new publishers have entered the market,
- The five largest publishers – Trinity Mirror (now Reach) (226 titles); Johnston Press (now JPI Media) (213 titles); Newsquest (211); Tindle (126) and Archant (75) account for 77.1% of all local newspapers in the UK – a net reduction of 2.2% from November 2015 figures.
- In addition to the net loss of titles, there were 30 separate instances of announced job cuts over the 17-month period involving the loss of 418 jobs.
- Newsquest, with 12 announcements affecting 139 jobs, led the way, followed by Trinity Mirror (at least 102 jobs) and Johnston Press (100 jobs). As well as job cuts, reorganisations affected a further 83 jobs, and six newspaper office closures were recorded, with journalists in some instances being moved long distances away from the communities they serve.
- The purchase of Local World by Trinity Mirror (now Reach) has both led to a substantial reduction of plurality across the local press (overall, and in particular geographical areas), and a programme of newspaper closures, staff cuts and office closures across the acquired titles.
- In total: six Local World newspapers have closed (including one daily, the Nuneaton News); there were eight instances of job cuts affecting at least 62 jobs, and likely many more among photographers; and two Local World offices have been closed – in Hertfordshire and Leicester.
- Some evidence has emerged pointing to deeper problems in the local newspaper industry: the decision by Johnston Press to sell, close or cut less profitable local publications while at the same time investing heavily to enter the national newspaper market; criticisms that some local papers no longer provide sufficient court and council reporting; local reporters criticising publishers over a perceived reliance on clickbait to attract audiences; smaller publishers handing off loss-making titles to non-profit groups; and newspapers devoting large amounts of space to online content with little or no local relevance.

- The BBC deal for 150 new local reporters, completing negotiations which began in September 2015, fails to offset the loss of over 400 journalists (and probably significantly more) from the largest publishers during approximately the same period.
- The use of £8m annually of the publicly-funded licence fee – is a fraction of the combined operating profits of the largest local publishers – and the scheme will not address the existing structural problems relating to the provision of local public interest journalism and the lack of plurality, proliferation of job cuts and lack of investment by the industry's largest commercial players.

(Media Reform Coalition, 2017)

The 2017 report builds upon the findings of The Centre for the Study of Media, Communication and Power, at King's College London which in 2016 also researched local newspapers' decline. It signposted to the dominance of the market by a small number of publishers.

This, in turn, the coalition report argued, has had a serious impact on democracy, "providing many readers with very little choice when it comes to choosing their local newspaper and leaving more than two-thirds of local authority districts not served by a local daily" (Media Reform Coalition, 2017).

Both reports point to the general and continuing trend of closures and mergers. They highlight a more pronounced hollowing-out of those that remain, due to job losses, the ongoing threat of redundancies and the stress of working in under resourced newsrooms.

Hyperlocalism

Brave New Words, by Kerry Maxwell, examines the changing dynamics of language including the emergence of new words. In her 2010 entry for the Macmillan Dictionary, Maxwell defined "hyperlocalism" as: "journalism which focuses on a very specific, local area".

She posits that "[i]n the UK, local news usually relates to a particular town, or often a wider geographical location such as a county. Hyperlocal news is much narrower, relating to a suburb or even a particular group of streets" (Maxwell, 2010).

Maxwell acknowledges that hyperlocal news is often gathered by amateurs rather than trained journalists. News is reported by local people and hyperlocal sites rely upon content provided by readers and may include personal blog posts.

If authentic local news is news created and published within local communities then the emergence of hyperlocal news sites might have appeared to be the perfect answer to the NUJ's concerns. It is hard to pinpoint a firm date, but from around 2005 the debate began about what hyperlocals might offer.

The first sites, essentially locally written blogs, emerged to a fanfare about how local news produced by local news enthusiasts could be the answer to the deficit left by declining local print titles and loss of journalism jobs.

In a guest blog post for the Carnegie Trust, (which has funded a number of hyperlocal news sites), Professor Richard Sambrook, Director of Cardiff University's Centre for the Study of Journalism writes:

> We should be in no doubt there is a serious problem to be addressed. Rural communities especially, but inner-city areas too, need binding together through debate and discussion of local issues. Citizens need to be better informed about the decisions being taken in councils and government on their behalf. Local accountability needs to be open and public. The decline of traditional local news sources puts all of this at risk.
>
> (Sambrook, 2014)

He further posits that the content of some hyperlocal sites are now 'holding decision makers to account and providing a crucial forum for information and debate about local issues'.

Whilst he acknowledges that the economic model necessary to sustain such sites is still unresolved he considers the impact of hyperlocals, coming new to an established media market, is significant.

Such sites are often run by volunteers, local activists and "armchair commentators". The postings are irregular and vary enormously in quality. But their potential reach in terms of online readers can significantly out strip that of their established print media counterparts.

Sambrook points to the need for more research into sites' sustainability but introduces the term "grass roots fifth estate journalism".

Community commentary and interest in local democracy is one thing but to label it journalism or suggest it is an adequate substitute for professional newsgathering is quite another. These sites are hybrids. They serve a valuable purpose offering local insight and independent viewpoints, but they are not journalism in the truest understanding of the term. There is no professional quality control funnel. They do not commit to fair, balanced and contemporaneous reporting by skilled, trained writers. They are the soundings of enthusiastic amateurs and should be recognised as such, lest we run away with some fantasy which transforms every neighbourhood into a hub of organically gifted "citizen journalists".

In his research report for the Media Standards Trust in 2014, Martin Moore from Bournemouth University explored the backdrop and development of hyperlocal news sites.

He reported then that there were around 496 active hyperlocal sites in the UK but acknowledges there to be limited research about the number and type.

These sites range enormously in distribution, scale, reach, type and regularity of output. There is, for example, a large variation in the spread of sites across the UK. Most sites are concentrated in metropolitan areas like London and Birmingham, with some large rural areas lacking any sites. 90% of the sites are in England. Across Wales there are fewer than 30 active hyperlocal sites. In Northern Ireland there are only three.

In terms of revenue and resources, most sites are 'in their infancy' and 'There is still … a huge disparity with legacy local media in terms of resources'.

Sites also vary considerably in terms of purpose and aims. Many were set up as a means of sharing of information within a community, and providing a forum for discussion.

However, from a 2014 survey we know that many hyperlocal sites are also performing similar democratic functions as local newspapers. The survey found that 81% of the hyperlocal sites that responded had covered local council meetings in the last two years, 79% had covered local government planning issues, and 75% had covered local businesses.

The same survey found that 'Seven out of ten producers see what they do as a form of active community participation, over half see it as local journalism, and over half as an expression of active citizenship.'

(Moore, 2014)

Even use of the word "covered" to reflect local attendance at council meetings implies that hyperlocal site writers fulfil the same function as would a regular journalist. Do they then have a clear understanding of local government decision-making? Do they understand the decision-making process in terms of paid officials and elected councillors? Do they have a fully formed understanding of their rights to access information about public accounts and to use the Freedom of Information Act to further bolster their requests on specific topics? At this stage it is not clear and it would be wholly unwise to ascribe the same level of professional focus to hyperlocal writers as to trained journalists. That is not to say that what these sites do is unhelpful. They are what they are, something else which brings a level of interest to local issues but it is not journalism and no replacement for the real thing.

One of the biggest obstacles to the continuance of such sites is that of funding to sustain them. They are mostly volunteer run; few if any now have paid professional editorial staff.

Dominic Ponsford, of *Press Gazette*, is firm on his own view of hyperlocals:

> We've done quite a lot of research on this, almost none of them employ professional journalists, one or two might manage to employ a full-time journalist. So they're sporadic, they're run as hobbies by enthusiasts, and they're not in any way a substitute for what's been lost.

A thorough review of much more research is needed to establish what the full potential of such sites might be but let's take a look at one typical example.

Pits n Pots

The Pits n Pots blog site using Wordpress was launched in September 2008 by Tony Walley of Stoke on Trent. Tony was and still is managing director of an aluminium and sheet metals stockist company, Service Metals Midlands in Stoke. He is also a keen sports fan and local radio enthusiast having presented programmes on sport and music.

He sought to promote discussion about the politics and issues of community interest in Stoke-on-Trent. Associate, Mike Rawlins joined Tony shortly after the launch to work on the "technical aspects of the site". He has since moved to Scotland and no longer contributes to the blog.

Tony has no journalistic experience or qualifications. By his own admission he says: "We were never the greatest writers or any threat to mainstream journalists. I have the greatest respect for journalists and what they do."

The idea for Pits n Pots came out of Tony's frustration at what he felt was a lack of "municipal" reporting. He recalls the local *Stoke Sentinel* newspaper used to have a designated reporter to cover all council issues but that was no longer the case. He recalls readership of local print media was in decline and local council issues were not being picked up by traditional local media. When I spoke to him in August 2017 he considered local municipal reporting to have reached "far worse" levels where local council issues were still going unreported. I asked to speak to someone at the *Sentinel* to seek their response to Tony's comments but no one was made available to my interview request.

The *Stoke Sentinel* was owned by the David Montgomery-led "Local World" group which was bought out by Trinity Mirror in 2015. We look at the Reach news development model in a later chapter.

Around 2010 Stoke on Trent was also being used as a focus and sometimes platform for far-right groups such as the English Defence League and the British National Party. The country was still reeling from the post 2008 banking crisis recession and Stoke was a receptive recruitment ground for those disaffected with mainstream politics.

Tony recalls lots of suspicion from the local council and local journalists: "They didn't understand what we were trying to do. We weren't a replacement for journalism but trying to fill a gap left by the lack of local municipal reporting." He recalls being "frogmarched" out of the Stoke City Council chamber for attempting to record a council meeting.

He and Mike also took the conscious decision to cover far right rallies and record and post film footage and interviews. "Other local media weren't going anywhere near them and we took the view that if we gave these people a platform they'd eventually hang themselves from the exposure."

Tony considers that he and colleague Mike's local connections sometimes gave them an advantage with stories and recalls one example of the BNP using a picture of a Spitfire plane at a local political rally. One of Pits n Pots' contacts spotted that the plane was not a British made version but one from Poland. This inevitably backfired on the BNP and as a story was one of many picked up by national media.

Pits n Pots became, albeit briefly, one of the best known hyperlocal sites in the UK. When it first emerged, it was feted by some mainstream media. Tony and Mike were invited to speak at conferences about Pits n Pots and how it had "helped change the face of local politics in the UK". Tony appeared on BBC Breakfast, and was interviewed by media about the rationale driving Pits n Pots. At its height the site was getting a regular 1500 visits a day, and at election times and when there were specific hard news stories, anything up to 30,000 views in a day.

By 2012, Tony's company was recovering and he had less and less time to give to the blog site. The last posting in the blog "News" section is given as July 31, 2012.

There are postings about local elections and council related stories such as a night time "task force" set up by City Council Leader Mohammed Pervez. Much of this text appears to have been plucked without change from a council press release. Then there are the self-styled "Eye Spy" postings that purport to offer an anonymous insider commentary on issues of local political interest. It is at best and perfectly valid as the view of one local businessman. It is neither revolutionary nor innovative and does not change the face of political commentary in Stoke or anywhere else. Neither does Tony claim anything of the sort, rather he reaffirms that it was set up to fill what he perceives as a coverage vacuum resulting from the decline of Stoke's very local media.

Funding and revenue is probably the main obstacle to the continuance of hyperlocal sites. Tony adds: "We never made any money from it, in fact it cost me money in the setting up and covering stories."

In another posting Mike writes: "Pits n Pots would not be the site it is today and be in the fortunate position to be supported by the Journalism Foundation if it wasn't for Tony having the idea to set it up initially."

It is understood the Foundation provided financial support to Pits N Pots. And so to the Journalism Foundation......

The Journalism Foundation

The Journalism Foundation was set up in December 2011, backed by Russian newspaper publisher, Evgeny Lebedev, to promote "free and fair journalism and expose corruption and . . . fund investigative journalism around the world" (Muir & Sabbagh, 2012).

It was led by a formidable lineup of the great and good. Chief Executive was Simon Kelner, former editor of the *Independent*. A board of trustees was chaired by Lebedev, chairman of the *Independent* and the *London Evening Standard* and included Baroness Helena Kennedy, the renowned human rights lawyer; Lord Norman Fowler, former chair of the House of Commons media select committee; and Sir John Tusa, former director general of BBC World Service.

Quoted in the *Independent*, Evgeny Lebedev said of the Foundation launch:

> At a time when, quite rightly, a light is being shone on malpractice in some areas of the British Press, I am delighted to give my backing to an initiative whose purpose is to demonstrate the positive aspects of journalism. Free speech has always been a touchstone issue for me, and an organisation intent on giving people around the world a voice is worthy of widespread support.
>
> *(Independent, 2011)*

The Foundation closed in less than a year.

In their article "Lebedev pulls plug on Journalism Foundation", *Guardian* journalists Hugh Muir and Dan Sabbagh allege the project came under pressure after Lebedev was charged with "hooliganism and battery offences in Russia" (Muir & Sabbagh, 2012).

They go on to write: "The venture, with headquarters in Mayfair, cost £600,000 with no significant legacy."

A "democratic deficit"

Emerging from these conversations is a term gaining recognition as a summary warning for wider UK society about the overall effect of such changes, that of a "democratic deficit". (Fairhead, 2015).

The term neatly frames the fear that if skilled and trained local reporters aren't actively looking at what is happening in local areas, particularly in publicly funded bodies; and if those organisations in turn are doing less proactive communications, then local democracy is not being held to account.

In February 2018, British Prime Minister Theresa May announced a government review into whether state intervention is needed to protect the role of local and national media. Speaking at an event in Manchester to mark 100 years since the Representation of the Peoples Act, Mrs May said:

> Good quality journalism provides us with the information and analysis we need to inform our viewpoints and conduct a genuine discussion. But in recent years, especially in local journalism, we have seen falling circulations, a hollowing out of local newsrooms and fears for the future sustainability of high quality journalism.

The Cairncross Review reported back in February 2019 (Elgot, 2018). A summary of key recommendations is set out in the chapter summary below.

Expert voices on the impact of media decline

Emily Bell

Emily Bell is director of the Tow Center for Digital Journalism at Columbia University's Graduate School of Journalism. She previously worked for the *Observer* and then the *Guardian* for 20 years.

In an article for the *Guardian* in June 2017, Emily emphasised the need for local reporting in the aftermath of the Grenfell Tower tragedy. More generally Emily comments:

> The causes of the failure of local journalism are well known: commercialism, consolidation, the internet, poor management. The fixes for that, cannot be found in an environment which is commercially hostile to small scale accountability, and for that we are all to blame.
>
> *(Bell, 2017)*

Former Guardian *Editor, Peter Preston*

In his own article a few weeks later, in July 2017, former *Guardian* and *Observer* columnist, Peter Preston reflected that things might have turned out very differently for Grenfell Tower residents had there been "properly resourced newspaper reporters".

He posed a series of telling questions for the local newspaper industry culminating in: "What if a press that investigates and champions cases on the streets where you live, still flourished, a vital part of democracy's response system?" (Preston, 2017b)

He returned to the subject a month later, as a new batch of newspaper closures was announced: "Local newsrooms with the critical mass to investigate, to turn over stones, are shrinking. Local journalism as one prop of democracy, grows weaker by the year. And that matters to communities and journalists themselves."

Matt Chorley, Editor of The Times' "Red Box" *column*

Matt Chorley's "Red Box" column makes essential early morning reading. In his column of September 9, 2017, Chorley uses a reminiscence about his early days as a trainee journalist on the *Taunton Times* (which closed in 2006), to set out his own concerns about the decline of local media (Chorley, 2017).

He bemoans the use by Google and Facebook of content produced by others, without paying for the privilege, adding: "The likes of Google and Facebook sell advertising around someone else's news stories, which they take for free and then promise to invest in robots that can write them for nothing in the future." More worrying is his warning:

> Every time a paper closes, lazy MPs, corrupt councillors, dodgy police chiefs, rip off businesses, and anyone in the dock can relax a little. This isn't just

nostalgia. The great and good didn't stop behaving badly because we all got Snapchat and iPlayer.... Grenfell Tower tells us what happens when poorer areas lose their voice in local media. Blogs aren't enough.

BBC fund for local journalists

A welcome development in addressing the gaps being identified in local journalism is the BBC's acknowledgment of the need to ensure good quality local reporting of public services.

In January 2017, the UK's foremost public service broadcaster, the BBC, released details of where licence fee-funded "local democracy reporters" would be based across the country, with jobs being phased in from the summer.

It has committed £8m a year to pay for 150 reporters, to work for local news organisations rather than the BBC. The journalists cover council meetings and public services and share their stories with the BBC.

James Harding, Director of BBC News and Current Affairs, said the move would strengthen local news coverage: "As more power is devolved across the UK, it's more important than ever that we cover, understand and hold to account local politicians and public services", he said.

So far, the BBC has allocated 20 reporters in Scotland, three in Northern Ireland, 11 in Wales and 104 in England, with plans to place the full 150 journalists by 2018.

About the scheme

The reporters, who must work for a "qualifying" regional publisher, will be responsible for local newsgathering and sharing their stories with the BBC.

To qualify, local titles must demonstrate they have a "previous track record" of public service journalism, as well as the ability to employ staff.

But the "exact nature of the reporters' duties in Northern Ireland is still under discussion", the BBC said.

In addition, the BBC will share audio and video material, after it has been transmitted, with local publishers under its NewsBank service, launching later in 2017.

It will also create a hub for data journalism, funded by the BBC with staff from local titles, with recruitment beginning in the spring (BBC, 2017).

"A drop in the ocean"?

Whilst this can be viewed as a positive development, the BBC fund has its sceptics. Dominic Ponsford, Editor of the *Press Gazette*, says:

> I think eight million pounds is useful, but it's kind of a drop in the ocean compared to what's been lost, thousands of journalism jobs have gone, and hundreds of millions a year in advertising revenue has gone to Facebook and

Google and the internet. So it's welcome, but it's going to fall a long way short of plugging the gap in terms of what's been lost.

(Ponsford, 2017)

Whilst the NUJ also welcomes the announcement, the union reminds us that the backdrop to this investment, negotiated and agreed with the NMA is more complex. In the NUJ's "Mapping Changes" research report it tracks that:

> During this period of negotiation to procure public funding of 150 local reporters, significantly more than 400 jobs have been lost or replaced across the local newspaper industry, including 100 at Johnston Press. The amount of money provided via the licence fee (£8m annually) is also a fraction of the profit margins of the largest publishers combined....
>
> The deal itself involves journalists being distributed across the UK, with the stories they produce being made available to commercial local news organisations as well as the BBC. It is not fully clear as of yet how the BBC will advertise and award these journalists in "bundles". The number of reporters is intended to increase to 200 in 2019. While the increase of funding for journalists doing journalism at the local level can only be seen as a positive, it is not clear to what extent this programme will offset the continuing and substantial loss of editorial jobs in local journalism across the major publishers. It is also not clear the extent to which licence fee money will be used to subsidise the core functions of local newspaper groups who have shown little appetite for investing in journalism even while maintaining healthy profit margins.
>
> *(Media Reform Coalition, 2017)*

The Bureau Local – "a message of hope"

The Bureau Local (TBL) is a venture by the not-for-profit Bureau of Investigative Journalism. TBL's aim:

> is to inform the public about the realities of power in today's world. We are particularly concerned with the undermining of democratic processes and failures to accord with fair, legal and transparent practices.
>
> We inform the public through in-depth investigative journalism, with no corporate or political agenda. Through fact-based, unbiased reporting, we expose systemic wrongs, counter misinformation and spark change.
>
> *(Bureau Local, 2018)*

Roy Greenslade, retired Professor of Journalism at City University in London, is former editor of the *Daily Mirror* and a regular columnist in the *Guardian*.

He describes this initiative as a: "message of hope, hope for the public and hope for democracy" (Greenslade, 2018).

The idea is to help local journalists reveal stories of public interest. TBL is to set up a network of journalists and technology experts from across the UK to discover and tell public interest stories. Since 2017 it has recruited 650 of them (Greenslade, 2018).

From a central London hub, it compiles and analyses data for network journalists that they can then use to support localised investigations. In turn the TBL central hub benefits from being able to analyse insight provided by regional journalists.

Just one example is the TBL's look at the problems caused by funding cuts for domestic violence refuges. It was prompted by a single story in Sunderland.

TBL researched data whilst reporters from as far afield as the *Yorkshire Post* and Archant titles in London contacted refuge managers. Although managers were at first reluctant to speak, once they were made aware of the nationwide scope of the research they agreed to help.

The result was front page stories, features, interviews and spin off stories in a variety of local and regional papers.

Public access to information

The UK Government rules on access to and reporting of council meetings and council information were updated in 2014. They now take account of the increasing appetite for recording council meeting using mobile phones and social media. This is now permitted. Some councils already use webcasts to afford easy public access to council discussions online. These don't always make riveting viewing but illustrate a willingness to support public access to such discussions.

> We now live in a modern, digital world where the use of modern communication methods such as filming, tweeting and blogging should be embraced for enhancing the openness and transparency of local government bodies. This will ensure we have strong, 21st century, local democracy where local government bodies are genuinely accountable to the local people whom they serve and to the local taxpayers who help fund them.
> *(Department for Communities and Local Government, 2014)*

The document also advises on access to background documents, to the use of Freedom of Information Act 2000 requests and to where councils can choose to exempt information from public view. Another very useful book on public access to information, particularly FOIA requests, is Heather Brooke's *Your Right to Know*, now in its second edition (Brooke, 2007).

On the face of it, the potential for public access is there, for members of the public, film crews, journalists, bloggers and activists. What is not clear is the extent to which such access is being used and by whom.

A perspective on the decline of this process of public scrutiny is starkly framed in a *Press Gazette* article featuring the former *Northern Echo* Editor, Peter Barron, in an article about the importance of and loss of local investigative *reporting*.

> Today, newspapers no longer have the staff to examine the agenda of each council meeting, let alone attend them. "Plenty of councils are looking forward to the demise of local newspapers because they hold them to account. They see them as a pain in the arse."
>
> (Wylie, 2016)

So is it just the case that journalists are coming over a bit Ned Ludd and hankering after the way things were done in the old days? Kissell's comments appear to suggest so. Or is there genuine concern about what is lost when a media organisation's priority is to balance the books rather than ensure the core function of robust local news reporting. There's a huge difference between running stories with local relevance to ensuring the key stories about issues affecting local people are covered consistently well.

What's at issue here is not an absence of local reporting but concerns about the extent to which such coverage has diminished. Check out the newsagents in any local high street and you'll find local papers still there.

What is not immediately apparent with local community newspapers (unless you know what you are looking for), is the extent to which coverage of public sector issues has been dramatically scaled back as a result of contracting newsrooms, cuts to print titles and a change of media ownership agenda to take account of the need to balance the books.

In summary there are less reporters, covering more stories, writing for print and online, producing video content with less time and more workload than ever before and they're dancing to a new online tune, which drives everything they do. Holding a torch up to public interest issues, takes time, lots of it and such time is a costly resource being prioritised elsewhere. (More in our chapter on the impact of social and digital.)

Summary of key issues

- Local media closures continue year on year and there's increasingly a lack of plurality with a dominance by four big media groups. Journalism skills continue to be lost along with diminishing scrutiny of public interest issues
- In February 2018 the UK PM announced a government review into whether state intervention is needed to protect and preserve the role of local and national media through the Cairncross Review. It reported back in February 2019 with nine recommendations. These included key options for the government to consider, including; establishing an Institute for Public Interest News; direct funding for local public interest news, with an evaluation and expansion of the BBC's Local Democracy Reporting Service; government innovation funding to

improve the supply of public interest news; and new codes of conduct to rebalance the relationship between online platforms and publishers.
- Positive new initiatives – BBC and the Bureau Local. The BBC fund for regional journalism has been broadly welcomed but its impact has yet to be assessed. The £8 million a year funding is also considered by some to be "a drop in the ocean" against what has already been lost.
- "Democratic deficit" – more and more media and political commentators are using this phrase to highlight the threat to local democracy posed by the decline in local and regional journalism
- Widespread concerns are being raised about the continuing loss of local and regional print titles and the consequent impact on journalist jobs and the monopoly of ownership by just four media groups
- Concerns are not just about job losses but on the lack of skilled and consistent scrutiny, which is locally based of our publicly funded services.
- More than two thirds of local authority districts are now not served by a dedicated local daily newspaper
- Whilst group owned local media titles purport to continue to cover local issues, there are fewer journalists doing more work, producing print and online content, plus servicing social media feeds. Consistent, informed and skilled scrutiny of local public services is less and less possible. Local news coverage is increasingly surface dressing for a community facing journalism much diluted. What is not known is what is lost by this diminution of the local news function
- Hyperlocals – over hyped? They are welcome but no substitute for the loss of journalism jobs and media titles. After being heralded by some as the answer to declining local media, they have yet to demonstrate a sustainable financial model. Whilst they offer a useful additional insight, local bloggers and amateur political commentators are no substitute for professional trained journalists
- The NUJ is lobbying central government to have local newspapers legally protected as 'community assets' to help prevent closures
- Google and Facebook in particular, continue to use content from other media organisations for free. This supports their own capacity to generate advertising revenue.

References

BBC News (2018a).'Trinity Mirror changes name to Reach after Express deal,' https://www.bbc.co.uk/news/business-43285531, March 5, 2018 (accessed October 23, 2018).

BBC News (2018b). 'Mirror and Express owner slumps to £113m loss', https://www.bbc.co.uk/news/business-45003639 (accessed July 30, 2018).

Bell, E. (2017). 'Grenfell reflects the accountability vacuum left by the crumbling local press', *Guardian*, https://www.theguardian.com/media/media-blog/2017/jun/25/grenfell-reflects-the-accountability-vacuum-left-by-crumbling-local-press (accessed August 4, 2017).

Brooke, H. (2007). *Your Right to Know: A Citizen's guide to the Freedom of Information Act*, 2nd edition. London: Pluto Press.

Bureau Local (2018). https://www.thebureauinvestigates.com/about-us*(accessed* March 26, 2018).

Cairncross, Dame Francis (2019). *The Cairncross Review,* www.gov.uk/government/publications/the-cairncross-review-a-sustainable-future-for-journalism (accessedFebruary 18, 2019).

Chorley, M. (2017). 'Closing papers is good news for lazy MPs and corrupt councils,' *The Times,* September 9, 2017, p. 29, https://www.thetimes.co.uk/article/closing-local-papers-is-good-news-for-lazy-mps-and-corrupt-councils-ktvqvt2zx (accessed February 22, 2019).

Department for Communities and Local Government (2014). 'Open and accountable local government', https://assets.publishing.service.gov.uk/government/uploads/system/uploads/attachment_data/file/343182/140812_Openness_Guide.pdf

Elgot, Jessica (2018). 'Decline of local journalism threatens democracy, says May', *Guardian,* February 6, 2018, https://www.theguardian.com/media/2018/feb/06/decline-of-local-journalism-threatens-democracy-says-may (accessed February 18, 2019).

Fairhead, Rona (2015). 'BBC Trust Chairman calls on BBC and wider news sector to work together to avert a democratic deficit in local news reporting', BBC Trust, 5 November 2015, http://www.bbc.co.uk/bbctrust/news/speeches/2015/ local_news_reporting

Giordano, Chiaro (2018). 'Johnston Press future secured after buyout by newly-formed JPIMedia', https://www.independent.co.uk/news/business/news/johnston-press-sale-latest-bought-by-jpimedia-future-secured-a8639036.html *(accessed* November 20, 2018).

Greenslade, Roy (2018). 'Local reporting ventures offer hope for future of newspapers', *Guardian,* March 25, 2018, https://www.theguardian.com/media/media-blog/2018/mar/25/local-reporting-tbij-bbc (accessed February 19, 2019).

Hansard (2017). 'Local and regional news', March 30, 2017, https://hansard.parliament.uk/Commons/2017-03-30/debates/B069F48A-DFC6-48A8-A1BD-BA9AB827E5E9/LocalAndRegionalNews (accessed February 22, 2019).

HoldtheFrontPage (2017). http://www.holdthefrontpage.co.uk/tag/local-world/ (accessed August 1, 2017).

Iliffe Media (2016). http://iliffemedia.co.uk/iliffe-media-to-acquire-13-titles-from-johnstone-press/ (accessed August 1, 2017).

Iliffe Media (2017). http://iliffemedia.co.uk/category/news/ (accessed August 1, 2017).

Independent (2011). The Journalism Foundation launches ', December 5, 2011, http://www.independent.co.uk/news/media/press/the-journalism-foundation-launches-6272241.html*(accessed August 1, 2017).*

Kissell, M. (2013). 'The decline of print doesn't mean the end of journalism', https://www.theguardian.com/commentisfree/2013/oct/29/decline-print-media-journalism-web (accessed July 28, 2017).

Maxwell, K. (2010). *Macmillan Dictionary,* https://www.macmillandictionary.com/buzzword/entries/hyperlocal.html (accessed July 16, 2018).

Media Reform Coalition (2017). 'Mapping changes in local news 2015–2017: More bad news for democracy?' Poole: The Centre for the Study of Journalism, Culture and Community, Bournemouth University, http://www.mediareform.org.uk/wp-content/uploads/2017/12/mapping-changes-in-local-news-2015-2017-interactive-research-report-march-2017.pdf (accessed February 24, 2019).

Moore, M. (2014). 'Addressing the democratic deficit in local news through positive plurality or, why we need a UK alternative of the Knight News Challenge', Media Standards Trust.

Moore, M. & Ramsay, G. (2016). 'Monopolising local news', London: Centre for the study of Media Communications and Power, King's College London.

Muir, Hugh and Sabbagh, Dan (2012). 'Evgeny Lebedev pulls plug on Journalism Foundation', https://www.theguardian.com/media/2012/nov/13/evgeny-lebedev-pulls-journalism-foundation, November 13, 2012 (accessed October 23, 2018).

News Media Association (2016). http://www.newsmediauk.org/write/MediaUploads/In% 20the%20Spotlight/NMA%20Economic%20Report/Final_Report_News_Media_ Economic_Impact_Study.pdf (accessed July 27, 2017).
Ponsford, D. (2017). Editor, Press Gazette, telephone interview August 2017.
Preston, P. (2017a). 'Sir Ray Tindle a local hero. We bid you a fond adieu', *Guardian*, July 23, 2017, https://www.theguardian.com/media/2017/jul/23/sir-ray-tindle-local-news paper-hero-hands-over-to-his-son (accessed February 24, 2019).
Preston, P. (2017b). 'A functioning local press matters. Grenfell Tower showed us why', *Guardian*, July 2, 2017, https://www.theguardian.com/media/2017/jul/02/grenfell-to wer-local-newspapers-authority-journalism (accessed August 4, 2017).
Private Eye (2012). 'Paul Foot Award', http://www.private-eye.co.uk/paul_foot.php? archive=2012 (accessed August 2, 2017).
Rusbridger, Alan (2014). '2017 signals major boost in deals for UK Media firms despite print cliff fall', *Sputnik International* (online), January 23, 2017, https://sputniknews.com/europ e/201701231049913585-uk-media-boots-deals/ (accessed November 1, 2018).
Sambrook, R. (2014). 'Local news and the democratic deficit', guest blog, Carnegie UK Trust, https://www.carnegieuktrust.org.uk/blog/guest-blog-local-news-and-the-democra tic-deficit/ (accessed August 1, 2017).
Stanistreet, M. (2017). 'Foreword' in 'Mapping changes in local news 2015–2017: More bad news for democracy?', Media Reform Coalition. Poole: The Centre for the Study of Journalism, Culture and Community, Bournemouth University, http.//www.mediareform. org.uk/wp-content/uploads/2017/12/mapping-changes-in-local-news-2015-2017-interacti ve-research-report-march-2017.pdf (accessed February 24, 2019).
UK Parliament (2017). 'Future of local and regional news providers', House of Commons Library, https://researchbriefings.parliament.uk/ResearchBriefing/Summary/CDP-2017-0103#fullrep ort (accessed February 24, 2019).
Wylie, Ian (2016). 'Running out of paper: "Plenty of councils are looking forward to the demise of local newspapers"', *Press Gazette*, http://www.pressgazette.co.uk/running-ou t-of-paper-plenty-of-councils-are-looking-forward-to-the-demise-of-local-newspapers/ December 23, 2016 – (accessed July 27, 2017).

Further reading

Archant http://www.archant.co.uk/articles/about-us-who-we-are/ (accessed August 1, 2017).
BBC News (2017). 'BBC funded local reporters to be spread across the UK', http://www. bbc.co.uk/news/uk-38843461 (accessed August 1, 2017).
BBC 'Today', *interview with Alan Rusbridger, editor of the Guardian and Andreas Whittam Smith, first editor of the Independent, December 24, 2009,* http://news.bbc.co.uk/today/hi/today/ newsid_7798000/7798624.stm (accessed July 27, 2017).
CN Group, http://www.cngroup.co.uk/about-us-2/ (accessed August 1, 2017).
DC Thomson, https://www.dcthomson.co.uk/about-us/ (accessed August 1, 2017).
Department for Culture, Media and Sport, *consultation report on 'Media ownership and plurality', 2013, 'Overview',* https://assets.publishing.service.gov.uk/government/uploads/system/uploads/ attachment_data/file/225790/Media_Plurality_Consultation_2013.pdf.
Greenslade, Roy (2011). 'Simon Kelner launches Journalism Foundation', https://www.thegua rdian.com/media/2011/dec/05/simon-kelner-journalism-foundation (accessed October 23, 2018).
HoldtheFrontPage, http://www.holdthefrontpage.co.uk/2017/news/yorkshire-post-tops-a bc-league-but-all-dailies-see-sales-decline/ (accessed August 4, 2017).

Johnston Press, http://www.johnstonpress.co.uk/products-services *(accessed* August 1, 2017).
MNA Media, https://www.mnamedia.co.uk/ (accessed February 4, 2019).
National Union of Journalists (NUJ), www.nuj.org.uk/about (accessed February 22, 2019).
Newsquest , http://www.newsquest.co.uk/our-titles/ (accessed August 1, 2017).
Pits n Pots, https://pitsnpots.co.uk/about-pits-n-pots/ (accessed February 23, 2019).
Press Association, https://www.pressassociation.com/about-us/group-overview/ *(accessed August 1, 2017).*
Tindle Group, http://tindlenews.co.uk/about/ *(accessed* August 1, 2017).
Trinity Mirror, http://www.trinitymirror.com/brands (accessed August 1, 2017).

5

VIEWS FROM THE FOOTHILLS

Carmel O'Toole

> "When I reflect on those years and the coverage we used to do, and the extent to which, for example, every single council meeting was covered, every agenda for every meeting was gone through, every day of the magistrates court there was a reporter from the Scarborough Evening News sitting there to cover every sort of case under the sun. Every department of the local authority had a reporter who was assigned responsibility for that area."
>
> *(Andrew Norfolk, June 2017)*

Many of the UK's most respected journalists began their careers on local newspapers. Here we take some personal perspectives on what it has meant to them. Plus, we explore the importance of local news gathering as an essential journalistic training ground.

Andrew Norfolk – Chief Investigative Reporter for *The Times*

Andrew Norfolk's two-year investigation into the targeting, grooming and sexual exploitation of teenage girls by organised groups of men, prompted two government-ordered inquiries, a parliamentary inquiry and a new national action plan on child sexual exploitation. In 2012 it also won him the prestigious *Private Eye* Paul Foot Award for investigative journalism. He is highly respected and one of the UK's leading investigative journalists (Private Eye, 2012).

His investigation revealed a crime model that police and care agencies refused to recognise – that most of the victims were white and a majority of those in identified abuse networks were men of Pakistani origin.

Andrew Norfolk's powerful articles revealed how the reluctance of agencies to acknowledge and confront a widespread form of abuse in deprived northern communities had broken families and shattered the lives of some of society's most vulnerable children.

FIGURE 5.1 Andrew Norfolk receiving his *Private Eye* Paul Foot Award from Editor Ian Hislop. The award recognised his investigative work on the child grooming scandal

I spoke to Andrew at his home in Leeds in June 2017, about his early days and the importance of local media.

Where he began

"At 24 years old I started as an indentured trainee on the *Scarborough Evening News*, which was then an evening newspaper with what was then the smallest circulation of any evening paper in the country. And as part of my training I went after, I think they sent me for a few days to an NCTJ college in Sheffield, and then I had to do a three-month block release, which I did in Harlow in Essex. Did all those preliminary exams in law and local government and central government, I had to get my shorthand up to 100 words a minute. And then go through final exams, and there was an interview about an incident at Oxtown, and you had to interview the police officer or the fire chief and then write it up. So although my starting salary was £6400 in 1989, they paid for all my training and in addition to that when I look back with everything that's happened in my career, and in some ways the most high profile story I've been involved in, so much of what enabled me to achieve working on that story and for it to turn into the success that it was, was grounded in stuff that I learned right back then. So many of the fundamentals.

". . . there were a team of really good young reporters on that paper in the early '90s, and there was a news editor who wouldn't let any of us rest on our laurels, who was actually grounded in the town, who if he thought you were getting above your station because you thought you could write quite well and had sort of made it would just keep kicking you and kicking you to get off your arse and go out and find some stories and bring them in yourself, not just expect everything to be handed to you on a plate. And I had a great time, but I think partly it was because it was a very small town, to fill that newspaper every day was a real challenge, but it really made you work for it. And in addition to that I did my very first bit of investigative journalism where they gave me two whole days to work on a story, which was a tip I'd had in a pub, and the day when that story appeared, which had the front-page splash, with 'Exclusive by Andrew Norfolk', and it gave me a thrill that even now I look back and I'm still slightly tingling, because nothing I've ever done since gave me that buzz that that first little story gave me."

So you'd have dedicated reporters assigned to departmental areas?

"Yeah, I remember a time when my brief was environmental health, and therefore I had to find a way to get to know the senior people there and try to build contacts with people lower down the chain. Then the traditional route into Fleet Street, as it still used to be called in those days, for somebody who was ambitious would typically have been to spend 18 months, a couple of years getting your hands dirty out in the sticks. I spent 11 years in regional journalism, I spent six years on the *Scarborough Evening News* because I absolutely loved it so much and I didn't really have an ambitious bone in my body. And then five years on the Yorkshire Post. Now that step up from *Scarborough Evening News* to the *Yorkshire Post* was initially, I was terrified, but again, I'll come back to the staffing levels in Scarborough now, but the head office of Scarborough was right smack in the centre of the town, on Aberdeen Walk. Anybody who's in town shopping or anything is walking past the front door, any time you make a mistake and somebody wants to pick you up on it, or any time anybody's got anything they want to talk about they just walk in, walk up the stairs, they come to your window and the secretary, and say 'I want to talk to a reporter'. They've moved to an out of town warehouse.

Which just so defeats one of the fundamental means of getting stories and being a newspaper to which the local community can relate. . . . When I started in'95 on the *Yorkshire Post* I was one of four reporters in the Sheffield satellite office, covering South Yorkshire. In North Yorkshire we had reporters physically based in Harrogate, York, Scarborough, I think there were two people in Hull. We had offices in Halifax, Bradford, Huddersfield, and then a really well staffed experienced head office in Leeds. Now I think I'm right in saying the Sheffield office doesn't even exist, and Harrogate's gone, I think York's gone, I know Scarborough's gone, I think there's still somebody in Hull, but I wouldn't be surprised, I do have friends who are still on the Yorkshire Post and it's just a completely different means of existing as a reporter and functioning, because the pressures are so much greater in terms of the sheer volume of work that one is expected to get through and therefore there's a danger it becomes more and more a question of churning out, less and less time to question and interrogate, less and less time to stand back and think, I'd had two years in the Sheffield office when I moved to Leeds, initially solely to work on what became the 'Donnygate' story. And that was the then editor of the *Yorkshire Post* Tony Watson, I think he's now managing editor of the Press Association, taking four reporters off diary for six months on a regional newspaper, just to work on one story."

Just outline "Donnygate"

"That was a classic, could have been written in any decade over the last 100 years, a classic local government corruption story. It was about corrupt builders paying bribes to (Doncaster Borough Council) councillors to ensure that land that they did not have permission for building had its designation changed against the advice of planning officers. And those bribes went from tiny pathetic little junkets to Donny races, to the chairman of the planning committee having a house bought for him. And it led to a major criminal inquiry and a lot of councillors were charged and some went to prison."

That started presumably with what you're describing as the nuts and bolts?

"…I think it was me in the Sheffield office on a Sunday, and it was a council agenda and it was a reference to a report about junketing, and it was initially just about junketing, the degree to which councillors, elected members were accepting hospitality at Doncaster racecourse which was owned by the council, I can't remember? And a very damning criticism of that, that I did a little story on. But then the initial impetus came from Leeds and from one of the reporters there who received a tip from a source that I think it still isn't known who that source is so I'd better not say, who realised actually there was something far more serious afoot and I was called up from Leeds to help initially with this team that was being put together to work on it. I know there are still some brilliant regional journalists, I know there are some brilliant and passionate newspaper editors out there, but I would be staggered if it's conceivable that any regional newspaper would commit four staff reporters to work for six months on one story these days, I just don't think it would begin to happen, it would barely happen on a national newspaper."

It's also about knowledge, do you think that awareness is still there?

"This is where because it's no longer my world I just don't know. But in another area of democracy which is criminal courts I do know, because for those first few years where I was doing the sex grooming stuff around the country I was sitting for weeks and months in criminal courts where I as a Times investigative journalist was the only journalist there. And here were stories that were really really important for the particular community involved, and yet they couldn't spare the time to send a reporter."

Going back to your time at the *Scarborough Evening Times*, part of the punishment for a crime is that it's reflected publicly in the media?

"Yeah, and I remember I think it was while I was there that, did this policy change nationally where they started publishing court lists, so even the most minor things like fines for not having a TV licence you would get a list each week, that definitely wasn't there when I started, I think it was by the time I left, and so we did, we published, and again that principle absolutely, it's part of the punishment and part of the incentive not to do wrong is to put your name in the local paper."

Did you have people asking you not to publish a story because they were embarrassed?

"I don't think that ever happened to me. But I don't know if this is relevant, but I think a year or two ago they asked me to go and address the national NCTJ conference, it was about Rotherham, and I spoke a lot about what I learned in Scarborough, and those basics that even we get these brilliant young boys and girls all with double firsts from Oxford or Cambridge, graduate trainees, however many thousand applications from which the three very brightest, and they're brilliant always, are cherry picked. And they're so bright, and some of them do go on to be just the best of the best and we're very lucky to have them. But some of them are so naïve, despite that wonderful intelligence, they haven't got any grounding, and it does make me sound like a dinosaur but I would almost force everybody before they work for a national newspaper to have had a minimum of two years learning that you never… you ask for somebody's name over the telephone and they tell you their name, no matter how simple that name is, John Smith, you must ask them how they spell both their Christian name and their surname, because if you get it wrong it absolutely infuriates the subject. Again this is just a digression, but we had satellite offices for weekly papers, there was a Bridlington paper, a Driffield paper, a Filey paper and the *Whitby Gazette*. And there was a reporter who was really sweet but not very bright in the Bridlington office who'd had to do a story, the fire brigade had had to be called out because he couldn't get a signal on his television properly, couldn't work out what was happening, and it turned out there was a pigeon caught in the aerial so the fire brigade had been called out to rescue the pigeon. And this had been picked up in the calls, and he'd rung they guy whose house it was who said in talking to him 'we were sitting there watching the television when suddenly the screen went fuzzy'. And so he'd had his little chat and he'd written his little story and it was on the day when they were going to press. He suddenly realised he hadn't asked who 'we' was. Maybe he did ring him back and he wasn't there, or maybe he just thought he didn't have time, maybe it was because he wasn't very bright, but what he'd done is looked up in the electoral register and saw that Mr Soandso lived with his wife Mrs Soandso at that address, and so he just assumed. And the paper came out, and the guy appeared in the office of the Bridlington Free Press and said 'you just said I was watching television with my wife, she died six months ago'. And they sacked him. That happens very often, but it's so helpful when that becomes so ingrained that you don't even think about it."

In the absence of that kind of scrutiny, what in your view is lost to community in terms of public interest?

"I guess it's the stuff we actually don't know about because there aren't any journalists any more to actually uncover it. I fear that local authorities, for example, become so accustomed to not being scrutinised and not being held to account.

I'm afraid to say that particularly applies in areas of this country where one political party has an overwhelming dominance, whether that is Labour or Conservative, but obviously because my years in regional journalism were in the north it tended to be, in Doncaster and Rotherham there was barely an opposition councillor. And if the local media are no longer there to go through the agendas and I know you sometimes get members of the public who take a particular interest in local democracy and try to raise a fuss, but if there's no outlet for scrutiny and opposition and questions and being put on the spot, and when you're actually about to take a decision you no longer need to consider is anybody going to ask any tricky questions about this, then I think the danger's self-evident."

Tim Minogue – Editor of *Private Eye*'s "Rotten Boroughs"

Journalist Matthew Engel, writing in the *Financial Times* in 2011, described "Rotten Boroughs" as "the national database of local government corruption" (Engel, 2011).

Essential reading for local government leaders and the citizens they serve, a typical column might include the arrest of a local authority chief executive, a punch up between elected councillors at a charity fund raising event; a senior council officer retiring to take up a lucrative private sector contract with a

FIGURE 5.2 Tim Minogue, Editor, "Rotten Boroughs", *Private Eye*, by Dara Minogue

company which has previously been handed council contracts; and a councillor refusing to resign despite admitting to stealing from his employer.

It does not inspire confidence in our public servants paid or elected but it is the only column of its kind in the UK that keeps a sharply focused spotlight upon UK local government misconduct.

Tim Minogue has been editing the column since 1999. I interviewed Tim in July 2017, about the column, his career and his views on the current media landscape.

He works as a freelancer, but *Private Eye* is his main source of income these days. He trained on local papers in the West country through the former Mirror group newspapers graduate training scheme. His training ground was places like Plymouth, Tavistock and Truro. The scheme was designed to offer a fast track to bright young journalists who were intent upon reaching Fleet Street and jobs on the nationals.

Fellow trainee alumni from that scheme, (although not all at the same time) have included the former Labour MP Chris Mullin MP, Nick Davies of the Guardian, (who exposed the phone hacking scandal) and the ubiquitous Alastair Campbell.

Tim says: "It was a very thorough training and you did do all the National Council Training of Journalists stuff, you did the shorthand and the law and everything, at the same time as working on the job on various local papers. And the idea of it was that the fast track bit of it came in where at the end you got a six week placement on one of the national papers." As well as the *Daily Mirror* in London, trainees could go to the *Daily Mirror* in Manchester, the *Daily Record* in Scotland or the *Sunday Mirror* or *Sunday People* in London. Tim got the opportunity to be a sub editor on the *Sunday Mirror* in London, and at the end of his attachment period, was able to do subediting shifts. Not long after that a job vacancy came up so he spent a few years working as a sub on the *Sunday Mirror* and then I went abroad for a couple of years and worked in Australia, came back, worked on the *Daily Mirror*. He went onto the freelance and did his first work with *Private Eye* in 1986 before taking on the task of editing the "Rotten Boroughs" column."

The importance of training

"It's important that you should be properly trained, and you should know the basics of defamation, and you should know how local government works.... A couple of years ago there was a very intelligent Oxbridge graduate came in here to do some work experience, because we have several graduates a year come in for a week or two to do work experience, and he was a very bright young man, and I realised he didn't know the difference between a councillor and a council officer. It's quite important to know those things, and under the old school of training you get to learn those things."

Rotten Boroughs

"'Rotten Boroughs' began in 1986. It was the case then and is the case now that the magazine is driven by the stuff that the readers send in, so in those days it used to be by post and by phone, and nowadays it's massively via email. And if there's a particular subject that people out there are concerned about, they'll contact us and give us tips and leads and everything.

I assume that there was so much coming in about local government that it was decided that it'd be worth having a slot or a page to itself in the same way that we've got regular things spots about health and the NHS, architecture, advertising, the press and broadcasting and other subjects."

Typical sources for stories

"Well it's sometimes, it's been claimed or quoted elsewhere that a lot of it's from local paper journalists who can't get stuff into their own papers. Now that has happened, but that's not the predominant thing, I'd say the predominant sources are ordinary people, readers who are upset about something that's going on in their area, either because they're just good citizens who are appalled by something that's going on, or because they themselves are involved and have an axe to grind, if it's a very egregious planning decision, or something seems a bit fishy, or a councillor has been caught out behaving badly, they will contact us and give us information which we can check out, or it may be that, we don't attempt to make every story completely exclusive, if it's a decent story in the local paper and it hasn't been reported elsewhere we'll follow it up. So some of the stuff is original and exclusive, and some of it isn't, and some stuff comes from councillors with an axe to grind, often very good sources are from disgruntled council officers and they're good because they will always supply you with, or point you out the documents that back things up. So it's a complete variety of sources really."

"National database for local government"

"Matthew Engel wrote a very nice piece in the *FT*, and one of the things he said in that is that Rotten Boroughs was the 'national database for local government corruption'. Which was a very nice thing to say, but actually completely exaggerated the scale of our coverage or influence, because this column has perhaps about six or seven items every fortnight, and those are culled from maybe 150 tips and leads over the fortnight, between 100 and 200, I've never actually counted. And of course, not all the 150 are worth doing, but maybe if we had the time and the bodies and the space in the paper we could, probably 40 or 50 of them could be stories that would be worth covering. Obviously, that would be way beyond what the readers or the editor could stand, but it is just like all news, it's a sample of what there is, and it's completely arbitrary really it's about what appeals to me, and what I feel like doing, and some of the stuff comes from reliable freelancers that we know as well so it sort of depends what the readers and the freelancers have sent in."

Have you noticed any change in the type of stories or in the number of stories coming through as a result of the changes in local journalism?

"I'd say the decline in local papers has been going on for quite a long time, I've been doing this for 18 years and what's happened, certainly the difference I've noticed is that when I started doing it there'd be a small pile of post, and a few notes from people who'd phoned in to ring back. And the tips might amount to 10 or 20 per issue, certainly very much less than it is now. There are a number of things that are influencing this, one is the expansion of email, so it's much easier for somebody to sit down and bang off an email to us if they're steamed up about something, I don't think we used email in 1998, 99, I think I had an email account of my own that I used, but we didn't have an office one, it sounds extraordinary but we didn't. So it's much easier for people to get in touch because of email, and they do, so that's different, and that increases the amount of material that's available. And dare I say it, I think the column has quite a lot of influence, and is probably better known now than it was in those days, so that will up the number of people who want to get in touch. And then the other thing, perhaps the contentious thing, it may be true that people are upset about something and they can't get it in the local paper, or the local paper doesn't seem to be interested, and I don't really want to start pointing the finger at different papers and everything, but it certainly is true in some places. I remember one council where the council leader had been convicted of various driving offences like driving without insurance, he was up in court for not paying maintenance to his wife, there were various conflicts of interest over planning things, and people were writing in to us about this, and I said what's the local paper doing, and they said they don't want to touch it. And then when we wrote about the guy, they followed up what we'd done. And there was another one a couple of years ago where the chief executive of quite a large local authority, we got an anonymous tip, because it was anonymous it took time to stand up, but this chief executive was having an affair with a female council officer, and they were having a reorganisation of the council and they were merging a couple of departments, and there were two women who were suitable internal candidates to head up this new department, and guess who got the job? The person he was having an affair with, it also entailed a large pay rise, a £16,000 pay rise. Now this information had been sent to the local paper, we knew it had, and they didn't touch it, and then we printed it and then they did a sort of 'oh it's all rubbish', the denials from the council guy saying all this stuff in *Private Eye* was rubbish, which of course it wasn't. But they hadn't gone near it, then they put exclusive on their thing, which was a bit galling. There are still lots of very good local papers, and people who make an effort and have an impact."

Tim reflects on the impact of news content moving online: "When I talk to local journalists it's very very depressing. You have to be able to use video, you have to take all your own photos, and somebody pointed out to me that lots of photos in local papers or rather on local websites, they'll be taken off Google Earth, it's turning up at the corners because it's just taken off Google Earth. And they're getting rid of subeditors, so the quality of the copy is extremely poor."

So what still drives you to do the "Rotten Boroughs" column?

"It's just like most of the journalism I've done, I do it because I'm probably not qualified to do anything else, and it's fun. And I enjoy it if something makes people sit up and take notice or if it's funny, and talking about those couple of stories earlier, if it causes somebody who's been misbehaving to resign that's… I don't take any great pleasure in scalps as it were, but if somebody's not really suited to what they're doing because of their other interests or their behaviour has marked them out as not suitable for public office then they stop doing that because of something we've done, then yeah that's quite satisfying."

He has praise for some examples of where local newspaper reporting is still having an impact.

Emma Youle at the *Hackney Gazette* won the 2017 *Private Eye* Paul Foot Award for investigative and campaigning journalism. This reflected her work on a series of articles about homelessness in the borough."

"… there are people there who are doing good stuff and sticking their necks out and being persistent. Because there are young people who want, it's a great job and there are young people fortunately who want to do it, and want to do it properly, but it's getting harder and harder. And it takes time yeah, which you're probably not allowed to have, that's the worrying thing. I mean my friend Nick Davies in his book *Flat Earth News*, in the early chapters of that he talks about the sheer number of stories people have to do on local papers, people are being required to file 10, 15, 20 items a day, and ok local papers you've always had quite a lot to do, but that's getting mad. And you're having to develop the video content and online yeah, not to mention all that other stuff."

Finally how important do you see the scrutiny of local government?

"Oh it's really important for healthy democracy. I think one of the things that's come out of the Grenfell fire is that they've not, as far as one can tell had a very proactive local press there, holding that council to account, and that may have added to some of the complacency that you will get with a council like that, certainly."

We take a closer look at the details about media coverage in Kensington and Chelsea in our chapter on the Grenfell Tower tragedy.

Eileen Brooks – from award winning journalism to council communications chief

Eileen was Head of Communications at Rotherham Borough Council from 1999–2005. Before that a journalist and Chief Reporter at the Yorkshire Post, for their South Yorkshire and North-East Derbyshire office. She now runs her own PR communications company, Stratiji.

Having started in journalism and then crossed over to local government public relations, Eileen is neatly placed to offer a dual perspective on local media and council communications.

Views from the foothills   115

FIGURE 5.3 Eileen Brooks by John Bates Photography

How was the story first uncovered?

"I started in journalism in the traditional old-fashioned way, with a three year apprenticeship at a local paper, the Rotherham Advertiser, which included two six week sandwich courses in journalism at Sheffield Hallam University, which was then the polytechnic. Then I went through the traditional route, which doesn't exist so much anymore, from local paper to evening paper to regional paper, and then people may go on to national papers which I didn't, the Yorkshire Post was my last paper. The difference between then and now is that my way of going into journalism means that you actually learn on the job, not just the theory, and you're embedded in a local area, which you know well in terms of institutions and people. And in those days, we're talking more than years ago, this was pre-internet, publication of council agendas and minutes was on paper, and they were eagerly awaited. We used to pick them up from the town hall as soon as they were ready, and a couple of reporters would literally pore over the stories, you would go through every line of them. Every council meeting and committee was covered in person, most parish council meetings in the evening were attended. Every magistrates court was covered. Now it's not unusual for full council meetings to have no journalist present, most magistrates courts have no journalists present, and even at crown courts staffing is so short that often journalists go for the opening and closing, and just dip in and out in between. This can be dangerous, as if you're not there all the time you can miss an instruction from the judge not to report something, and I've seen this happen with television reporters."

One of Eileen's biggest stories and one for which she was awarded the "Regional Independent Media Scoop of the Year", whilst still at the *Yorkshire Post*.

Her investigative work focused on an anti-poverty forum contributed to by 150 other local councils. Rotherham Borough Council's Deputy Leader Garvin Reed was shown to have used over £170,000 of forum funds, intended to alleviate poverty, to bankroll his own lavish lifestyle including paying prostitutes and luxury hotel bills. The investigation led ultimately to him being jailed for three years.

Eileen picks up the detail: "It was a national organisation, and there was a subscription paid by different local authorities in quite deprived areas. The aim was to get together and talk about poverty and how they could alleviate it. But in actual fact what happened was the deputy leader and a few of his colleagues and friends were actually spending the money on jollies and prostitutes, and none of it was going to help alleviate poverty. And they ended up going to court, and they ended up in prison. It was fascinating to work on, but I would say that I was helped all the way by contacts that I'd built up over the years who would give me confidential information in the knowledge that I would never reveal my sources, and I would always report what they told me accurately. You can only build up trust and contacts over a period of time by getting to know people on the ground, you can't do it by swanning into an area where no one knows you."

"I got a phone call from a contact at the council to say the police had raided the deputy council leader's office that morning, and he told me a little bit more about it, obviously all in confidence. So by the time the council had called a press conference later in the day I had a bit of a head start and knew a little bit more about it."

So that process of relationship building was one of the reasons you were tipped off?

"Yes. And another of my good contacts, I think it's ok to say this now, was the police."

As the investigation went on, did you look at council minutes, or were there formal papers you needed access to?

"Yes, we looked at all the formal papers in relation to the poverty forum. We sort of hung out outside their offices talking to people who came out, I did things like telephoning, I'm not sure about this actually but I'll tell you, I don't know whether you can use this, I would ring the hotel where I knew where they'd stayed, I'd ring it and pretend I was the secretary booking them in again, and can I book them in at the same rate, and they told me what they'd paid last time and how many people were in the room. This was devious but the information was in the public interest and could not be obtained in any other. Certainly I was never worried about that at the time, but I think there are now more restrictions on data protection, and maybe the hotel shouldn't have told me but they did."

This was in the days pre FOIA, where your ability to get information about public sector spending was much less?

"Yes it was. It was much less, you were dependent on what they told you. And if they didn't tell you, you had to find out by other means."

The picture we're building is you learn your craft, you do your training, you build up your contacts?

"And build up trust as well, which brings us back to Grenfell Tower. I'd like to come back to that, because one of the themes that's emerging is the national media swamped in immediately.

How do you see that as being difficult?

"Well they haven't got the understanding of the area, they haven't got a relationship with local people. A local reporter would probably know somebody who lived in that tower, there were so many people there. They would certainly know somebody who knew somebody, and it's a bit of cliché, it's always said that national journalists don't have to face people again, whereas local journalists do have to live in that community so they have to behave, and they have to be fair."

Because you might be going into a residents' meeting two weeks down the line?

"Exactly, yeah."

One of the things that's emerged in our research is the move of newspaper offices out of town, people can't just pop in?

"No, when I worked at the *Advertiser* it was right in the middle of Rotherham, and we had a desk, a reporters' desk, and people would come in to reception and say 'can I speak to a reporter please?' and a reporter would be sent out to speak to them at this desk. And we just got loads of stories and information. (The *Advertiser* office is now based seven miles outside of Rotherham on an industrial estate.)"

And is it fair to say that people would feel that was part of the local community structure, and would you feel part of the local community, that you're championing local people's interests?

"Yes, absolutely, definitely. And there's a line maybe you could use about the Rotherham Advertiser, Rotherham Borough Council is a Labour council, almost all elected members are Labour, and so the Rotherham Advertiser used to call themselves the unofficial opposition. And they would give the council a hard time, as you know."

How long would you say it took you from joining the local paper to feeling competent at what you were doing?

"A couple of years I think, and then I probably would say, when I worked at the *Star* and then I got the job at the *Yorkshire Post* people did say to me who'd gone the same route that you will find it a step up and that even more will be expected of you in terms of balance and accuracy, and that was true because if you hadn't got both sides of the story you'd get a call from the subs to say 'it's one side, what's the other side?'. And that was a really big thing at the *Yorkshire Post*, you had to get both sides of the story. I don't think people bother with that now. The BBC do because they've got to be by law, they've not got to be biased, and that's a problem with social media, there are no checks and balances on social media."

Give me a couple of examples of something a sub editor might pick up on?

"I suppose the mantra is 'when in doubt, find out', some people say 'when in doubt, leave out', and they would phone us, on the *Yorkshire Post* it would be during the evening, and they would phone and say this doesn't make sense, or you've mentioned this person but you've not explained the context, why are you mentioning this person, you've spelt this name in two ways which one is the right way? There was so much more attention to detail than there is now. I read some local papers now and I think 'oh god', I do read some papers and it's so sloppily written with whole paragraphs repeated. And then every word in a newspaper was proof read before publication, I don't think proof reading is done thoroughly these days."

On falling circulation figures

"When I worked at the *Yorkshire Post* everybody was really keen to put on the circulation and do good coverage and get good stories, that has now all gone, the *Yorkshire Post* hasn't even got an office in Sheffield any more. And I can remember going to editorial meetings and it was called Project 100,000, aimed at increasing our very healthy circulation of 80,000. We were trying to get it about 100,000. To put that in context, I came across these figures the other day, daily circulation of the *Yorkshire Post* apart from Saturdays is just 18,991 now. Less than a fifth. The Saturday paper sells a lot more because it's got a magazine, but that's only 47,261. So it averages out at 23,000, which is just awful."

(Average daily circulation for print and digital editions at the Leeds-based title fell 3.6pc in the period July to December 2016 to stand at 25,178.) (HoldtheFrontPage, 2017)

In terms of the investigative work that you did, how important do you think your early training was?

"It was really important, because you had to know who to ring and how to approach things. I would also say the big thing, you need time to do it. So I was allowed time just to concentrate on the forum, but that's because we'd got the staff to be able to do it. It takes time, and you don't produce a story every day, whereas now I think reporters are expected to produce a quota of stories each day or each week."

Not too long after you went over to the other side? (in her PR role at Rotherham Council)

". . . it was something I hadn't done before, so again I was learning on the job and had to learn very quickly. But it was invaluable to have been a journalist before becoming a PR practitioner, because you know how a journalist's mind works, and there are so many people who don't. You think it's fairly logical, you see something and you think 'yeah, that's a good story', and other people don't think like that, and that's quite a surprise. What also surprised me was that people were terrified of journalists, terrified of talking to them about the most mundane things, because they thought they would be misquoted or splashed all over the front page, so there was a job there to be done."

What's your view on how important it is to let people know how their money's being spent?

"It's absolutely crucial, because as soon as you start doing things in secret, that's when bad things happen, and corruption happens. I remember, the (former) Head of Communications at Derbyshire County Council, Rod (Cook) saying to me, when I went to pick his brains, before I started in the job, and he said: 'Look, with an organisation this size, there will at all times be somebody doing something they shouldn't be.' And that's true. You do need, councils, institutions, health, the police, they need the scrutiny of journalists and it just isn't there, because there aren't enough journalists."

And does that make you worried about what's happening?

(On the Grenfell Tower tragedy):
"Somewhere on a piece of paper it will say that they made a decision to save so many thousands of pounds by putting an inferior kind of cladding on.

Now I know it's not been proved that it's all down to the cladding, but that will have been on a piece of paper somewhere. If you had proper scrutiny by journalists in that area, they would have picked that up, that would've been a story, and that could've stopped that happening."

On declining media plurality

"One important point is the plurality of ownership now, because when I first started out in newspapers they were all separately owned, so the *Yorkshire Post* had an owner, the *Advertiser*, the *Star*, *South Yorkshire Times*. Now, as you know, most of them are owned by the same company, Johnston Press, so you get journalists going out and covering a story for half a dozen different papers, there's no rivalry there, there's no incentive to uncover the story, uncover the truth, because it's going to appear everywhere. And because it's all run by accountants now, and to accountants, this was said to us, why does it make sense to have a reporter from the *Yorkshire Post*, a reporter from the *Star*, a reporter from the *Morning Telegraph* all at the same event, all coming back and then writing the story? They couldn't see that those papers had different readerships."

And that each one of those journalists might have uncovered something different, and would be competing to do so.

"Yes, would cover it differently."

How concerned should we be about the loss of those journalistic skills in terms of holding up a spotlight to public sector organisations?

"I think we should be very concerned, because if people aren't learning the skills then the skills disappear, and without them institutions, the council, the police, they can't be held to account in the same way. Yes, people can get an FOI, but even to submit an FOI you have to have a little bit of basic knowledge about what's wrong here, what's the information you're trying to get? So you do need some basic skills to formulate a successful FOI. And they're time consuming, they're quite narrowly focused aren't they, they will give you the answer to the question you've asked, but they won't give you any additional information. So I think it's a tragedy."

FIGURE 5.4A, B Front pages of the *Whitby Gazette*, *Scarborough News* and the *Burnley Express* series newspapers are reproduced with kind permission of the publishers, Johnston Press (now JPI Media). Photography by Carmel O'Toole

And do you think it almost inevitable that things will be going on that don't become publicly apparent without that scrutiny?

"Yes, definitely."

Andrew Mosley – Editor at the *Rotherham Advertiser*

FIGURE 5.5 Andrew Mosley, Editor, the *Rotherham Advertiser*

Andrew Mosley edits one of the fast disappearing numbers of independently owned and run local newspapers. The *Rotherham Advertiser* offices which used to be based in the town centre, are now seven miles out of town on the Manvers industrial estate. That is on the border of Rotherham with Doncaster, in South Yorkshire. Like many of the media professionals we have interviewed, Andrew began his working life on local newspapers.

He paints a more upbeat picture in which he is managing to buck some the trends typical of many group owned media titles. He describes his success thus far in resisting leaping from the "digital cliff" and (for the moment at least) a newsroom where print still comes first. He was happy to share his experience of the pleasures and pitfalls of life editing a local newspaper in today's ever more competitive market.

Can you tell me something about the roles and the scope of your responsibilities?

"I edit the *Rotherham Advertiser*, our paid for newspaper, and we also have two free papers, the *Rotherham Record* and the *Dearne Valley Weekender*. I'm responsible really for delegating jobs to reporters, photographers, sub-editors, and read every word of each newspaper, so if there's any mistakes in there they're my fault, I like to think. Deciding what goes on the front page, what goes where, attending management meetings, liaising with the local authorities, council, police, education authorities, that sort of thing. Going out doing the ambassadorial duties, talking to community groups, charities, presenting awards, trying to really represent the paper in the community as well as making sure that what we do in paper and on our digital forums and social media forums is up to date and as good as it can be."

Can you tell me briefly how long you've been in this role and working in journalism?

"I've been here since June 2012, moved over from being features editor and assistant editor in Bolton in Lancashire, on the *Bolton News*. I've been in journalism since 1991, and I started on the *Craven Herald* in Skipton so I moved back to Yorkshire via Devon and Lancashire."

What's been your experience of changes to the media over the last 5 to 10 years?

"I think twofold really, there's been extra pressure on the media through websites to start with, then other forms of social media coming in with Facebook, Twitter etcetera. And at the same point pressure on jobs, so you tend to find that owners of newspapers specifically the larger groups want to reduce staffing but get more out of them, which I think stretches your ability to provide a quality product, and I think that's evident in some of the products that are put out by the larger newspaper groups who've cut staff massively, maybe sent their subbing out to subbing hubs, maybe Newport, so you've got people in Newport subbing a paper in Yorkshire. And I think they maybe don't have the commitment to that paper or the knowledge of the area, and I think that's evident in the quality of what you get, but yet you've got newspaper owners and chief execs expecting the same results. And I think that's put a lot of pressure on journalists, and I think the people who are running papers as opposed to people who were running them 25 years ago when it might have been the editor don't really understand what a newspaper is about and why people bought it in the first place. Aside from that obviously there's outside pressures on newspapers, such as there's hundreds of TV channels, there's hundreds of websites, people are getting their information elsewhere and quicker, and we've had to react to that. And I think newspapers generally have been quite slow in reacting, and when they did react they went over the top, they sold their papers down the river for a digital product without really researching how to monetise that, and I still don't think they have. So I think the pressure from that has been to say well we need to make cuts, so more jobs are going, but they expect more, and so what they get is actually less."

You referred to some of the bigger groups, what's the ownership status of the Rotherham Advertiser?

"It's an independent paper still, we're family owned, we're owned now by Nick Alexander who's under the title of Regional Media Limited. We split this year from our print group, so we're standalone now as a publishing business."

So one of the few in the country then?

"Yeah, the *Barnsley Chronicle* as well, and I think the *Oldham Chronicle, Kent Messenger*, and a couple of others, but there aren't many."

[Reach] has hundreds of titles

"Yeah, and I'm not sure how many [JPI Media] is either, but that can't be that far behind. I came from that with my previous two jobs, I was at Northcliffe in the *Express* and *Echo* in Exeter, and then Newsquest at the *Bolton Evening News* in Lancashire."

Can you tell me something about the news judgement process as it's evolved to take account of these changes?

"Specifically here, when I came here, and part of the reason I did come here, is that we haven't leapt off that digital cliff, and I thought that's quite interesting, there's still a decent quality paper putting out around 100 and odd pages every week, and not going online first with everything. So we were in some people's eyes behind the rest of the country, but I think that's actually turned out to be a good thing, because we haven't committed ourselves and thrown the paper out, which a lot of papers have, so we haven't experienced the massive decline in circulation that a lot of papers did. We were also aware that we did need to do something digitally, so we slowly developed the website, and over the last year we've more than doubled our hits and unique users whilst also, we've had a 4% drop in circulation, which we'd obviously rather not have, but industry-wide for a paper still selling over 20,000 I think it's the top performer in the country. The problem we've still got, even though I think we've trebled our monetising of the website and social media, it still doesn't make up for what you're losing in print. And I think that's been the big job, to balance what we're putting out digitally and what we're producing in the newspaper. So the decisions we made, we weren't going to give our front page stories away, we weren't going to give any of our major stories away that we didn't think anyone else had got, unless of course there's a murder happens on a Monday, you can't hold onto it until a Friday like the paper used to do. So I think we've made the decision social media wise to concentrate on breaking news, early morning traffic news, anything overnight, a bit old style really, like you did with your paper, your police calls, your fire calls, get them online early doors. Anything that's actually useful to the reader, rather than something they don't really need to read that day, they don't need to read a story that we might have about cuts to a school or a hospital, it can wait until Thursday or Friday, because it's not happening that day. We've not gone down the celebrity route, we've not gone down clickbait, so I think we're trying to give local people something that benefits their day, something they need to know, something that can help them avoid a traffic jam, find out what's going on, causing the disruption in their town centre, that sort of thing."

How do analytics factor into your setup?

"I've been to visit some other papers where they do that, where they've got big screens up around their offices and they're telling you what the age group that's hitting certain stories is, how many people are looking at a certain point, and they look at those and transfer those stories to their newspaper. Which I find a bit odd, because their best performing digital stories end up in their paper, and they think, I've been told, that that makes for a better product. But I don't believe that, because I think you can grab a certain audience for your digital product and for your newspaper, I don't think they have to be exclusive, I think some people will read both, and you have to give people a bit of a flavour of what you're going to be putting in your paper on a Friday without giving the whole game away. So we are quite aware of that, and we're quite aware that if we put a full story online on a Monday there's no point putting it in full in the paper on Friday, because people have read it already, because virtually everybody now is on social media, so you've given the game away. So I don't really want to do that, I want to drive people back to the paper, and equally from the paper to the website."

I guess some of the content that will engage people online, like videos, isn't necessarily a news story?

"No, this week one of our reporters went to a new go-carting centre in Tinsley, and we put that out on Facebook, and it's had 3200 shares, which surprised us really. But that's not going to be your most read story in the paper, even though it's in the paper, a version of it, but I'm quite happy with that, that's got people to our website, and they've had a look around at other stories, maybe seen what we've got to offer in the paper and they might have a go at buying it [laughs]. And also that's hit younger readers as well perhaps, which maybe you don't always, so they might come back and have another look at your website, and in future years they're aware of the brand, they're aware it's the *Rotherham Advertiser*."

So it's making a more harmonious relationship between web content and print?

"Yeah, that's what I've been trying to do out there, and things like sport, whereas say even three years ago we were doing a traditional two page Rotherham United match report, coming out on a Friday six days after the game, and it seemed a bit pointless. But if you get that on the web straight after the game then we get reaction in on Friday's paper and look ahead to the next week, and we try to do a bit more of an online magazine style thing for next season, a bit of a sort of Sky Sports News match day special. We've not worked out the full implications of that and how we're going to do it, but it'll be totally different to what we do in the paper, so then hopefully people who are interested in that will want to read what we've got in the paper."

Has your budget been cut for editorial in the time you've been here?

"Since I've been here we've had one redundancy, and we had a part time reporter who left who hasn't been replaced. I think there were 17 editorial staff when I started including myself and we've got 15 now. 16.6 and we've got 15 now. We've done cost cuts, but they've generally been looking at things like utilities and what we've been using, and how we've been using the building and how we do things, rather than cutting back on our editorial system and our staff, we've been trying to avoid that. A lot of papers have stopped their sports reporter going to away football matches or to rugby games, and we've tried to preserve that by looking at savings elsewhere. So we've even looked at things right down to toner cartridges that the photographers are using, to try and relook at everything we do to cut back costs there before we have to go anywhere else, things we don't need to spend on particularly."

What about feature writing?

"We haven't actually got a full time feature writer, so what I've tried to encourage people to do is anyone can write features. So if they go out and do a news story and come back, and I think hang on that'd be better as a feature than just a straightforward news story. Some are more aware than others, but we're quite free with that, if somebody's got an idea I'm quite happy to book a double page spread in for next week's paper early on, and we'll continue doing that. I think feature writing's important if it's the right type of feature, and I don't think the right type of feature is just an interview with a celebrity who's not from round here just because they're turning up in the area. I think it's something that affects the area, something that affects people who live here."

In terms of cutbacks yours is nothing like the scale I've been finding in other areas, which area of editorial has been most significantly affected?

"We've kept up with the sport. The people we've lost, we lost a full time news reporter, and a part time news reporter who did district, so somebody else has had to absorb those jobs. We haven't been affected subbing wise, we had a person leave but they were replaced by a reporter, then another reporter took on part time subbing so we tried to mix the jobs up a bit more so they weren't as affected as they could have been. So I guess reporting because we're doing a lot more digital, so that's had an impact as well, so when you lose your person and a part time person then the rest of what you've got here are doing more."

In terms of the way people are badged, how does that work?

"We all do digital work, and we all do print work, so whoever's doing whatever, and we say shall we put it on the net, no I don't think we need to, yeah we need to do that. We've got somebody who joined us recently came over from JP and so they were aware of what had been going on there, so they're a bit more digitally sharp than the team we had here before, and he's taken on quite a lot of those responsibilities, galvanises people to do that, but also the reason he left Johnston Press was because of their digital first policy, so he's quite cautious as well, so I think that's helped us strike a bit of a balance on taking us forward digitally and not over committing us."

So whilst the team's aware of the pros and cons of digital, is print first here?

"Still print first. I think when I came there was a complete anti digital stance here, and where I'd come from being at Newsquest it was just moving the other way. And I think gradually we've evolved, but with the commitment to be still print first, and to make sure that we're not giving our stuff away for free, because why would you, I never have understood that."

And it's borne out by the size of the paper?

"We're 96 this week – I try to keep it just over 100, so generally depending on the advertising it'll stick over 100 if we can. It's gone up and down, I've got a few ideas for next year that'll possibly increase it as well in some ways, with added value content that may save money otherwise, with magazines that we do that we think we can bring in paper to save on glossy costs, but will actually be part of the *Rotherham Advertiser* brand and will boost what we're doing in paper. Like the *Yorkshire Post* do a weekly magazine on Saturday, whereas we can't maybe match that, we can perhaps do that sort of thing and make it a local, we do Chase magazine and we can perhaps bring that into the paper on a monthly basis maybe, and do leisure and lifestyle in that, without taking up the news pages. I've not actually told the MD or the owner that yet, but it's my plan that I've been putting together this week [laughs]."

What issues around staff culture, skills and training has the new emphasis on digital raised?

"Quite a lot at first. The first person that left after I started here was the person responsible for the website, they were also a sub as well. They took total control of it though, so when that person had gone it was quite difficult to persuade people that they needed to be part of this, and it really did gradually evolve and it's been mainly over the last year that people have really taken it on board. People have got more into Twitter, they've got more into Facebooking, and so that's just become second nature now, but they still write their stories first for the paper, then we have a look at where it's going for the internet, unless it is a breaking news story. So people are aware now of what works well digitally, and on a weekly basis we analyse what's done best, why we think it's done best, what we think we could've done better. Like last Saturday, could we have gone into Rotherham to spend the day filming the EDL protest, yeah we could have done but what would that have got us, it's the seventeenth in a couple of years, would that have got us loads of views for the cost of having a person out there for a day? Probably not, we've got it in paper, we had a story online, and so it's really measuring the value of the amount of time you spend doing that. After the previous one where we had the slight ruckus about the police performance on the day of the march we had a couple of front pages out of that as well, so it is a big issue, and I went down on the day to have a look around at what was going on, and I found it quite depressing really that 500, 600 police there, the high street railinged off, and not that many people there really, and it just seems a bit of crying shame really to have 120 marchers and five times as many police, which we're paying for big time in a town that hasn't got a lot of money, and then police are having to make cutbacks, shops closing in the town centre, there's new shops open trying to make a living. So we have to give that what it deserves whilst not maybe pandering to 120 people and giving them the publicity they want, it's the effect it has on the town rather than that. And so we did make the decision not to spend the day videoing it because we've done that before several times, but to give it generally the coverage that it deserved."

Have you been encouraged to pool resources with other papers?

"The interesting thing about the *Dearne Valley Weekender* is that frees over the last couple of years, and there's been a couple of stories on the front page recently, are dying to a degree, but the *Weekender* comes in at around 40 to 48 pages a week, and it's all exclusive content, it's not one of those frees where they just reproduce some of the previous week's paper, we actually have people working on it and producing stories for this area. And with the *South Yorkshire Times* closing down I'd say the *Doncaster Free Press* and the *Sheffield Star* possibly not committing quite as many people and staff to this area, it's kind of just here at the moment. And the Dearne Valley's not the most wealthy area, and we're probably the only paper that's committed to the Dearne Valley, so we're pursuing that and we're thinking of taking that perhaps further towards Doncaster, at the moment it's largely Wath, Mexborough, Swinton, Denaby, and there's nobody else covering those areas, and so that's kind of a free paper that's not covered anywhere else, it's not covered in our paid for, and it's not covered in any other papers unless there's a murder really, when everybody turns up. So I think that's quite an interesting model, because it's quite rare really to have a free paper that's, it's not staffed, but all the reporters work on it."

But it's bespoke content for that title?

"It is yeah, and we have had discussions as well about outsourcing production and things like that, but I'm quite keen to avoid that because I've been there before. It depends what part of production you're outsourcing, if you're outsourcing your subbing then I'm not keen on that. I just don't see that it works, it hasn't worked anywhere else, it's ok, it might save you a bit of money in the short term, but does it not cost you in the long term when people start to realise that your content's not quite as good, the look of your paper's not quite as good because it doesn't have an identity any more. If you look at the JP papers they all look pretty similar, and every page looks pretty similar because of the templates, so you end up with a murder looking the same as a charity fun run because it's got the same space, the same boxes, and you end up flipping over the pages and you think hang on what was that? And you turn back."

This is the template system where pages are planned days in advance?

"And if you haven't got the picture you wanted because they didn't turn up for the picture, you end up with a head shot, which would be 2cm big, taking up three quarters of the page. I mean people will say our paper doesn't look the most modern in the country, and perhaps it doesn't, but I think it's got its own identity, and I think the day the papers stopped representing their town with their look as well as their content, was a bit of a sad day. I used to work on the Craven Herald in

Skipton which was my first paper, and it used have a full front page of adverts, but they weren't adverts for shops they were adverts for events. And when they stopped that when they got taken over first of all by Westminster Press and then Newsquest, it just looked like everything else. And the sales are now less than 10,000 and they were 20,000 and I think that's sad, it lost its identity."

You were saying this is about 20,000 now, how does that compare to a couple of years ago?

"It's gone down probably between about 3 and 5 per cent a year, we're still committed to trying to stop that, but looking at the ABCs last week there were some as far as 20 or 30 per cent down. Even the *Star*, you're looking at it going down to 17,000 and over the last few years that's probably gone down half in the time I've been here, just less than five years. I think they'll tell you that they're reaching a record audience, which they maybe are, but I don't know how much of that you monetise. I was told this morning that we'd trebled our internet revenue, does that make for what you're losing in print, and does that make up for the amount of hours you're putting into producing that content."

In terms of local correspondents, in some of the others they're now refashioning these roles as community content curators, is that something the *Advertiser*'s done?

"We have photographers who work for us, but they work for us for free, they generally represent the clubs they're working for like athletics clubs, football clubs that sort of thing. And we have community correspondents who produce our district news section and correspondents who might send us athletics news that sort of thing. It's actually a bit of a discussion we're going through at the moment with the owner of a local club who thinks we can have a community team, and I'm not sure how well that works. Derby have got a community photography team of about 100 I'm told, who go out to jobs and do pictures for them, but you'd have to be pretty confident in their ability to cover a murder scene, the legalities of what they're doing, and I'm not confident in going down that road. And I think it's a long-term thing rather than a quick fix solution and I don't think you can suddenly say yeah we'll stop having photographers and reporters and we'll have 100 community journalists. Because they don't do it properly, I'm not having a go at any our district correspondents but you sub the district pages and however many times you try and give them style pointers and hints it doesn't happen, and why should it, they're not fully trained. I don't mind going down the road slightly to have readers sending in their opinions on restaurants, films, music, books, that sort of thing, but I'm not confident about sending people out to cover breaking news stories and that sort of thing, you're getting rid of the quality aren't you. The first time you get a big legal coming onto your desk you'll be the one to blame, it won't be the people who've made the decision that that's the route you have to go down."

So you haven't gone down the template route

"We've discussed templates for the frees to a certain extent, and we have discussed it for certain pages in the *Advertiser* but it would be things like the district pages, perhaps things like the clubs pages we do, they wouldn't be for news pages."

To what extent is local government coverage a priority?

"It's still a big priority, we don't have a full time local government correspondent but we have Gareth Dennison who wrote the front page today who attends all the council meetings, goes through all the council agendas, keeps in contact with the councillors and follows all their issues and the hospital issues. So he tends to cover all that and that's his main duty and he's on top of that. And I've made sure really that he has enough time to do that, because I think a lot of papers have stopped going through agendas and stopped that, and Gareth's good because he goes to all the meetings and the councillors I've spoken to that I meet elsewhere they all know him, they all ring him, they all write in with tip-offs. So we've kept on top of that, whereas I know a lot of papers haven't, I've worked in places before where we've been reduced to occasional meeting with the chief exec and a couple of others who've explained why the decisions that they've been making have been made and the positives behind them. And we've gone with that, and I've found that really frustrating. In a previous place I've worked they were closing down the libraries and the story we ran was that there would be a library service within a mile of every reader, because they were doing mobile library services, it's not quite what people wanted though is it, but it was the council spin, and I don't think we've ever gone down that route. People still say oh yeah the Advertiser is in the council's pocket, you're going to get people saying that, certain local self-styled political websites will tell you that. Which I find quite astounding, every time you have a front page that's not about the child sexual exploitation, oh the Advertiser's gone with this, they're letting them off the hook, and I think have you not read the paper, have you not seen it's been on the front page 28 times in the past two years or whatever. I used to find it more frustrating than I do now, I used to want to write back to these people and say actually have you read this page, that page, that page and that page? And the council didn't particularly like us before, and maybe that means you're striking the right balance if you've got people who think you're in their pocket but yet the council don't like you.

We still go, I've got a meeting next week with Sharon Kemp the chief executive, and we still go through those, she'll say any issues you've got, and we'll say we've got this, this and this that we wouldn't mind answers to. And she'll say these have been my issues with your paper. And it's not cleared the air as such, it's just a sense of where you're both coming from and why you did what you did, and people understand that, and why they could've got a better story out of it by maybe reacting a bit quicker or saying something different.

And sometimes why we could've done it slightly different, and yeah maybe we could've done. And I think that works ok."

So are you confident you're giving local government sufficient attention?

"Yeah, and one thing I do is every morning I go on these political websites and have a look around, I get emails from people quite regularly saying do you know this about the council? So we do have a few insiders coming to us and I always get Gareth or whoever to follow those up, so I think we find out most things. And in one way it's more difficult to find out, but in another way there are so many more avenues, there's Twitter, there's people posting things all over, and a lot of the time it could be rubbish, but equally sometimes there's a bit of a germ of truth in there and we will always follow it up and I don't think we let them off the hook, whatever some people might think."

Do you find that you use the Freedom of Information Act regularly?

"Yeah, a lot."

Is that because you find there are barriers to getting bits of information, or because it's a good useful tool anyway?

"Both. Sometimes we'll ask a question from the press office and we don't get the answer so then we'll put the FOI request in, that's not just the council that's the hospital as well quite a lot."

Does that work?

"Yeah it does, you don't always get your answer on time, but you'll get a certain response and then you'll get your answer, so I think yeah it does work. I think it costs local authorities quite a lot of money to operate through that, so I think to be fair to them they're probably quite keen to avoid it, so they'd rather give you to a degree the answer that you want, or an answer that gets some way in that direction, than force you down that route and force them down that route."

The clock's ticking as soon as you submit isn't it?

"Yeah, it is. And obviously the person who receives that request has then got other people to drag in to get the answer. But I think it does, we've had quite a few front pages out of FOI requests."

And in terms of your relationship with the press office, how does that work – is it helpful or obstructive, or a mixture of both?

"I think it's a mixture of both. If you go back to when I started, and that's probably before there were council press offices, so if you had a planning story, you'd ring up and get straight through to the director of planning who would answer your questions, or not depending. But you'd get an answer of some sort. And that seems to me in some ways more sensible because sometimes you get to the press office, they can't get hold of the director of planning or he doesn't want to speak to you, and it's then become more difficult to get a direct answer. And I think sometimes for a local authority that doesn't work, but I think that might be a culture thing now because that's changed over years, the director of planning or whoever doesn't expect to speak to the press. In some ways at least you've got a direct contact straight away, and you can say right we are running this story this Thursday, we need it by this time, if you don't get an answer back we're going to go with it. So they can at least get through to that person and speak to them. They'll also do a bit of research for you, we also meet with the press office or a representative whenever we go to meet the chief exec, so we'll go through the good and bad points of that. And I think to a degree our relationship with the council press office is probably not that bad, it's pretty decent, I think it's actually probably improved over the past year, 18 months."

That's interesting, because they've restructured haven't they in about that time?

"Yeah, admittedly some of that might have been when the council were going through the really difficult patch just before Martin Kimber left, they seem to have got a bit more, there's a bit more openness about them now."

The lack of transparency was one of the criticisms of them

"Yeah, and we used to have regular meetings, but it was kind of I can't tell you off the record or on the record quite a lot, and you'd come away thinking why did we do that? Whereas I think we meet now, and Sharon Kemp will say this is the answer, can't print it yet but this is what is happening, and she's quite honest I think in how she tells you things, and what's really going on. She'll say obviously what I'd like to say is this, but it's not necessarily what's going on. Yeah, I think we're better than we were, I'd say the hospital similarly has got more open, I'd say our main problem is probably our relationship with the police. They've got quite a few people working in their press department, they do seem under quite a lot of pressure, and I think they find it difficult to operate as they'd want to maybe."

There must be lots of sensitivities at play?

"There are, we've found that over our coverage over the EDL (English Defence League) marches. After the march that brought about the prosecutions from the Wellgate riot and what happened in court about policing and their research and their planning for the day, we got quite a backlash from reporting that, even though it's what was said in court, and I was told by one person we'd set back policing in South Yorkshire by five years, and my answer to that was wasn't that you? So we've had a bit of a tiff after that, as you might like to call it – do your research before you've gone into court and answered your questions, it's going to go in the paper if you haven't."

It sounds like you feel like you've got a healthy balance, from your personal point of view, is that an important priority for a local paper?

"Yeah massively for me, having come from Newsquest before and Northcliffe before that where I saw it gradually slipping. That frustrated me a lot, these kinds of meetings where the chief exec would tell you what to write, and the reporter had to go with a senior member like the editor or the deputy editor, and they'd be quite friendly with the chief exec. And I found that a bit disconcerting and uncomfortable, that we'd come away with a story that I never felt was the story, but it was what we'd agreed to write. And at one point we were not publishing anti-council letters because of various advertising implications, and I found that really really uncomfortable, and it affected how I felt about where I worked, and where I wanted to be, and when I started looking around for other papers and other jobs the Advertiser actually stood out as being something that still did that. The less staff you've got the less ability you've got to do that, which is what we'll always say to people who want to make job cuts here, but I still want that to be a priority. You've got to entertain as well, but you've got to give that right balance, and I think if you look at our front page today you've got the young lad having his 2–3 million YouTube hits and going on a US chat show, but we've obviously go the chief commissioner of the council who's paid £800 a day quitting not long after he said the job's only been half done."

And your letters pages are full of council related...

"Yeah, it's a nightmare! And every week you're aware of what you're putting in and what you're not putting in, and I'll get on Friday why's my letter not gone in, we're sick of the right wing letters that get printed, you favour the right wing letter writers. No, I don't, we're getting more of them at the moment, then somebody from the right wing will say you're clearly Labour biased, we can tell by the letters that are printed. And that used to bother me, and now I think well if they're both coming from both sides we've got to be doing something ok, and I do try and print both sides, and a lot of the time it's people complaining they've not sent their letter in until Thursday morning. So we do have quite a lively letters page, which I think is interesting. Probably there's only one week a year where we have to resort to not printing genuine political letters, we might have to have the odd charity appeal and that sort of thing – most weeks we can quite easily fill and have an overspill onto the website. And there's a good amount of letter writers as well, you get some who write every week, some three a week, I don't know how they think they're going to get three letters printed a week. There's a mix, there's [name] and [name], and [name] is another one, and they're all writing quite regularly – they're all of an ilk, one's slightly more irritating than the other two [laughs]."

Is there anything you want to add about the biggest challenges ahead?

"I think since I've been here, my first week here was the Dennis McShane (former Rotherham MP) expenses thing and I thought that's a lively start, and not long after that there was that national story broke when the council took some adopted kids off some UKIP voters, and then we had the CSE (child sex exploitation) scandal. And I remember my mum saying since you moved to Rotherham it's all happening, every time I turn the TV on there's Rotherham [laughs]. We talk about local authorities, but then we've had big fall outs with the football club and we've been banned from there, so all those things have been quite difficult, and I've gradually got used to dealing with that, it used to worry me and now in some ways you quite enjoy it. And I think the challenges are to avoid pressures internally and externally to reduce what you're doing, to look at different ways of what you're doing, to be told by some people that people would rather just get the information and they're not too bothered about the quality – can you look at community photographers, can you look at community reporters, well I'd rather not. Eventually it might come that I'm told I have to, but we're looking at the moment at restructuring, which in a lot of people's minds means you're going to cut people, but I've put three plans together that don't involve any job losses, they're the three that I'm going to be presenting to the next board meeting. They include looking at doing extra products, and extra things from the staff that we've got, because to my mind we should be looking at expanding what we do rather than reducing it, because once you start doing that there's not really any way back. So I think that's probably the biggest challenge internally."

Interviews conducted March–June 2017

References

Eileen Brooks, Journalist and PR Consultant, author interview, August 2017

Engel, Matthew (2011). 'I'm sceptical, not cynical', *Financial Times*, September 16, 2011, https://www.ft.com/content/25d9d058-de08-11e0-a115-00144feabdc0 (accessed September 18, 2018).

HoldtheFrontPage (2017). 'Yorkshire Post tops ABC league but all dailies see sales decline', https://www.holdthefrontpage.co.uk/2017/news/yorkshire-post-tops-abc-league-but-all-dailies-see-sales-decline/ (accessed September 18, 2018).

Private Eye (2012). http://www.private-eye.co.uk/paul-foot-award/2012 (accessed February 22, 2019).

6

TODAY'S NEWSROOM

Adapting to digital

Carmel O'Toole

"It's all about algorithms and analytics."
(Maggie Radcliffe, Editor of the Broadchurch Echo *[ITV crime drama* Broadchurch*])*

You know when a theme finds itself reflected back in popular culture that something significant is happening in wider society. In ITV's hugely popular crime drama *Broadchurch*, which concluded in 2017, the role and importance of the fictional local newspaper the *Broadchurch Echo* features in all three series.

Maggie Radcliffe, the Editor, played by actress Carolyn Pickles, and as created by writer Chris Chibnall is a veteran journalist. She is a champion of public interest issues and truth crusader. She is every cub reporter's dream heroine and the town's very own Woodward and Bernstein.

Maggie reflects depressingly to a ruthless new managing editor about what's happening in local print media. Her succinct summary of what now drives the news agenda is an indicator of how much news gathering has changed, and the increasingly common awareness of the scale of these changes (Chibnall, 2017).

Sam Hoyle was script editor across all three series. She explains: "Maggie is tough and honest and rigorous and principled. She is what you want our journalists to be."

Bridport and the West Dorset coastline were catapulted to stardom as the setting for the TV drama. Chibnall hails from Bridport. Sam says there were some obvious local parallels for him to draw upon for his writing, between the *Bridport News* and his fictional *Broadchurch Echo*. The high street office had closed, and the news production process had been centralised, reflecting some of the changes we explored earlier in our local media chapter.

In this chapter we take a closer look at what is happening in real newsrooms. We hear from journalists, editors and managers about the role of online and social content and how it is changing the way local news is identified, and the new priorities emerging in the news making agenda.

As previously mentioned in Chapter 5, Trinity Mirror group changed its name to Reach in March 2018 after the multi-million-pound takeover of former Northern and Shell title the *Daily Express* and *Daily Star*. My interview with Chris Walker took place just prior to this change in March 2017.

Chris Walker, Trinity Mirror, North West

Chris Walker is Senior Managing Editor for Reach (formerly Trinity Mirror), North West region, which covers Merseyside, Cheshire and North Wales. He has worked in journalism for over 43 years and been in his current role for 19. The role has changed hugely since he took it on. When he started, it was to manage the *Liverpool Post* and *Echo*.

Now he manages a team of around 170 editorial staff, split with 90 in Merseyside, 40 for North Wales and 25 Cheshire. These are mainly journalists but include some admin support and the "new beast" – "Community Content Curators" (CCCs). These are what would have been known historically as local or village correspondents.

Community Content Curators – a new journalistic hybrid

The CCCs gather and coordinate very local content including local MPs' columns, charity news, and such as when, as Chris explains, people send in "pictures of children and pets dressing up for Halloween".

A new kind of hybrid between local amateur correspondents and trainee journalists, they produce content for print and online and use social media to promote these stories. They do work, some of which, historically, might well have been done instead by local journalists. They are paid for their content, sometimes still based on the equivalent centimetre column "lineage" of print content they produce.

"Whether it should have been done by journalists in the past you can have a debate about," says Chris, who adds: "They are part of the way that local and regional newspapers have sought to compensate for the inevitable reductions of staff."

The benefits of CCCs, Chris considers, are that they free journalists to produce the content "which enhances the brand."

As a reporter, Chris covered local and national politics. He reported on Liverpool City Council 25 years ago when perhaps two full pages might be set aside for council news. Today the *(Liverpool) Post* has a political reporter whose remit is across the region's political stories not just the city council. There is also a City Desk that picks up on such as local planning issues.

He maintains that the level of focus for news coverage is much as it was and that there is still the reporting expertise to spot strong local council related news.

Reach Newsroom 3.1

Everything goes online first. News desk and the team of, what are now called, not journalists but Multi Media Reporters – anyone creating content, are told "don't worry about the paper. . . . Your sole focus is on getting the best possible content online."

"The purity of the model is, if it's not going to drive an audience online, it doesn't get written." He acknowledges this means that "inevitably lots of the grout stories which would have been covered in the past don't get written" if they aren't going to drive readership online, however "worthy" they might be.

Once the online version is published then a small team of production journalists gets a print ready version. Some content for online does not lend itself for print and either needs to be re written or different content used.

"Without doubt that has changed the way stories are written, because we are driven by analytics." Content is different from 10–15 years ago when stories would be based on "journalistic feel" or news value judgement. Stories are written differently to take account of the need to appeal to online readers.

Two news room conferences are held each day. At the morning conference, a content analyst will produce all the figures about the previous day's content. News and real time analytics are displayed on a big screen in the newsroom, so staff can see what readers are watching.

Stories attracting a significant audience will dictate where further content is then focused.

"It is difficult . . . because people will sometimes view something online in their thousands which we would no way regard as news." Puppies chasing squirrels?

There is also much greater emphasis on video content that brings in more revenue than print. This can be news related film such as CCTV of crimes that do attract online audiences but also have a news based back-story. This allows them to work well for both online and print.

There is a new relationship then emerging between content areas, where one feeds the other and the presentation of content has to be refocused to work for the nuances of both media.

Skewing the news agenda?

This increasing emphasis on online video content, particularly where it relates to crime and is an issue picked up by Liverpool City Council's former Chief Executive, Ged Fitzgerald.

He considers that whilst it might reflect content that people want to see online and in print, it is costing the local economy dearly. Ged believes it is unfairly skewing the local news agenda and he says "absolutely disproportionately features and give prominence to guns, gangs, criminals and all those kind of bad news stories."

This creates the impression of the "city within the city" and negatively affects the council's drive to support regeneration and attract inward investment.

> ". . . we have lost count of the number of the number of potential deals that we've had lined up on the economic side that have been deterred, put back or even cancelled, by virtue of the online exposure that the *Echo* does.

FIGURE 6.1 Ged Fitzgerald, former Chief Executive of Liverpool City Council. Picture courtesy of Liverpool City Council

. . . you get people doing the research to inform decision making, and they say we've come across this newspaper that has all this stuff in it, what's going on? And actually, the crime numbers are no worse than any other major city in the country, and certainly not in the world, but that's not the impression and the perception that is therefore created."

Indeed in response to the Parliamentary question about crime statistics in 2012, Liverpool emerged favourably. Birmingham, Manchester, Leeds and Sheffield all having worse figures for burglaries and car crime per person (McTague, 2012).

Budget cuts

Chris estimates that in the last 10 years his editorial budget has more than halved. The percentage terms cut is even greater, when you take inflation into account and cuts to other departments: "The fall in advertising revenue in particular has been absolutely huge, and if we hadn't taken those sort of measures the *Echo* would probably here but there probably wouldn't be a great deal else around it."

Former Merseyside local weekly print titles such as the *Southport Visitor, Formby Times* and *Crosby Herald* would have had between 60–70 editorial staff.

"Now there's an editor of the *Southport Visitor* and the Merseyside weeklies and website. There are just three dedicated reporters, and they have no photographer, where they probably would have had about eight and there is no discrete editorial production team, they are dealt with by the general production team which also does the *Echo* and anything else."

User-generated content, published first online, fills significant parts of those titles. Then a small team of journalists will do the crime, the public interest, council and planning stories.

The locally produced editorial content which has been hardest hit by cutbacks is that of news features. Chris says; "Features don't exist anymore as we know them."

Now a Shared Content Unit based in Liverpool centrally produces such as lifestyle and travel features which are offered to Local World and Trinity Mirror editors as far apart as Cornwall up to Newcastle. This has replaced local feature writing.

Chris reflects on a current generation of news consumers who grew up not expecting to pay for online content, but where the comparative low revenues from online as compared to print in its heyday, are miles apart.

He also points to the licence fee funded BBC online content:

> "If we were starting again no one would provide content for free, but how do you react to the fact that the BBC provide all that content for free? And it's very difficult for commercial organisations like ours to charge when a publicly funded organisation like the BBC can put it all out there and people get it for free."

Staff culture skills and training

Chris reflects:

> "When I was a trainee all you needed to focus on were the traditional core journalistic skills of being able to recognise a good story, tell it in a way that was easily understood by readers, coax reluctant interviewees to tell you what was going on, have a brilliant news sense, be able to spot a story buried in page 55 of a council report."

Today's multi-media reporters need all those traditional journalistic skills. They also need to be great at identifying and promoting stories from social media channels.

With the increasing emphasis on filmed content, journalists are given extra training to produce this. Gone is the traditionally "sharp dividing line between writing and taking pictures." All Chris's journalists are expected to be able to produce visual content.

Producing stories for Facebook, Twitter, Instagram and other social media is also an essential part of his journalists' role, to drive their audience online.

Relationship with local government – Liverpool City Council

> "There always has been and always should be a friction there, but there should also be a mutual respect and a mutual willingness to cooperate where it's useful, and an acceptance that a certain percentage of the time our interests and their interests will coincide,"

says Chris. He considers local government today to be "much more anti-democratic", with less transparent decision making and based on a model much closer to that of Central Government.

Working on the basis of being a critical friend, and a mixture of combative and partnership Chris considers this approach is not always understood.

> "We're having a relative period of calm at the minute, but it seems like the mayor (Joe Anderson) is always emailing us, because his perception is that if you're not absolutely for him you're against him. When he was leading the opposition he had a very different view."

Chris says it's harder now for journalists to talk directly to local government officers. Press offices can be more obstructive. Information requests are channelled through a central press office and are likely to result in contact with elected councillors with portfolio responsibility rather than in talking to officers.

His journalists now also increasingly have to resort to using Freedom of Information Act (FOIA 2000) requests to get answers to information, where this might have previously been yielded more simply via the press office or local council contacts.

Nancy Fielder – Editor, *Sheffield Star*

Over in Sheffield, Nancy Fielder has brought boldness and ambition to her role as Editor In Chief at JPI Media's *Sheffield Star*. There is much common ground between her and Chris Walker with falling print circulation, more traffic online than to print and ever- increasing pressures upon staffing and budgets. The key task of ensuring both local community relevance and helping The Star become more sustainable is a tough one.

Nancy took over the helm of the city's daily paper, the *Sheffield Star* in April 2016. From September the same year that role expanded to include the weeklies *Doncaster Free Press*, (DFP) and Sheffield Telegraph. Her staff team overall is 38.

Originally from Sheffield, Nancy has worked in local print journalism for 18 years.

Eight staff members are specifically "news", who go out and identify stories. There are then two more in sport. There's a communities team that focuses on user-generated content for the weeklies, the Telegraph and DFP. Then there's Nancy, a news editor, a head of print, head of digital and deputy head of digital. There are also editorial assistants.

Nancy created a team of specialists including Health and Court writers. The communities team picks up supplied content and a news team that goes out to generate news. This has meant the *Star* is less reliant upon syndicated materials and better placed to generate genuine local news.

Facing falling print circulation, shrinking staffing figures and the growing online audience, Nancy has taken a bold approach to address these issues. The revenue from print still pays for the *Star*, but year on year that financial model looks more imperilled. Longer term the management strategy is to generate more income from the *Star*'s online presence.

FIGURE 6.2 Former *Sheffield Star* offices for sale in 2017. Photography by Carmel O'Toole

"We've got a much bigger audience online than in print, so yesterday the *Star* will have sold around 16,000 copies, and online we had roughly 130,000 unique users. They're coming in and looking at one story or two stories or three stories, but still the number of eyeballs there's just no comparison."

She paints a picture of when she took over of a newsroom culture stretched by lack of staff and heavily reliant upon emailed and public relations content. There was a palpable sense of panic to fill pages. A phone culture prevailed and journalists were not going out and generating stories.

PR and supplied content was being used, often without editorial changes and she was keen to introduce a new and more challenging approach.

> ". . . if you're not getting people out of the office and you're not getting good content, why are we bothering? And if you look through a lot, particularly the smaller weekly ones that've got, to be fair to them, hardly any staff, some of them have got no reporters actually attached to them, they rely predominantly on press releases, so that's not journalism."

Nancy set about changing the newsroom culture. She had to acknowledge the need for some early planned content and pages but was emphatic about wanting journalists to get out of the office and actively seek and develop news stories which would reconnect the *Star* with the local community: "So we've done quite a lot of restructuring so that some of the paper can be produced really quickly so that the front end pages are done by journalists who just go out and get stories."

Over at the *Sheffield Telegraph*, the *Star*'s weekly sibling print title, there's been a shift to user generated content but of the "local expert" kind: "....actually the *Telegraph* is very loved, so there are a lot of people willing to say I'm an expert I'll write about it. And actually that's gone really well, you kind of wondered if there'd be a backlash."

This has also enabled good quality features content, something fast disappearing from other print titles and groups. There is also crossover content from *The Star*.

How has the shift to online changed how your newsrooms works?

Just as is the case at Reach, everything goes to online first.

> "The major difference is now the reporters write straight to the website, which sometimes I would rather not do, but I can't see any way around it, and then the copy goes to the head of content, so everything's online first and the head of print decides what goes where in the paper."

Online readers expect to see local news reflected much more quickly and the nature of what is covered online is different too. Nancy cites a story of a Sheffield man who had texted that he thought his plane was going to crash. He was nowhere near Sheffield, but this was getting lots of attention online: "...there's a lot of reacting to stuff that you might not have been bothered with back in the day".

Changing the relationship with PR companies

Local newspapers are the bread and butter targets for public relations agencies and officers. Achieving coverage in key local media has historically underpinned the success of communicators. It is evidence that they have persuaded local journalists of their skills and the relevant news value of their work.

One of the first things Nancy did when she took over was to visit local PR agencies and tell them the days of using some of their commercially focused PR content for free were over.

She muses that PROs would sell the prospect and benefits of media coverage to their clients to whom they were charging a fee. They would then work to persuade local journalists to use their provided content but for free. With the onset of tougher financial times Nancy is resolved that this will no longer be the case for her media. She now charges agencies for commercially related content.

The third-party advocacy of local media is a valuable commodity for PROs. They reflect achieved coverage in their client reports about coverage achieved. Historically a crude way of quantifying the value of what a PROs does, has been through calculating the Advertising Value Equivalent, (AVE) of coverage achieved. So a front page lead generated from PR activity can look very impressive indeed. To have to pay for page one coverage would be very expensive compared to monthly PR agency retainer fees. It's an old fashioned measure and considered by the PR industry organisations such as the Chartered Institute of Public Relations, (the CIPR) to be wholly unsatisfactory. More complex metrics and models which measure the impact rather than the output are now more routinely encouraged. But clients can still be impressed by the easy metrics of coverage achieved and whether the CIPR likes it or not, A.V.E. is still a measurement used.

Nancy explains:

> ". . . actually newspapers have been incredibly naïve for a long time, and when it comes down to it, Sheffield needs journalists, it doesn't necessarily need PR. And some of the PR companies took it really badly, 'are you trying to put us out of business?' No I'm not, we're just saying we need a slice of this pie or where are you going to publish your stories?"

It is a bold strategy and one not without its risks. The relationship between media and PR has always been a bittersweet one with journalists resentful and resistant to PR "puffery". But then over stretched newsrooms and time poor journalists have often been grateful recipients of well written and well targeted copy. They can be just as reliant upon PR content as PROs are on their willingness to provide it.

She considers this is just one of several essential conversations she has to have with The Star stakeholders, to generate a better understanding of why she is taking the approach she has set out.

> "I think local newspaper, newspapers in general have created their own problems, because we've kind of hidden from it for a while, we've cut ourselves so badly, we've had to rely on PR, we haven't had any of these difficult conversations, and I think to some extent a lot of the reporters don't have a clue how badly their newspapers are doing. There's a lot of the weekly titles that are only selling a few thousand, and they're shrinking 20 percent year on year, while I'm not a mathematical genius but give them three years and they're not selling a single copy…."

Nancy has consciously championed a return to basic journalistic skills in her editorial team. Journalists cover local courts every day and council meetings. They delve into council agendas and reports to root out the stories that can so easily go uncovered.

These are skills and knowledge that are broadly in danger of being lost for lack of exposure and opportunity.

> ". . . we lost sight of that for a long time. And it does delight me when the press officers go 'where have you found this?', and you go it was in your own policing agenda. Because they're not used to it, but that's a really sad indictment of how journalism has been for a long long time, and in Sheffield they didn't expect things to be uncovered by the methods that journalists have relied on for decades. So it delights me when that happens."

She has also sought to champion issues of public interest, taking a campaigning stance on stories such as local library closures, the local hospital struggling to cope, and in more recent times the controversy over Sheffield felled trees.

Where the easy approach with Sheffield trouble hot spots might be to reinforce local stereotypes about crime and anti-social behaviour, Nancy has encouraged a more open attitude from her journalists.

> "A lot of what we do now (is) because of pride in Sheffield. When I first started there were a couple of really bad incidents in Gleadless Valley, but do you know what, the people of Gleadless Valley actually love being there. Most of them wouldn't move even if you said you can have a nice house in Fulwood. And so what we're trying to do is actually reflect that as well, because again that's just the same as the council. We can kick Gleadless Valley, we can say don't ever go to Parsons Cross, but that's not the experience of the people who live there. So we went down and said 'what's it really like?' Most of them were 'we quite like it here, we'd like a bit more money, we'd like our parks to have a lick of paint', and so that's very much what we're trying to do."

This gives local people their voice back and builds trust. When in turn a news story breaks, communities are more likely to trust and talk to *Star* reporters. The *Star*'s declining print circulation hasn't turned around as a consequence but it has slowed since this approach was adopted: "… people say you're back in the communities, you're back out there, and you kind of get us, you understand".

With this proactive approach to news gathering Nancy is confident her news team would have picked up on the community warnings around safety at places such as Grenfell Tower: "I think there's a very good chance we would've picked it up because our reporters are now, we've removed email, they're looking for stories all the time and they're actively searching."

She is careful, however not to overclaim and admits that identifying residents' concerns and successfully calling out the grave risk posed by conditions at Grenfell in time to prevent tragedy, would have been much less likely.

The impact of social media

Within Nancy's news team are digital reporters who scan social media for Sheffield related stories, stories that have "gone viral" or are beginning to build online attention. They are effectively "chasing hits". These stories are often not suitable for use in the print edition and used solely online.

The focus is mainly Facebook and Twitter with an age group of readers "in their 40s". *Star* reporters sometimes now cover stories they wouldn't have touched in the past. Nancy gives an example of a story about a fire in Worksop (almost 20 miles away):

> ". . . top story at the beginning of the week was there was a massive fire, it was actually in Worksop but because you could see it from Sheffield, you would never have done that in the day, there was a fire outside your patch but you could see the smoke. But people were interested in it."

There's a stark contrast between the tone and focus of print and online content.

> "The paper is much more positive, and you don't necessarily get negative stuff on the front, or if you do we try and put it in context, which I think is really important. And all the communities features, and the regular things about volunteers, and all the campaigning we do, you don't get that feel on the website even though it's there.
> . . . People want to know about bad stuff online, that's what they want. You can see it, whether they like to admit it or not, that's what they get."

Andrew Mosley – Editor, *Rotherham Advertiser*

One of the country's dwindling number of successful independent newspapers, the *Rotherham Advertiser*, is a paid for weekly, print and online title which tops 100 pages most weeks. It is edited by Andrew Mosley who is emphatic about his editorial priority of "print first".

He also looks after two free weeklies, the *Dearne Valley Weekender* and the *Rotherham Record*. The *Advertiser* and sibling titles are owned by Nick Alexander, as Regional Media Limited.

It shares its independent status with a declining number of other title such as the *Barnsley Chronicle* and *Kent Messenger*. Andrew's list of fellow independents did include the 163- year-old *Oldham Chronicle*. However, this title closed in summer 2017 only to be later rescued from permanent closure by a local radio group (Mayhew, 2017).

We've looked at Andrew's route into journalism in our earlier chapter on local and regional media changes. Here we focus in on his perspective on the impact of online and social media.

Not leaping off the "digital cliff"

He is emphatic about not leaping off the "digital cliff" and of that being key to his decision to go to the *Advertiser*.

> "I thought that's quite interesting, there's still a decent quality paper putting out around 100 and odd pages every week, and not going online first with everything. So we were in some people's eyes behind the rest of the country. But I think that's actually turned out to be a good thing, because we haven't committed ourselves and thrown the paper out, which a lot of papers have."

Still selling over 20,000 papers a week puts the Advertiser amongst the most successful local print titles in the country. Like the majority of regional print titles it has been losing print circulation year on year but at a rate of around 3–5% compared with others losing 20–30% according to the Audit Bureau of Circulation.

The online *Advertiser* was developed slowly alongside a model for monetising the online and social media content. Hits and unique user figures grew quickly:

> "Over the last year we've more than doubled our hits and unique users whilst also, we've had a 4% drop in circulation, which we'd obviously rather not have, but industry-wide for a paper still selling over 20,000 I think it's the top performer in the country.
>
> I was told this morning that we'd trebled our internet revenue, does that make up for what you're losing in print, and does that make up for the amount of hours you're putting into producing that content.
>
> The problem we've still got, even though I think we've trebled our monetising of the website and social media, it still doesn't make up for what you're losing in print. And I think that's been the big job, to balance what we're putting out digitally and what we're producing in the newspaper."

Andrew and his team make a clean distinction between what is used for print and for social and online. They don't give major stories away first online but save for the Friday print edition. "Unless of course there's a murder happens on a Monday, you can't hold onto it until a Friday like the paper used to do."

The social media concentrates on breaking news, early morning traffic information, anything overnight.

> "Anything that's actually useful to the reader, rather than something they don't really need to read that day, they don't need to read a story that we might have about cuts to a school or a hospital, it can wait until Thursday or Friday.
>
> We've not gone down the celebrity route, we've not gone down clickbait, so I think we're trying to give local people something that benefits their day, something they need to know, something that can help them avoid a traffic jam, find out what's going on, causing the disruption in their town centre, that sort of thing."

Andrew has visited other local media offices to see their use of news room analytics and he takes the view:

> "I think you can grab a certain audience for your digital product and for your newspaper, I don't think they have to be exclusive, I think some people will read both, and you have to give people a bit of a flavour of what you're going to be putting in your paper on a Friday without giving the whole game away."

Andrew wants to use online to help drive readership to the print title and equally to drive audience to the website. He is relaxed about the way some popular online content departs from traditional news value.

> "This week one of our reporters went to a new go-carting centre in Tinsley, and we put that out on Facebook, and it's had 3200 shares, which surprised us really. But that's not going to be your most read story in the paper, even though it's in the paper, a version of it, but I'm quite happy with that, that's got people to our website, and they've had a look around at other stories, maybe seen what we've got to offer in the paper and they might have a go at buying it."

He is keen to develop a more harmonious relationship between print and online. Online has specifically changed the way the *Advertiser* covers sport.

> "Whereas say even three years ago we were doing a traditional two-page Rotherham United match report, coming out on a Friday, six days after the game, and it seemed a bit pointless. But if you get that on the web straight after the game then we get reaction in on Friday's paper and look ahead to the next week."

Andrew sees his biggest challenge ahead to be ensuring being able to cover the stories which need covering whilst balancing the need to expand, offer extra products and to provide well received content online. He thinks that is about doing things differently but not about dumbing down the quality of content.

Summary of key issues

Online first – the increasing move to producing content for "online first" is changing the essence of news making, with the new priority of delivering online content which the widest possible audience wants to read. This is less likely to reflect public interest issues. At Trinity Mirror, the biggest UK media group, Multi Media Reporters are told "don't worry about the paper…Your sole focus is on getting the best possible content online."

Loss of news value – journalists' "nose for news", or traditional news sense is being downgraded overall as an essential skill. News value is being overridden by "hits chasing" where journalists scour social and online for trending stories which drive the website content priorities. This includes stories that previously might not even have been considered relevant or newsworthy.

"Worthy stories" – about issues of public interest, increasingly don't get written because they aren't perceived to attract and drive online audiences.

Skewing the news agenda – bad news works better to maximise online audiences. In Liverpool real concerns are expressed about the negative public perceptions this sets up for wider audiences, and the deterring of inward investors. Crime stories supported by such as CCTV footage dominate online and in turn are translated for print use.

References

Interviews

Adrian Roxan, interview with Nancy Fielder, Editor, *SheffieldStar*, July 20, 2017.

Carmel O'Toole, *interview with Chris Walker, Regional Managing Editor, Trinity Mirror, March 2, 2017*.

Carmel O'Toole, *interview with Liverpool City Council Chief Executive, Ged Fitzgerald, March 29, 2017*.

Carmel O'Toole, *interview with Andrew Mosley, Editor, Rotherham Advertiser, March 3, 2017*.

Secondary sources

Chibnall, Chris(2017). *Broadchurch*. Episode 7, Series 3. London: Kudos Film and Television, Imaginary Friends.

McTague, Tom (2012). 'It's calmed down: Liverpool one of the safest cities to live in – that's official', *Mirror*, October 27, 2012, https://www.mirror.co.uk/news/uk-news/liverpool-one-of-the-safest-cities-to-live-1401463 (accessed March 9, 2018).

Mayhew, Freddy (2017). 'Oldham Chronicle to "restart production" after newspaper save by local radio station', *Press Gazette*, October 12, 2017, http://www.pressgazette.co.uk/oldham-chronicle-to-restart-production-after-buyout-by-local-radio-station/ (accessed March 28, 2018).

7

CASE STUDIES

Grenfell, child sexual exploitation and Sheffield tree-felling

Case study 1: Grenfell Tower

"Somewhere on a piece of paper it will say that they (Royal Borough of Kensington and Chelsea Council, RBKC), made a decision to save so many thousands of pounds by putting an inferior kind of cladding on……if you'd had proper scrutiny by journalists in that area, they would have picked that up, that would've been a story, and that could've stopped that happening."

(Eileen Brooks, Journalist and PR Consultant, August 2017)

One way of illustrating the power and potential of local media to make a difference is by taking a closer look at examples of key events.

In this chapter we examine the 2017 Grenfell Tower fire tragedy, the horrific Child sexual exploitation (CSE) in Rotherham, South Yorkshire and the community versus city council row over the felling of thousands of mature Sheffield trees in 2016–18.

In each case there's a troubling dynamic between the local authority, local people and local media. There's also a strong narrative about the diminishing resources available to local media and the increasing loss of skilled journalists scrutinising what's happening in local communities.

The events

Just before 1 a.m. on June 14, 2017, the London Fire Brigade took the first of hundreds of calls from the 24-storey Grenfell Tower in North Kensington. The first crews were reportedly on site within six minutes, with fire fighters in breathing apparatus ready to go inside to try to rescue people already trapped by the blaze (Heffer, 2017).

152 Case studies

FIGURE 7.1 Grenfell Tower community memorial: 24 hearts representing each of the 24 floors of the building. Photography by Mark Gordon

By 8 a.m. it was confirmed 50 people had been taken to hospital and there were a "number of fatalities" following the fire. London Fire Commissioner Dany Cotton described the blaze as "unprecedented", with more than 250 firefighters and 40 fire engines attending the scene.

The fire affected all floors of the 24-storey building from the second floor up, and at its height 40 fire engines and more than 200 firefighters were at the scene (London Fire Brigade, 2017).

At 9.45 a.m. firefighters were battling the flames to reach the 21st floor and the first questions began to be asked publicly about what had caused such a catastrophe. Accounts began to emerge of advice to residents to stay in their homes in the event of fire. London Mayor Sadiq Khan said questions needed to be answered.

Temporary shelters were opened for now-homeless residents. The names of those missing and feared dead began to emerge. By Monday June 19 the death toll had risen to 79. A week later that figure had risen to approximately 80. The Metropolitan Police said it might be weeks before a full and accurate total number could be confirmed.

By 4 p.m. on the day of the fire, RBKC's housing management company, the Kensington and Chelsea Tenant Management Organisation (KCTMO), admitted it had been aware of residents' fire safety concerns. Blog posts from the Grenfell Action Group clearly signposted a lack of information and advice for residents to "stay put" in their own homes unless their flat was affected.

In November 2016, eight months before the fire, a residents' blog post had prophetically warned:

> It is a truly terrifying thought, but the Grenfell Action Group firmly believe that only a catastrophic event will expose the ineptitude and incompetence of

FIGURE 7.2 Grenfell Tower, February 2018. Photography by Mark Gordon

our landlord, the KCTMO, and bring an end to the dangerous living conditions and neglect of health and safety legislation that they inflict upon their tenants and leaseholders. We believe that the KCTMO are an evil, unprincipled, mini-mafia who have no business to be charged with the responsibility of looking after the every-day management of large scale social housing estates and that their sordid collusion with the RBKC Council is a recipe for a future major disaster. [. . .]

FIGURE 7.3A, B Community murals at Grenfell, February 2018. Photography by Mark Gordon

> It is our conviction that a serious fire in a tower block or similar high density residential property is the most likely reason that those who wield power at the KCTMO will be found out and brought to justice.
>
> *(Grenfell Action Group, 2016)*

Within days of the incident the Metropolitan Police (the Met) then flagged crucial gaps in the information provided by the KCTMO.

> The Met was given a list of those recorded as living in Grenfell Tower by the tenant management organisation on the first day, however by the end of that day the Met identified the list was not accurate. Detectives have been examining every possible source of information, from government agencies to fast food delivery companies to understand who lived in Grenfell Tower [...]
>
> The terrible reality is that . . . there are 23 flats where despite investigative efforts, the Met has been unable to trace anyone alive who lived there. At this stage, it is presumed that none of the occupants from these flats survived the fire.
>
> *(Metropolitan Police, 2017)*

FIGURE 7.4 Community child mural at Grenfell, February 2018. Photography by Mark Gordon

Cause of the fire

Police soon advised that the fire had started in a fridge freezer in a fourth-floor apartment (London Evening Standard, 2017). But further safety tests soon also pointed to the flammability of the building's external cladding as a key contributing factor in the fire's swift spread.

A BBC investigation then suggested that cladding fitted to Grenfell Tower during its 2014 refurbishment was a cheaper and more flammable version than that originally proposed and which residents were advised would be the case. Documents obtained by the broadcaster show the zinc cladding originally proposed, had been replaced with an aluminium type, which was less fire resistant, saving RBKC nearly £300,000 (BBC News, 2017a).

In the aftermath of the fire the cheaper cladding subsequently failed fire safety tests. Official concerns sparked a nationwide safety check into high-rise tower cladding materials.

Corporate manslaughter investigation

In a letter to Grenfell residents around July 27, Met police advised they had seized a "huge amount" of material from RBKC council and the KCTMO:

> After an initial assessment of that information, the officer leading the investigation has today notified the Royal Borough of Kensington and Chelsea and the Kensington and Chelsea Tenancy Management Organisation that there are reasonable grounds to suspect that each organisation may have committed the offence of corporate manslaughter under the Corporate Manslaughter and Corporate Homicide Act 2007.
>
> *(BBC News , 2017b)*

Public inquiry

On June 29 2017 the Government announced an independent public inquiry would be held into the fire, led by former judge, Sir Martin Moore-Bick. The inquiry was charged with examining the circumstances leading up to the tragedy. It would seek to establish the facts and make recommendations on action needed to prevent a similar tragedy happening again.

Evidence examined would include reports by the police, the fire brigade, safety experts and others including Grenfell residents. The inquiry formally opened on September 14, 2017. (Grenfell Tower Inquiry, n.d.)

Resignations

The public outcry following the fire led to the resignations of RBKC Chief Executive, Nicholas Holgate; the Conservative Council Leader Nicholas Paget-Brown, the Conservative, Deputy Leader with key responsibility for housing, Rock Feilding-Mellen and Robert Hall the chief officer at the KCTMO housing organisation (Bilefsky, 2017).

Calls for Paget-Brown's exit had intensified after a council meeting he led, ended in chaos and acrimony when he tried to exclude reporters, saying that their presence might "prejudice" a government inquiry into the tragedy. The journalists had obtained a court order admitting them to the meeting.

Local media

Seamus Dooley, National Union of Journalists (NUJ) acting general secretary, said: "Reliable, quality journalism and trusted news sources become acutely important when people are forced to endure tragic and devastating events such as the Grenfell Tower fire."

The terrible tragedy at Grenfell prompted mass media interest and first-hand coverage of the unfolding events. National and international print and broadcast media shot to the scene in their droves to record the incident, the unfolding controversy about how this had happened and to question those involved and directly affected. What was conspicuous by its absence was the role of local media.

Dominic Ponsford, Editor of the *Press Gazette*, suggests the number of local journalists has fallen by at least a half in the last decade. He has chronicled the issue of the lack of local media coverage about Grenfell. He highlighted that despite the openly available warnings from Grenfell residents on their blog site, which should have been essential reading for local journalists. No journalists picked up the November 2016 prediction about the catastrophe to come: "The RBKC has a population of 160,000 but just one dedicated weekly newspaper – the *Kensington and Chelsea News* – and one dedicated reporter, who also covers two other London boroughs across five titles, *Press Gazette* understands" (Ponsford).

Called *Kensington and Chelsea Today* it focuses on arts, culture, business and finance with a "monthly roundup" of local news.

"News" is part of the London Weekly News series, owned by Capital Media Newspapers, which has a circulation in the borough of just over 7,000, according to the media circulation database, JICREG.

> Capital News Media acquired the title, along with others covering west London, from Tindle Newspapers in 2016 as part of a management buyout. The company also owns the South London Press (SLP) and Dorset titles the View From series and Pulman's Weekly News.
>
> Kensington and Chelsea could easily have ended up with no local media at all after Trinity Mirror's decision to close the Chronicle series, including titles covering Kensington and Chelsea, Fulham and Westminster in April 2014 with the loss of 15 jobs.
>
> But Tindle newspapers decided to relaunch the Kensington and Chelsea News along with a series of other historic west London titles in late 2014, before selling them on. [. . .]
>
> Geoff Baker was news editor for the Kensington & Chelsea News from its relaunch under Tindle up until he was made redundant through cuts in April 2017. His only reporter left the company a few months earlier.
>
> Baker, 61, who has 40 years' experience in the media and previously worked as Paul McCartney's PR man, also covered four other west London titles in his role.

He told Press Gazette: "To be honest I didn't run a story on residents' concerns [at Grenfell Tower] and that was because they hadn't got in touch with me about that particular tower."

He added: "If someone had phoned me or sent me a release I would have done it, but it just didn't come on the radar, simple as that. Just because there's so much else to do if you are doing it on your tod. To my huge regret, I wish that I had… Whether that would have made the council change their minds I very much doubt it.

I definitely should have taken much more interest or had more time to take the interest and put more stuff on the front page and kicked up merry hell because the [Grenfell Tower] situation is wrong, by any measurement.

It was simply that I didn't have the time to pull out all the stops because all the stops were already pulled out on other things."

(Mayhew, 2017)

RBKC is also covered by the *London Evening Standard*, which no longer has a specific local government correspondent but does have a City Hall editor.

Specialist housing media

Press Gazette also highlighted that one news title which did report on tower block fire safety concerns ahead of the Grenfell disaster was *Inside Housing*, the weekly specialist magazine for UK housing professionals.

News editor Peter Apps carried out an investigation into a tower block fire in Shepherd's Bush, which broke out in August last year, for the specialist news title as part of its monthly investigative journalism series Spotlight.

Apps used Freedom of Information requests to gain information from Hammersmith and Fulham Council and the London Fire Brigade (LFB) about how the fire had spread across five floors of the tower block after a faulty tumble dryer set alight on the seventh floor.

The investigation revealed that panels attached to the outside of the building which came apart when burnt, exposing flammable insulation material and plywood to the blaze, were "likely to have assisted the fire in spreading up the outside of the building" and led to the LFB warning all London boroughs about their use.

Apps told Press Gazette: "After the Shepherd's Bush fire, journalists weren't pushing on the answer to that question [of why the fire had spread so quickly]. All the focus was on the tumble dryer. It shows a role for specialist media to keep an eye on these things."

(Mayhew, 2017)

Grant Feller is a journalist and corporate media consultant; when he began his career on the Kensington News and Chelsea News, the two titles had an editorial team of ten and faced competition for stories from the Kensington and Chelsea Times and the Evening Standard (which then devoted more resources to local borough stories).

This was in 1990, before competition from the internet destroyed the old newspaper publishing model and in particular took away most of the classified advertising revenue.

Asked whether he thought the concerns of residents would have been picked up by the Kensington News in 1990, Feller said:

"One hundred per cent yes, we would have picked up on that.

If we hadn't found that story ourselves we would have been bollocked by the editor. Any local newspaper journalist worth his or her salt would have been all over that story because of that blog.

But today there is no-one there. There is a newspaper that cares for Londoners, reflects London and does its bit for London – and that's the Evening Standard. But it doesn't do these types of stories.

We would have known about that local group's concerns because we were very much in the local community. We would have pored over the council meeting agendas and asked questions of the councillors and the officers.

"But today there is no-one there. Those people can do what they like because there's no journalists looking at what they are doing. That's why local journalism is so important."

Feller . . . recalled writing stories himself about the poor living conditions in Grenfell Tower.

He said: "It was dilapidated, had really bad wiring and was a horrible place to live. I remember writing stories about it very many times. If there was a story of local residents complaining about the council, that was our bread and butter."

He recalls from his time on the Kensington News "we were out all the time, finding stories – it was a very active job".

And he worries about what has been lost through the decline in the local press, which has been particularly severe in London.

Writing on Linkedin, Feller said: "We talk about community and religious leaders as being the lifeblood of neighbourhoods, but we forget that local newspapers are too. They are an essential ingredient in the fabric of society, a cornerstone of democracy. Or were..."

"Local newspapers and their websites are still making valiant efforts to report community stories but staffing levels mean that there's little time for patient, revelatory journalism.

"And, in fact, many 'local' journalists don't even work in the districts that they write about – and I doubt very much whether they devour those council agendas in the way that we used to."

(Ponsford, 2017)

In a *Guardian* article in August 2017 the veteran journalist Jon Snow said reporting on the deadly Grenfell Tower fire made him feel "on the wrong side" of Britain's social divide and warned that he and others in the media had become too far removed from ordinary people's lives (Ruddick, 2017).

The Channel 4 news presenter used a speech at the Edinburgh Television Festival to say the episode made him conclude that there was a lack of diversity across the media, which should have been more aware about the dangers of the high-rise block.

The Grenfell episode demonstrated, Snow said, that the media was "comfortably with the elite, with little awareness, contact or connection with those not of the elite" and that the fire had shown this lack of connection was "dangerous" (Ruddick, 2017).

When Snow visited the area around the tower in west London, in the immediate aftermath of the fire, he was surrounded by angry locals who complained that no media had shown interest before.

The journalist said:

> "Amid the demonstrations around the tower after the fire there were cries of: 'Where were you? Why didn't you come here before?'
>
> Why didn't any of us see the Grenfell action blog? Why didn't we know? Why didn't we have contact? Why didn't we enable the residents of Grenfell Tower – and indeed the other hundreds of towers like it around Britain – to find pathways to talk to us and for us to expose their story?
>
> In that moment I felt both disconnected and frustrated. I felt on the wrong side of the terrible divide that exists in present-day society and in which we are all in this hall major players. We can accuse the political classes for their failures, and we do. But we are guilty of them ourselves.
>
> "We are too far removed from those who lived their lives in Grenfell and who, across the country, now live on amid the combustible cladding, the lack of sprinklers, the absence of centralised fire alarms and more, revealed by the Grenfell Tower fire."
>
> *(Ruddick, 2017)*

The newsreader and journalist said he has been left "haunted" by the fire and also revealed that he knew one of the victims – 12-year-old Firdaws Hashim, who had won a school public debating competition of which he was a judge just weeks before the disaster (Ruddick, 2017).

Emily Bell, Former *Guardian* Editor and Director of the Tow Center for Digital Journalism gave her own perspective of media failure around the Grenfell incident:

> The Grenfell Action Group blog carefully documented their repeated complaints to the council. Other reporting is scarce, and where it exists, hard to find.
>
> Grenfell Action Group blogposts form the most reliable archive of concerns about the area's social housing, and yet they were unable to make the council act on their behalf. Even in the aftermath of what the group describes as 'social murder', it continues to publish posts on other housing tenants and issues in the area [...]

The causes of the failure of local journalism are well known: commercialism, consolidation, the internet, poor management. The fixes for that, though, cannot be found in an environment which is commercially hostile to small scale accountability journalism, and for that we are all to blame.

(Bell, 2017)

Key findings

- The Kensington and Chelsea Borough had no specific news media covering local and community issues at the time of the Grenfell Tower fire. Media title *Kensington and Chelsea Today* is arts and culture focused, offering only a monthly news roundup
- Public warnings by the Grenfell community months ahead of the tragedy, about extreme safety risks, were not picked up by local media
- Numerous media commentators consider the absence of local media scrutiny to be a key factor in the tragedy

Case Study 2: Child sexual exploitation in Rotherham – with Andrew Norfolk, Chief Investigative Reporter, *The Times*

No one knows the true scale of child sexual exploitation (CSE) in Rotherham over the years. Our conservative estimate is that approximately 1400 children were sexually exploited over the full Inquiry period, from 1997 to 2013.

In just over a third of cases, children affected by sexual exploitation were previously known to services because of child protection and neglect. It is hard to describe the appalling nature of the abuse that child victims suffered. They were raped by multiple perpetrators, trafficked to other towns and cities in the north of England, abducted, beaten, and intimidated. There were examples of children who had been doused in petrol and threatened with being set alight, threatened with guns, made to witness brutally violent rapes and threatened they would be next if they told anyone. Girls as young as 11 were raped by large numbers of male perpetrators.

(Jay, 2014, 'Executive Summary', p. 1)

Professor Alexis Jay is a former senior social worker and academic. In 2014 she was commissioned by Rotherham Council to lead an independent inquiry into the issue of child sexual exploitation in the town. She was subsequently (in August 2016) appointed by the UK Government to chair the national "Independent Inquiry into Child Sexual Exploitation".

A critical factor in bringing such a concentrated spotlight onto this issue was the skilled and sustained coverage by Andrew Norfolk, Chief Investigative Reporter for *The Times*. After dipping into and out of the topic across a protracted time period, Andrew was encouraged by his editor to be able to focus exclusively on this story.

FIGURE 7.5 "Feared no more", *Rotherham Advertiser* front page story, Friday February 26, 2016, coverage of trial linked to Rotherham's Child sexual exploitation issue, 2016. Reproduced with kind permission of Andrew Mosley, *Rotherham Advertiser* Editor

Case studies 163

FIGURE 7.6 Rotherham Borough Council offices. Photography by Carmel O'Toole

Up until then there had been but pockets of mainly local and regional media coverage of the criminal prosecutions resulting from CSE in cases stretching across the UK. These tended to concentrate on the specific court proceedings relevant to their area. The CSE issue is by no means confined to Rotherham and Rochdale. An honourable mention should go to local and regional media, the *Rotherham Advertiser*, *Sheffield Star*, *Yorkshire Post* and BBC Radio Sheffield for their work on this story.

But it was Andrew's sustained coverage that gave the issue the coherence and forensic attention it so desperately needed. He pieced together a fragmented jigsaw of evidence from different parts of the UK and started to notice a pattern, links between them. Many would argue his work forced the hand of Rotherham Council to bring Jay's high profile and respected independent external scrutiny to the issue

Much has been said and written since the scandals in Rochdale and Rotherham were brought to light. A common theme to both and the multiple other cases of child sexual abuse in other parts of the UK, was the reluctance of child protection agencies to acknowledge the crime's association with specific racial or cultural communities.

We know now that in Rotherham, a small but toxic group of men from within the British Pakistani community and linked to some local taxi services were central to the situation. They predominantly but not exclusively, preyed upon vulnerable white girls. This was similar to the picture in Rochdale, where specific British Pakistani run, local fast food takeaways were used as grooming centres to attract and abuse vulnerable young girls.

A second key barrier to child protection agencies taking timely action was an embedded culture within police and social services of blaming the victims for their involvement. Young vulnerable girls who had "entered into" relationships with older men were too often perceived to have been complicit in their own abuse.

> "Certainly there is evidence that police officers on the ground in the 1990s and well beyond, displayed attitudes that conveyed a lack of understanding of the problem of CSE and the nature of grooming. We have already seen that children as young as 11 were deemed to be having consensual sexual intercourse when in fact they were being raped and abused by adults."
>
> *(Jay, 2014, p. 69)*

Child protection agencies feared sparking a cultural tinderbox and being accused of racism. This made them coy about calling the abuse spade a spade. Crime was, and remains, the issue. The fact that some abusers were Muslim and others not, is just part of the complex narrative. It should not have been an excuse for agencies sit on their hands to ponder an acceptable form of framing the story, while young girls' lives were being ruined.

Louise Casey is a former deputy director of homelessness charity, Shelter, now a British government official specialising in social welfare. She was appointed in September 2014 by the UK Government to inspect Rotherham Council's governance of Children and Young People's Services and to look at taxi and private hire licensing. She fully endorsed the findings of the earlier Jay Report and these were central to her research.

Casey reported back on a council "in denial":

> Terrible things happened in Rotherham and on a significant scale. Children were sexually exploited by men who came largely from the Pakistani Heritage Community. Not enough was done to acknowledge this, to stop it happening, to protect children, to support victims and to apprehend perpetrators.
>
> *(Casey, 2015, 'Foreword', p. 4)*

She also painted a dismal picture of the culture within the council:

> Interviews with staff and Members of RMBC highlighted a pervading culture of sexism, bullying and silencing debate. The issue of race is contentious, with staff and members lacking the confidence to tackle difficult issues for fear of being seen as racist or upsetting community cohesion. By failing to take action against the Pakistani heritage male perpetrators of CSE in the borough, the Council has inadvertently fuelled the far right and allowed racial tensions to grow. It has done a great disservice to the Pakistani heritage community and the good people of Rotherham as a result.
>
> *(Casey, 2015, p. 10)*

Concerns about abuse links to local taxis

Concerns about the involvement of local taxi drivers in the CSE issue had been reported for some years, not just in Rotherham but in other areas where CSE had been investigated. This extract from the Casey Report is typical of stories captured by Rotherham Council to try to more effectively log details of incidents.

> ... she caught a taxi to her boyfriends and she was let off the fare as she didn't have much money. He took her to McDonalds and bought her food ... she realised he was much older, in his late 30s. He took her out to XXX in his taxi – she believes another young woman was locked in a room – he tried to have sex in the car ... she has given the details in a statement to the police... . It's not safe to use taxis.
>
> (Casey, 2015, p. 110)

Andrew Norfolk – on years investigating child grooming

Spending several years of his life immersed in the detail and harrowing personal stories of the victims of child sexual abuse, had clearly impacted upon Andrew when I spoke to him at his Leeds home in June 2017. "*The Times* has been very good to me," is as much as he wanted to say, but the heaviness in his eyes and voice was telling.

His account of the experience of reporting on this issue, over a prolonged period is measured, but at times more animated by his frustration and anger at what victims were subject to. He also has criticism for the conduct of social services and police in their misreading and mishandling of information repeatedly made available to them.

Limited media interest in abuse cases

Andrew described often finding himself as the only media representative in court to bear witness to and chronicle the shocking detail of the police investigations. The full horror of what happened in Rotherham to an estimated 1400 young girls has now been widely publicly acknowledged. Many were under 16 and some nominally supported by or in the care of the local council.

As a further populist indicator of the importance of his work to the public awareness and police action on this issue, Andrew was featured (played by an actor), in the harrowing 2017 BBC 1 drama about the Rochdale child sexual abuse story, *Three Girls*. It told the story of three abuse victims aged between 13 and 15, all of whom became pregnant by their abusers. These crimes spanned from 2008 to 2011.

Andrew's reporting on the CSE issue began in September 2010 but the issue was being flagged years earlier.

Andrew begins:

> "Ann Cryer in Keighley, Labour MP had spoken publicly about her concern about the situation in Keighley, which when you look back was exactly the

model of grooming and exploitation and abuse that it turns out had pretty deep roots in towns and cities across the North and the Midlands, and as we now know places like Oxford and Bristol and anywhere else you care to mention. And so I dipped my toe into it in around 2004–5."

He explains that Cryer had got the then, Home Secretary, David Blunkett, involved because of two mothers desperate for help for their daughters who'd got "sucked in" by CSE groomers.

Cryer's office told him of the names of 30 men, all described as "Asian", preying upon girls who were all white and young and underage. But there was an instant dilemma for Andrew. It was the same dilemma that had held social services and police officers from properly tackling the issue: "…hearing it, writing it down, and thinking how on earth can I report this story, because it's the far-right wet dream. And so I didn't do my job, I just did a very brief balanced piece and moved on."

But Andrew continued to be aware of the CSE story coming through reams of daily agency copy and local newspaper cuttings about court cases. He started noticing a pattern.

> It would be a court case that was only getting reported in that local area, and there would be two or more men, and they were being convicted of offences where they were meeting, it was always girls, they always seemed to be 12–15 age group. They didn't know them through anything except an initial meeting in a public place, on a street corner, shopping mall, bus station, train station, and then this befriending process was happening and alcohol and drugs.
>
> I'd been up to Scotland for a golfing weekend in the Borders, and 5 Live Drive was on in the car, and they went over to Manchester Crown Court at the end of a trial where nine guys had been convicted of exactly these sorts of offences against one child, one 14 year-old girl.
>
> … it was a BBC radio reporter outside the court who was talking to … Peter? in the studio in London who clearly knew nothing about it either. She didn't say anything about the men other than there were nine men, she didn't name them, which you wouldn't normally expect to in a radio report. But Peter was obviously saying 'this sounds absolutely horrific, these offences have been committed in Rochdale and in Manchester against this one girl, who were these guys, did they have anything in common?' And there was this embarrassed silence on end of the line from the reporter."

When Andrew got back to his office he checked whether his personal hunch about the common factor was the case:

> "… it kept overwhelmingly being Muslim names, and men. And sure enough it was, and the next day I sent this long email to my news editor and said look you've got to give me some time, and that was in early September 2010."

He spent the next three months trawling. Andrew knew he would have to have rock solid evidence if he was going to be able to call out such a controversial issue.

> "I'd kept whatever records I had as these things had come in, but obviously we needed to try to look and find every case that we could where two or more men had been convicted of offences like that against girls of that age group and see who these men were. ....
>
> The very first one was Leeds, 17 cases from 13 different towns and cities, and it was 55 men in those 17 cases being convicted. And three of them were white, 52 were Asian, and I think a couple of them were Indian, Hindus and Sikhs. But 48, 49 out of 55 were Muslim names, and then when I started looking into the background, overwhelmingly from the Pakistani community, not from, for example, the Indian Muslim community. So you're thinking right, this is factual information, and of course each one had been reported as a one off."

"Wall of silence" from police to charities

> "That's the point where you need to start talking to people, people who should know what they're talking about, charities who specialise in working with victims, police forces, prosecuting role, local authorities with social services departments or children's social care whatever it's called, with a responsibility, because so many of these kids were from tough backgrounds. And initially it was just a wall of silence."

But the issue was being talked about. Far right and nationalist groups, the English Defence League and the British National Party were talking about the issue. Channel 4 had commissioned a documentary about Bradford social services that included Ann Cryer's concerns.

Andrew continues:

> "Julie Bindell had done a couple of really good pieces for the *Sunday Times*. When I started trying to talk to, from government level down, from the Home Office down, and police forces and council, nobody would talk, and the worst of all was Barnardo's which set up the very first specialist project in the country in Bradford in the mid 90s, that was how long ago they'd been aware of it, and they would not even speak to me off the record. Because I was reading all the research that they'd done and there was so much about the victims, how many were 11 years old, how many were 12 years old, their backgrounds and how the meetings had taken place, and there was absolutely nothing to do with the perpetrators, it was like they weren't even interested. It was like all these kids running to the edge of a cliff and jumping off, and they're there a charity like Barnardo's trying to catch them as they're falling off, but not beginning to wonder why the kids are running to the edge of the cliff in the first place, and it became increasingly frustrating.

4th January 2011, and we did our splash, four pages inside and the headline on the first day was 'Revealed: Conspiracy of Silence on UK Sex Gangs'. There was a double page spread graphic showing every single place where these places had been, how many men had been convicted, who the victims were, who the men were. And we spent a lot of time in particular towns in the West Midlands talking to young Muslims for their perspective."

This had an immediate impact. Within a few days the government announced a national inquiry. Then a few days later the issue exploded. Former Labour Home Secretary, and Blackburn MP, Jack Straw was interviewed on BBC2's *Newsnight*. He said some young Pakistani men in his constituency regarded white girls as "easy meat" (BBC News, 2011).

Andrew says it then: "just went ballistic . . . until then nobody was speaking to me. From that day everything changed, and the emails started arriving and the phones started going."

The Chief Executive of Barnardo's (who Andrew had been asking to interview for months), contacted him and said he was so relieved that *The Times* had covered the story because they'd been concerned for some time by the significant over-representation of men from certain minority ethnic groups in this type of offending.

Then members of the public starting contacting Andrew. "An anonymous email from Rochdale arrived, which told me of this bungled inquiry that had collapsed that had led to the same girls being horrifically abused for two more years and finally though nobody knew about it they started a second investigation, and that all of course turned out to be spot on." (This was later chronicled in the BBC 1 drama *Three Girls*.)

A further key turning point came as Andrew was heading away on holiday:

> "So I'm at Manchester airport and I'm going through my emails, and there was an email from the guy in Rotherham who was the grandfather of a girl, and I can't remember the exact wording of it, but I remember standing in the rain at Manchester airport thinking I have to ring this guy straight away."

Andrew's subsequent meeting with the man and his daughter, the mother of a 13 year-old girl "absolutely shattered every preconception I had about Rotherham and how they were dealing with this".

The granddaughter had gone to school one morning and gone missing. The school had phoned her mum and she had contacted the police, who said not to worry, they were sure she would return "when she gets hungry or it's time for tea". By early evening the girl had still not returned.

The police went to the house early evening, still being very reassuring. At 2:30 the following morning, there was a 999 call to the police from a woman living on the opposite side of Rotherham who said she could hear a young girl screaming in the house next door to her.

Andrew goes on:

> "2.30 the cops arrived at that house, they found two girls, a 13 year old and a 15 year old, with four or five adult Pakistani men. The girls were drunk, the 13 year old is wearing a pair of knickers and not much else, she's abusive and leery, and they arrest the 13 year old girl and take her to the cells, and they charge her with being drunk and disorderly, they don't question the men about what these two children are doing in the flat in the middle of the night drunk, barely wearing any clothes, and she was convicted of being drunk and disorderly."

From his conversation with the girl's grandfather Andrew discovered that Rotherham social services had been aware of the case and involved in the girl's care. He said something felt really wrong.

He turned his eye again to Rochdale. There through his painstaking scrutiny of council minutes, and those of local child safeguarding boards, and despite some records being made secret, he found enough evidence to show that people had known and been discussing this issue as far back as 2006/7: "So I tried to set up a meeting with Rochdale Council, went through the head of their press office, and they did eventually agree to see me, but were incredibly wary."

They would not allow Andrew access to minutes of their child safeguarding board citing client confidentiality and Data Protection. At the same time Andrew became aware of a case in Blackpool, involving Lancashire police and Blackpool council, and a 14 year-old girl who had gone missing. He tried, unsuccessfully to set up an interview with both the local authority and Lancashire police.

An award-winning project there had identified and reported back on "hotspots" where girls were going and being exploited. There was one street where line of kebab shops and fast food restaurants was known by the girls and local Police as "Paki Alley". "The kids would go there when they were hungry or whatever or they wanted some free booze or a slice of pizza or a fag, in return for one good deal deserves another type of thing." None of this had been made public.

One of the themes that Andrew kept encountering in his contact with social services and Police forces was this reluctance to talk about the role of specific racial groups, for fear of being branded racist.

> "It's such an awful accusation to have thrown at you, it's career ending, if you're a senior police officer just after the Macpherson[1] hearing branded the police institutionally racist, there is also the liberal guilt, a fear of being racist and not really understanding different cultural practices."

Another issue, identified initially in Rochdale, was what Andrew describes as the contempt that social workers and police officers had for these girls. This was nothing to do with racism, rather the idea that these young girls were consenting to what was going on –"asking for it". "If they were running away from a children's home and being picked up by these guys, and the police officers are taking them home and five minutes later they're back with the same guys…" (Norfolk, 2017).

His work has placed him within a cultural minefield where there was a lack of understanding of the psychology of the grooming process, a lack of training, general awareness of what grooming was and a lack of resources to tackle it.

Rotherham whistle-blower Jayne Senior

A huge turning point for Andrew's reporting on the abuse issue in Rotherham 2012 was contact and information from former local youth worker, Jayne Senior. She had managed Rotherham Council's "Risky Business" project, set up to support vulnerable young girls at risk of sexual exploitation. Jayne subsequently published her own account of the town's CSE issue in her book, *Broken and Betrayed*. Widely praised for her actions in exposing the issue, Jayne was awarded the MBE and was elected as a borough councillor in 2016.

So in September 2012, *The Times* laid bare a 10-year history in Rotherham. "We splashed it, we did a double-page spread inside, and the very next day we splashed again and this time we told the story of that one girl, the first girl I'd met."

A week before publishing, Andrew had contacted the Council press office setting out what he was going to be covering. He wanted to give them and the council the opportunity to cooperate and respond in advance of *The Times* publishing.

He sent a 4000-word email, setting out everything *The Times* would be running with. Everything was drawn from either council records or those of projects funded by the council or South Yorkshire police. A similar email was sent to South Yorkshire Police.

He thought that, when presented with evidence of such hugely disturbing allegations, the council or police would immediately announce a public inquiry:

> "The response … basically, on behalf of both the police and the council was complete denial. And the inquiry they ordered was to try and get South Yorkshire police to launch a criminal inquiry to find out who'd leaked the information."

Some of the case study evidence in Andrew's coverage beggars belief. One story that proved to be a tipping point in terms of pressure upon police and the council, involved a 14 year-old girl. She had run away from home to be with her older abuser "boyfriend". He was married with children of his own.

The then Deputy Leader of Rotherham Council was Jahangir Akhtar (a relative of the boyfriend). Akhtar was described in the Casey Report as "an intimidating and powerful figure". He was a former taxi driver with a criminal conviction for his role in a violent restaurant brawl (Norfolk, 2015). He resigned shortly after this story was published.

Akhtar took on the role of "go-between". The girl's adult abuser was permitted to arrange to meet him at a local petrol station for her then to be handed over to the police.

> "To return a missing 14-old girl, her abuser gets to take her back to a petrol station and hand her over to the police and not face any action, because Mr Fixitall in the Pakistani community has saved the day.
>
> ... when she finally goes into foster care because her parents think it will make her safer because she just keeps jumping out of the bedroom window, she's allowed to go on holiday to the seaside and he's allowed (the 'boyfriend') to go with her. The arrangement with the foster carer is that he can pick her up at the end of the street in the morning, as long as he brings her back at night and drops her at the end of the street that's fine."

Council announces independent inquiry

Andrew believes that story tipped the scales. Within days Rotherham Council had announced an independent inquiry into the issue and the Jay Report was commissioned.

He consents to taking some credit for the impact of his work. Andrew, however, also considers that Professor Jay's report, "exploded anything I'd done out of the water 100,000 fold. ... rather than it just being the British media, or the Rotherham public and wider British awareness, suddenly it's the *New York Times*, it's the *Washington Post*, it's newspapers in China, in Russia, in Australia, New Zealand. Half the Western European countries turned up with film crews that next week in Rotherham. That figure of 1400 girls in one small town, and Jay's saying the overwhelming majority of perpetrators identified were from the Pakistani community."

Operation Stovewood, the National Crime Agency's (NCA) independent investigation into Child Sexual Exploitation and Abuse (CSEA) in Rotherham, is now responsible for investigating reports of non-familial Child Sex Exploitation and Abuse between 1997 and 2013, the time period covered by the 2014 Jay Report.

By the end of November 2017, Operation Stovewood had identified more than 18,000 lines of inquiry requiring investigation and had engaged with over 250 identified victims and survivors. There are currently 36 specific investigations within the scope of this investigation (South Yorkshire Police, 2018).

Summary of key issues

- Andrew Norfolk's sustained and forensic investigation into the CSE issue is widely credited as having turned the tide of institutional resistance, forcing Police and local council to acknowledge the scale and significant of this issue in Rotherham. It led to two important independent inquiries into the CSE issue and the National Crime Agency's "Operation Stovewood", which have in turn brought about important improvements and changes to the way such cases are dealt with locally and nationally.

- Andrew learned his journalistic craft on local newspapers, a training ground he is happy to acknowledge. He was given time and resources by *The Times* to follow the wider UK story. Local media coverage of each area's issue and prosecutions was crucial in helping Andrew to build a coherent picture of what was happening across the UK. In the case of Rotherham, local media included the *Rotherham Advertiser*, the *Sheffield Star, Yorkshire Post* and BBC Radio Sheffield all covered the story. The same applied to cities across the UK where this abuse had also been happening.
- After the *Jay* and *Casey* reports wholesale changes were ordered by Government into the running of Rotherham Council. Elections for all council seats were ordered for the following year resulting in new council members and a new Cabinet line-up. A team of Government appointed commissioners was sent in to review and run the council until it could demonstrate effective standards of governance.
- The role of media in bringing the perpetrators of this horrendous issue in Rotherham and Rochdale has proved crucial to bringing Government pressure to bear on the public agencies responsible for protecting child welfare. It is also a fine example of the role of national and local media in championing local democracy.

Case Study 3: Sheffield City Council, Amey, a PFI contract and a question of trees

The case of Sheffield City Council and its contract with Amey that has led to the Sheffield Trees saga is less one of the failings of the media – indeed this particular story has been covered at length in both the local and national media.

This saga points more towards the increasing question marks over the use of private contractors for the delivery of public services. The growth of PFI contracts and the widespread use of private contractors has seen the ever more complicated relationship between local government, local residents – and central government – turn into a complex labyrinth where who is accountable to whom is, at times, impossible to fathom.

The sage of Sheffield's trees began in 2012 when Sheffield City Council signed an agreement with private contractor, Amey, to renew roads throughout the city at a cost to the taxpayer of £2bn over 25 years.

The project, named "Streets Ahead", had been negotiated by the previous Liberal Democrat controlled council but the new Labour administration decided to go ahead with the deal and signed it.

Private Finance Initiative (PFI) contracts of this nature have become commonplace in local government as devices to allow major projects to be funded without an immediate outlay from the public purse.

PFI contracts give public bodies the opportunity to undertake large capital projects but put the initial burden of borrowing on the private sector supplier by underwriting the financing but leaving the private sector to borrow the money from banks and other lenders.

The private company secures a long term contract which usually involves a long term maintenance element which, in turn, gives the company a chance to earn a profit on the scheme.

FIGURE 7.7 The Vernon Oak is one of the celebrated trees of Sheffield earmarked for possible felling – protestors have placed a value on each tree marked for felling. Photography by Adrian Roxan

Sheffield City Council was no stranger to the concept, having used PFI schemes to rebuild a number of schools across the city.

The "Streets Ahead" programme was negotiated at a time when Sheffield's roads were in a parlous state with potholes appearing on roads throughout the city leading to regular claims from motorists for damage caused to their cars.

Amey acclaimed the contract as the second of its kind in the country following a similar deal with Birmingham City Council. Amey's press release of 31st July 2012 (Amey, 2012a) confirmed the terms of the contract:

174 Case studies

FIGURE 7.8 Sheffield Town Hall. Photography by Adrian Roxan

Amey will now be tasked with delivering one of the biggest highways projects in the country and providing the improvements which are needed to support the Council's ongoing plans for the regeneration of the city. They will be responsible for bringing Sheffield's highway network up to a high standard within the first 5 years of the contract and then maintaining that standard for the remaining 20 years of the contract.

Amey's press release added:

The contract will see Amey improving and maintaining the city's highway assets as well as providing street cleaning and grounds and tree maintenance and carrying out all winter maintenance duties.

There will be a significant investment in the first five years known as the "core investment period" when the majority of the improvements works will be carried out. This work will involve improving roads and pavements, replacing street lighting columns and upgrading them and traffic signals with the latest LED technology, strengthening and repairing bridges and structures, improving flood prone drainage and replacing highway trees where necessary.

Nick Clegg, then MP for Sheffield Hallam constituency and deputy prime minister in the coalition government was pictured on the Amey website welcoming the scheme. In a press release from Amey on 25th May, 2012 (Amey, 2012b), Nick Clegg said:

> Refurbishing local roads, pavements and streetlights up to a decent standard has long been a top priority for local people. I know that Sheffielders across the City will welcome the end results of this project, which will be the largest of its kind in Sheffield's history.
>
> I'm proud to be part of the Coalition Government that is providing Sheffield with the investment to make this once in a lifetime opportunity possible.

The irony of the former Liberal Democrat leader and local MP enthusiastically welcoming the project would not be lost on future protestors – many of them from the Lib Dem party locally – as the true "end results" for trees on many roads became clear.

Significantly towards the end of the press release quoting Clegg, Amey set out the detail of their work as part of the contract:

> Under the Sheffield contract, Amey will take responsibility for improving and maintaining 1,900km of road, 68,000 streetlights, 500 traffic signals, 600 bridges and other structures, 2,400 retaining walls and 35,000 highway trees across the city. Amey will embark upon a five-year renovation programme to upgrade the city's highways infrastructure; then work to maintain improvements for the duration of the 25-year contract.

It is not possible to know whether the sensitivity of the reference to "improving and maintaining ... 35,000 highway trees across the city" was understood at the time but this particular part of the contract was set to haunt both Amey and Sheffield Council as the true implications of the contract's delivery began to emerge.

Initially, a year into the contract, Amey was celebrating its progress with quotes on its website (22nd August 2013 (Amey, 2013)) from leading council figures:

> Key achievements during the first year of 'Streets Ahead' include:
> - Resurfaced roads and pavements: 185 miles
> - Street light upgrades: 4,000
> - Energy saved from new street lights: 40%
> - Street cleaning litter collected: 75 tonnes per week – the equivalent weight of nine double decker buses
> - Grass cutting: more than 2.8 million square metres of grass verges maintained each year – amount of grass cut equivalent to around 4,500 football pitches
> - Roadside drainage gullies cleaned: 63,500

- Distance travelled by city gritters last winter: Equivalent of five times around the world.

Cllr Julie Dore, Leader of Sheffield City Council said: "'Streets Ahead' is progressing really well and we are starting to make the difference we all hoped for – better lighting, smoother roads and an improved environment. The project is on programme and budget and will be great for Sheffield."

Perhaps by now the implications of tree felling was beginning to occur to both the Council and Amey as any reference to trees is omitted from the list of key achievements.

Indeed references to the "Streets Ahead" contract all but disappear from Amey's media list of press releases with just one further press release posted – in 2017 – celebrating that "people in Sheffield are happier with the city's roads and transport than they have been for a decade, a leading national survey suggests".

> Of 112 UK local authorities participating in the annual National Highways & Transport Survey (NHT) Public Satisfaction Survey, Sheffield has made the biggest overall improvement in satisfaction levels over 10 years and, thanks to Streets Ahead, satisfaction with the condition of Sheffield's roads has doubled since 2010.
> *(Amey, 2017)*

But by this point, and perhaps in explanation of this attempt to smooth over the level of bad publicity, Sheffield's "Streets Ahead" programme – and the relationship between the Council and Amey – had achieved national notoriety as a result of concerted campaigns by local residents.

The problem – and a problem that just wouldn't go away – was the vexed issue of how many of the 35,000 highway trees were going to be left standing by the end of the road improvement programme.

The contract's delivery soon began to hit problems as it became clear that part of the renewal would involve the removal of trees on a number of roads across the city. Residents started to object and a number of active protest groups formed with the main co-ordinating body being Sheffield Tree Action Groups (STAG).

STAG was quick to point out that an independent study, conducted five years before the Amey contract was signed, had set out the state of the 35,000+ highway trees in Sheffield:

> Elliott Consultancy undertook an independent survey of Sheffield's 35,057 highway trees. Although Elliott observed that 74% of trees were 'mature', he judged that 25,000 (71%) of the total tree population were healthy and safe enough to require no work. Approximately 10,000 trees did merit some further action including:
> - **241** trees requiring works so extensive that replacement could be considered
> - **995** trees that should undergo more extensive surveys which, in a small proportion of cases, might indicate the need for removal
>
> *(STAG, n.d.)*

So 1,236 trees were identified as needing either replacement or further assessment. STAG were quick to point out that more than 5,000 trees had been felled under the Streets Ahead programme by the end of 2016 and this was not the end of this practice.

The key arguments between protestors and "Streets Ahead" revolved around "expert" advice on the question of whether trees needed to be removed in the interests of safety – or, as the protestors claimed, Amey's profits from maintaining roads and pavements when the core scheme of resurfacing was complete.

Protestors maintained that Amey was felling trees that it thought would cause damage to roads or pavements over the following 25 years – when Amey has the contract for repairing them. Hence the accusation that the tree felling programme was largely motivated by saving money rather than protecting the environment.

What then followed was nothing short of a public relations nightmare for the council as local residents organised protest after protest in attempts to block Amey's tree felling programme.

Perhaps the news story that kick started the "Sheffield trees" saga was when contractors – protected by police officers – appeared at 5 a.m. on a cold November morning in 2016 in Rustlings Road in the more affluent west of the city and, after rousing residents to move their parked cars, began felling trees.

Residents, some still in their pyjamas, either refused or began to protest at the tree felling leading to arrests and accusations from across the political spectrum in the local and national media of "police state" tactics.

Nick Clegg – yes, remember he appeared on the Amey website saying Sheffield residents would welcome this project – was quoted in the *Guardian* on 28th November 2016:

> "It was, said Nick Clegg, 'something you'd expect to see in Putin's Russia, rather than a Sheffield suburb'". Council contractors and police had descended on a particularly desirable street in his Hallam constituency under the cover of darkness, "dragged" people out of bed to move their cars and detained peaceful protesters – "all to chop down eight trees", he wrote in a local paper [*Sheffield Star*].
>
> So far five people have been arrested in relation to a long-running and increasingly bitter battle over the fate of Sheffield's trees, including a 70-year old emeritus professor and a 71-year-old retired teacher, both women. On Thursday two men will become the first of the city's tree protesters to appear in court, charged under trade union legislation, following a protest on 2 November.
>
> *(Pidd, 2016)*

After initially defending the contractors, the Council was forced into an embarrassing admission. In a press statement on 25th November 2016, Councillor Bryan Lodge, Cabinet Member for Environment at Sheffield City Council, said:

> We would like to offer an apology to the people of Sheffield who were affected by the way in which we took the trees down on Thursday of last week, and particularly those living on Rustlings Road, who will also receive an apology in

the post. We are sorry for the disruption and distress caused by the work starting at 5am and the decision not to publish the Tree Panel report in advance.

There were reasons relating to public safety why the decision was taken to fell the trees at 5am and not to publish the report earlier, but we have heard the message loud and clear that this was not the acceptable course of action. We have reflected on this and will not do work in the same way. To be specific, we commit to publishing the Independent Tree Panel reports in a timely manner, with full and transparent information about how we have come to decisions. We can also give assurances that no work will begin before 7am.

As we continue to carry out work as part of the largest investment there has ever been in the city's street trees, and to protect the city's 36,000 street trees for generations to come, it is important that we take necessary measures to ensure that we protect the safety of our workforce, and the public. But we know we got it wrong last week with the way the work was started. We have listened and are sorry for the mistakes that we made.

(Sheffield City Council News, 2016)

But the saga would not go away. The council retaliated with a factsheet entitled "Myths about Streets Ahead", saying that most of the accusations levelled about unnecessary tree felling were unfounded and that new trees were being planted to replace those being removed.

But the damage had been done and the very "myths" that the council looked to dispel, were the ones that took hold of the public consciousness.

Local news stories continued to appear on a regular basis across the media and the national media also continued picked up the scent of story with all the ingredients of a "David v Goliath" confrontation.

The council claimed that the trees needed to be removed while the residents refuted this challenging the evidence and seeking alternative solutions to widespread tree felling.

By this point, with the council on the defensive, an independent tree panel of experts was appointed to adjudicate on whether trees needed to be removed but even this intervention failed.

Accusations from protestors then ensued that the independent experts' recommendations were being ignored. According to STAG, the panel recommended in one report that 312 trees surveyed did not need to be felled but the council ignored this advice and saved only 75 of these. The Independent Panel was eventually disbanded.

Key issues of accountability

The slew of media stories that portrayed a council being forced to defend a contractor begged the question as to who was in charge. The council as the commissioner of the contract or the contractor in pursuing the contract agreed with the council?

Inevitably the answer is buried in the detail of the contract that was not fully shared in public due to "commercial confidentiality" – an aspect of this kind of third party arrangement that ensures little opportunity for public debate or scrutiny.

Indeed local campaigners attempted to use the Freedom of Information Act to elicit more information on the nature of the contract but the information eventually released by Sheffield City Council was redacted to the point of telling them little of the detail.

The national outcry was further stoked by the intervention of central government through the offices of Environment Secretary Michael Gove who chose, in August 2017, to condemn the council's actions.

The irony of a Conservative Government minister condemning a Labour council for using a Conservative model of public private partnership was not lost on commentators.

As an example of the high level of confusion created by the increasing role of this "third party or partner" in the landscape of local government, it raised further questions.

Yet this was a contract being funded by the taxpayer to provide an improved public service – the question of accountability was clearly laid out. Should the Council be responding and accounting for its actions on such a partnership? Or had it ceded not just the responsibility for the renewal of roads but also the responsibility of accounting to the public for the actions being taken?

Just as importantly, who were the councillors representing? They would claim the interests of Sheffield as a whole but they are elected representatives. Protestors put forward substantial evidence that many of the trees, which the people who elected them wanted preserved and which were not covered by the contract's stipulations, did not need to be felled. So when it comes to the accountability question, the direct relationship between elected representatives and those they are elected to represent is compromised by the clauses in a contract with a third party – in this case, a private contractor.

In early 2018, reports began to emerge of Amey employing private security personnel who were accused of heavy-handed actions in breaking up protests at further tree felling. The impression of a contractor now acting on its own – without reference to the council – raised further questions about the accountability of the contractor to the council employing it.

A wider question also emerges from this saga. Central government, since the days of Margaret Thatcher, has been looking to exert ever-increasing control on local councils.

That control was further exacerbated both by the Labour Government focus on governance and efficiency between 1997 and 2010 and, more fundamentally, by the austerity programme of the Coalition Government from 2010 onwards – a programme kept in place by the Conservative administrations that succeeded it.

With such tight control of every local authority action, through the tightening of purse strings, local councils have had to be creative in looking at ways to both protect their services but also deliver on improvements for local residents.

Sheffield is just one of many to resort to the PFI route as a way of releasing money into its budget without having to go to the Government, cap in hand, knowing the answer would be no.

As a result, many local councils, just like Sheffield, have been forced into arrangements where who is accountable for the delivery of these "arrangements" is far from clear.

There can be little doubt that in the battle between central and local government for control of local government, central government has prevailed. The diminution of local democracy – that local people elect a council accountable to them for its actions – is the undoubted outcome.

The last word goes to George Monbiot, writing about the Sheffield trees saga in the *Guardian* in October 2017:

> If the contract were changed, the council insists, there would be "catastrophic financial consequences". Exactly what these are is impossible to know, because the relevant sections of the contract have been blacked out. This, the council tells me, is because such details are "commercially confidential or commercially sensitive to either Amey or the council."
>
> It is hard to see why. It seems to me that the information is more likely to be politically embarrassing than commercially compromising. In a twist that comes straight out of a Franz Kafka novel, the schedule to the contract (#30) that explains why parts of it have been deemed "commercially sensitive" has been withheld from public view. The hybrid nature of PFI provides a never-ending excuse for denying information to the public.
>
> *(Monbiot, 2017)*

Note

1 The Macpherson Report, ordered by the then Home Secretary, Jack Straw, was published on 24 February 1999. It found that the Metropolitan Police Service investigation into the murder of London teenager Stephen Lawrence was "marred by a combination of professional incompetence, institutional racism and a failure of leadership by senior officers" (Home Office, 1999).

References

Grenfell

BBC NEWS (2017a). 'Grenfell Tower: Cladding "changed to cheaper version"', http://www.bbc.co.uk/news/uk-40453054 (accessed October 17, 2017).

BBC News (2017b). 'Grenfell Tower: Corporate manslaughter considered by police', http://www.bbc.co.uk/news/uk-40747241 (accessed October 17, 2017).

Bell, Emily (2017). 'Grenfell reflects the accountability vacuum left by crumbling local press', *Guardian*, June 25, 2017, https://www.theguardian.com/media/media-blog/2017/jun/25/grenfell-reflects-the-accountability-vacuum-left-by-crumbling-local-press (accessed February 22, 2019).

Bilefsky, D. (2017). '3 officials resign amid outcry over Grenfell Tower', *New York Times*, June 30, 2017, https://www.nytimes.com/2017/06/30/world/europe/grenfell-tower-london-fire-uk.html (accessed October 17, 2017).

Grenfell Action Group (2016). 'KCTMO – Playing with fire!', https://grenfellactiongroup.wordpress.com/2016/11/20/kctmo-playing-with-fire/ accessed October 17, 2017).

Grenfell Tower Inquiry (n.d.). https://www.grenfelltowerinquiry.org.uk/news/ (accessed October 17, 2017).

London Evening Standard (2017). 'Grenfell Tower fire cause: Faulty fridge freezer sparked blaze and insulation failed safety tests, say police', June 23, 2017, https://www.standard.co.uk/news/london/grenfell-tower-fire-faulty-fridge-sparked-blaze-police-confirm-a3571501.html (accessed October 17, 2017).

London Fire Brigade (2017). 'Incidents', http://www.london-fire.gov.uk/LatestIncidentsContainer_grenfell-tower-fire-update-15-june-2017.asp (accessed October 17, 2017).

Mayhew, F. (2017). 'Journalists missed concerns raised by Grenfell Residents' blog – but specialist mag sounded alarm on tower block safety', *Press Gazette*, June 21, 2017, http://www.pressgazette.co.uk/journalists-missed-concerns-raised-by-grenfell-residents-blog-but-specialist-mag-raised-alarm-on-tower-block-fire-safety/ (accessed October 17, 2017).

Metropolitan Police (2017). https://www.met.police.uk/news/grenfell-tower-incident/ (accessed October 17, 2017).

Monbiot, G. (2017). 'Look to Sheffield: This is how state and corporate power subverts democracy', *Guardian*, October 24, 2017, https://www.theguardian.com/commentisfree/2017/oct/24/sheffield-state-corporate-power-subvert-democracy-pfi (accessed November 1, 2018).

Heffer, Greg (2017). 'Grenfell Tower: A timeline of one of Britain's worst tragedies', *Sky News*, July 5, 2017, http://news.sky.com/story/grenfell-tower-a-timeline-of-one-of-britains-worst-tragedies-10937186 (accessed October 17, 2017).

Ponsford, D. (2017). 'Former Kensington reporter says local press would have picked up on Grenfell fire-safety concerns in pre-internet era', *Press Gazette*, June 22, 2017, http://www.pressgazette.co.uk/former-kensington-reporter-says-local-press-would-have-picked-up-on-grenfell-fire-safety-concerns-in-pre-internet-era/ (accessed October 17 2017).

Ruddick, G. (2017). 'Jon Snow: Reporting on Grenfell made me feel on wrong side of social divide', *Guardian*, August 23, 2017, https://www.theguardian.com/media/2017/aug/23/jon-snow-grenfell-mactaggart-media-diversity (accessed October 17, 2017).

Further reading

KCTMO (2017). 'Fire at Grenfell Tower statement', http://www.kctmo.org.uk/news/343/fire-at-grenfell-tower-statement-28-july-2017 (accessed October 17, 2017).

Ponsford, D. (2017). 'Grenfell Tower fire disaster suggests more journalism is needed in London – not less ', *Press Gazette*, https://www.pressgazette.co.uk/grenfell-tower-fire-disaster-suggests-more-journalism-is-needed-in-london-not-less/ (accessed September 25, 2018).

CSE case study

BBC News (2011). 'Jack Straw: Some white girls are "easy meat" for abuse', https://www.bbc.co.uk/news/uk-england-derbyshire-12141603January 8, 2011, Jack Straw, child sex grooming (accessed September, 25, 2018).

Casey, Louise (2015). 'Report of Inspection of Rotherham Metropolitan Borough Council', February, 2015, https://publications.parliament.uk/pa/cm200809/cmselect/cmhaff/427/42703.htm (accessed March 28, 2018).

Home Office (1999). 'The Stephen Lawrence Inquiry', https://www.gov.uk/government/publications/the-stephen-lawrence-inquiry (accessed February 22, 2019).

Jay, Alexis (2014). 'Independent Inquiry into Child Sexual Exploitation in Rotherham, 1997–2013', 'Jay Report' – Professor Alexis Jay, OBE, 2014.

Norfolk, Andrew (2015). 'Jahangir Akhtar: Kingpin who "had influence over police"', *The Times*, February 5, 2015, https://www.thetimes.co.uk/article/jahangir-akhtar-kingpin-who-had-influence-over-police-0kdgx9d8kxz (accessed February 16, 2018).

Norfolk, Andrew (2017). Author interview.

South Yorkshire Police (2018). http://www.southyorkshire.police.uk/help-and-advice/z-crime-types/child-sexual-exploitation (accessed February 23, 2018).

Sheffield tree felling case study

Amey (2012a). 'Sheffield's £2 billion highway maintenance PFI project reaches financial close', https://www.amey.co.uk/media/press-releases/2012/july/sheffields-2-billion-highway-maintenance-pfi-project-reaches-financial-close/ (accessed July 27, 2018).

Amey (2012b). 'Clegg supports Amey's £2 billion Sheffield highways project', May 25, 2012, https://www.amey.co.uk/media/press-releases/2012/may/clegg-supports-amey-s-2-billion-sheffield-highways-project/ (accessed July 27, 2018).

Amey (2013). 'Streets Ahead celebrates its first year with miles of road improvements', August 22, 2013, https://www.amey.co.uk/media/press-releases/2013/august/streets-ahead-celebrates-its-first-year-with-miles-of-road-improvements/ (accessed July 27, 2018).

Amey (2017). 'Satisfaction with Sheffield's city's road surfaces doubles', November 7, 2017, https://www.amey.co.uk/media/press-releases/2017/november/satisfaction-with-sheffields-city-s-road-surfaces-doubles/ (accessed February 23, 2019).

Pidd, Helen (2016). 'Sheffield trees dispute prompts "scenes you'd expect in Putin's Russia"', July 31, 2012, https://www.theguardian.com/uk-news/2016/nov/28/sheffield-trees-dispute-scenes-putin-russia-nick-clegg-arrests (accessed July 27, 2018).

Sheffield City Council News (2016). 'Rustlings Road trees', November 25, 2016, https://sheffieldnewsroom.co.uk/news/rustlings-road-trees/ (accessed February 23, 2019).

STAG (n.d.). 'History', https://savesheffieldtrees.org.uk/history/ (accessed July 27, 2018).

8

SUMMARY AND CONCLUSIONS

Carmel O'Toole and Adrian Roxan

Where now for local democracy?

This book, based around its original research, tackles the difficult subject of defining the best structure, culture, and political system to furnish a healthy democracy at a local level in the UK. It identifies two particular elements that contribute to creating an effective democratic dynamic – the provision of information by which electors can judge their representatives through local councils and the coverage through the media that scrutinizes councils.

The principles of democracy with a particular emphasis on accountability are set out in chapter two. There are many different models of democracy with no particular variant holding sway in any debate on each model's effectiveness and integrity. However, the overriding factor is that political events – driven by the policies of different political parties in government – have shaped, and even distorted, what a purist might describe as genuine democracy.

This book focuses on one particular political and economic event – the aftermath of the financial crash of 2007 triggered by the speculative policies of a number of banks within the sub-prime mortgage market in the United States. This sparked the now infamous "credit crunch" in the UK and led to a period of financial uncertainty unparalleled since the stock market crash of the late 1920s.

In charting the period from 2010 onwards, the research suggests that, whatever the economic arguments for and against the fiscal policy of austerity adopted by the Coalition Government elected in 2010, that policy led to a negative impact on the health of local democracy.

Chapter 3 begins with an exploration of the history of "modern local government", tracing its origins and journey through such pivotal moments as the industrial revolution, the impact of two world wars and the emergence of the hegemony of neoliberalism from the late 1970s onwards.

But the core of the original research conducted by the authors revolves around the two particular impacts – the reductions in local government expenditure leading to challenging circumstances for local council communication functions; and the changing nature of the local media reporting on local councils with a focus on local newspapers.

Chapter 5 examines a further element of this complex picture which must be added – the rise of the digital age and the increasing move of news in the form of the printed word from the medium of paper to online platforms. It is a challenge to make definitive judgments on the factors that have contributed to any diminution of local democracy when putting this element into the equation. However, some conclusions can be drawn and this chapter is designed to draw on the lessons that can be identified and provide a framework for the reader to draw on the evidence presented.

The changing face of council communications

It is important to acknowledge that there is a political debate about the value of local authority communications. The first Communities and Local Government Minister of the Coalition Government (DCLG), Eric Pickles, is famous – indeed infamous in local government circles – for his attack on "town hall pravdas" and his assertion that local councils should not be spending public money on "propaganda". How he squares this with central government spending money on such communications is unknown but perhaps is more symptomatic of one of the key themes of this book – the historical battle between central and local government for control of the narrative around local democracy (Department for Communities and Local Government, 2010).

Of course, semantics is always in evidence when politicians use different terminology to describe the same event. For those critical of the reductions in local government expenditure, these are called "cuts" but for those who take a less critical view of austerity, these are "efficiency savings".

Whatever these semantic debates, it is important to analyse from the research conducted what might constitute in Mr Pickles' mind "propaganda" and what might be classified by others as providing information and conducting conversations vital to the principles of local democracy.

The findings presented by the research set out a landscape of local councils of all shapes, sizes, and political control needing to reduce the amount of communication, consultation and information with the people they are charged to represent and serve.

Most of the councils interviewed reported that consultation with local residents had largely ceased or become focused on an annual exercise around the setting of the council's budget. So one vital aspect of democracy – continuing dialogue between those elected and those they represent – has been diminished.

The only other survivors in this area of consultation were reported to be when specific decisions were being considered affecting a small group of residents with particular needs.

Mr Pickles' desire to see a reduction – or even elimination – of "town hall pravdas" or council newspapers, as others call them, seems to have worked. Many of the interviewees reported that they had either scrapped their publications or reduced them down in size and frequency.

One unseen irony of this trend is that the local newspaper printers locally printed many of the council publications and so the campaign by some proprietors to reduce local council publications has cost them money in their pocket. But it can be no coincidence that this desire to see council newspapers reduced in frequency or eliminated completely comes at a time when local newspaper proprietors have been campaigning against the BBC and local council publications, which they see as a threat to their continued existence.

The BBC reported that "The government has announced a review into the future of the newspaper industry, warning the closure of hundreds of regional papers is fuelling fake news and is 'dangerous for democracy'. But is it too late to save local newspapers?" (Hutton, 2018).

Indeed such a campaign has been running for more than 10 years as the *Guardian* reported in October 2008 when reflecting the words of National Union of Journalists' General Secretary Jeremy Dear:

> Speaking at today's Federation of Entertainment Unions debate at the Houses of Parliament, Dear said complaints about the corporation's wish to boost its local online activity "did not make sense", because the BBC was not competing for advertising.
>
> "You have two very different beasts. [Former regional publisher, now owned by Johnston Press] Northcliffe has carried out a significant reduction in staffing, giving less resources to local news in order to maintain a 28% profit level," he added.
>
> "The only reason I can see why they [regional newspapers] would object to it is if the BBC was taking all the advertising that they could get online. That's not the case. I'm slightly bemused by the argument that newspaper owners are using," Dear said.
>
> He added that newspaper campaigns against the BBC were driven by "commercial self-interest".
>
> *(Dowell, 2008)*

On the other side of this coin was the recognition that social media platforms require a more intensive form of delivery leading to councils being pushed into a 24/7 cycle of communication whether they had the resources and inclination or not.

There is no doubt that some reported that the initial drive from the Coalition Government to cut back on local government expenditure was a welcome "kick up the backside" to challenge some inefficiencies and slow responses to the changing communication environment.

As this book goes to press, councils are into their ninth year of "austerity" with no sign of any relief from the relentless drive to reduce local council expenditure.

Despite the sight of Northamptonshire County Council's fall from grace with the serving of the first section 114 notice (a halt to all but statutory expenditure) for a couple of decades, the squeeze on local council finance goes on.

Indeed some local government commentators suggest that 2016/17 onwards was always going to be the point when the real effect of the austerity programme would begin to bite as all possible "efficiency savings" are exhausted. The pressure of the impact of rising social care costs, the crisis in the provision of social housing and the first real term cuts in school funding were creating the perfect political storm.

But the overwhelming story of cutbacks in local council communication has to be placed alongside the demise of the local newspaper and, with it, the arrival of digital forms of communications.

Council communicators reported a significant reduction in the number of journalists on local newspapers, leading to less public scrutiny of council activities and so less information to the voting public. The sense is conveyed by a number of interviewees that many newspapers had become conduits to print "oven ready" material provided by local bodies including the council.

The changing nature of local government

In Chapter 3, the enhanced role of the private sector in local government is described – first through the imposition of Compulsory Competitive Tendering (CCT) under the Thatcher Government in the 1980s and then through the subsequent policies of Best Value and the use of PFIs under the Labour Government from 1997–2010. This practice has gathered pace since 2010, with councils looking to be ever more creative in bringing money into their area without needing to service such debt up front.

It has taken the collapse of one of the major outsourcing companies, Carillion, in 2018 for critics of PFIs and other such schemes to emerge and declare that such practices were past their sell by date. However the genie is out of the bottle as most of the schemes involve a long-term contract with debt being paid back over typically 25 years. In other words, council taxpayers will be paying for these schemes for many years to come.

These private sector alliances – perhaps more than any other initiative in the last 50 years – have had a profound effect on the concept of local democracy by putting so much of the delivery of local services in the hands of private companies.

The profit motive has led to the further embedding of the trend of turning the population into customers and consumers – some would argue moving further away from the principle in any democratic model of the informed and active citizen.

Electors are asked to judge their councillors in local government by the efficiency of the services they are elected to deliver – the governance versus government dynamic explored in Chapter 2. But are electors in a position to make such a judgment when so much of the delivery is not controlled or led by their locally elected representatives?

As the Sheffield Council trees case study shows, there are some fundamental questions as to who controls the both the delivery and accountability of the road surfacing contract. With £2.2 billion of public money being devoted to this contract, these are not insignificant concerns. With many of the PFI (and other) private contracts being signed in an era of austerity, there are serious concerns that councils are desperate to find ways to fund vital projects that cannot be financed through normal expenditure routes.

In these desperate circumstances, contracts are signed which will require meticulous negotiation – and more importantly – scrutiny as they are delivered. But councils are strapped for cash and so oversight through contract compliance functions has also been cut back.

Take the example of Amey: the contractor being used in the Sheffield "Streets Ahead" contract to resurface all roads in the city. A simple search of Amey's website reveals that this one contractor has contracts to provide services with more than 40 local authorities across England, Wales, Scotland and Northern Ireland. There are 418 councils of all types – county, district and unitary – which means that this one contractor has already secured contracts with 10 per cent of them. Waste management is one of the biggest areas of outsourcing, with research from the European Services Strategy Unit in 2014 (ESSU, 2014) reporting that local councils had let 45 contracts worth nearly £45 billion.

So a further significant question is whether councils are able to control such contracts – in Sheffield's case it will last 25 years – against private sector companies who, in many instances, have had the council staff with the expertise transferred to them for the duration of the contract.

The Sheffield trees saga is characterized by increasing attempts by those involved to shift responsibility for the implementation of the tree-felling programme from the council to the private contractor Amey. As protestors were arrested in March 2018, the impression that Amey and the police were calling the shots, with the council a reluctant participant, was hard to counteract.

The phrase "tail wagging the dog" came to mind, with many commentators aghast at the failure of the council to assert itself in the face of a private contractor – with help from South Yorkshire police – taking an increasingly aggressive and punitive approach.

Whatever the rights and wrongs as to whether a large number of trees needed felling in Sheffield, the subsequent furore exposed the extent to which some councils have been forced to embrace arrangements with private sector providers which have compromised their ability to control areas of service delivery which they were elected to oversee.

Of course, some councils have enthusiastically embraced this approach.

Patrick Butler, the *Guardian*'s social policy editor, writing about Northamptonshire County Council's financial crisis in February 2018: "it has crashed after rigid adherence to the Tory ideological rulebook for local government. Northamptonshire embarked on a 'next generation' reform plan in 2014. Services would be outsourced or turned into profit-making companies. The council would

> drastically shrink in size and be run like a business. 'The old model of local government no longer works,' it declared" (Butler, 2018).
>
> Butler, reporting in 2014 on the implications of the Coalition Government's expenditure strategy for local councils, wrote that the contribution from central government to Northamptonshire budget would fall from a third of its overall spend of £410m in 2013 to less than 10 per cent by 2020.
>
> The Council was asked to find a further £148m in savings in 2014 which its chief executive, Paul Blantern, described as "getting towards the impossible".
>
> Blantern describes the proposed new council approach as analogous to running a business – operating "almost like a PLC". The council becomes a holding company, setting the strategy, while services are provided by subsidiary firms, free to make a profit (to be reinvested in the service) and sell services to other councils and businesses. The watchwords are suitably commercial: "strategic commissioning", "market-making", and "brand protection".
>
> Perhaps prophetically, the then Chief Executive of the Council, Paul Blantern ended Butler's article by saying "there is no other option but to be bold: We are going to have a damn good go at it. I'd rather we go down trying than [do nothing] and go bankrupt" (Butler, 2014).

Impact on accountability

The themes outlined in this book of a rapidly shrinking public sector, a diminished local media, and the mixed impact of the inexorable move into the digital age ask some questions about accountability.

In Chapter 2, David Beetham argued that democracy is about control over the decision makers and for such control to be exercised, Beetham suggests that authorisation and accountability are the key planks for the achievement of some sort of effective concept of democracy (Beetham, 2017).

Authorisation comes through the electoral process where representatives are elected and expected to enact the policies and pledges they have made in seeking office. This book will not address the question as to whether representatives meet this last criterion. But accountability is the key issue here. When electing local authority councillors in 2010, no one can have anticipated that the task for many of these elected representatives would be to oversee 40 per cent reductions in expenditure over the following decade. However, electors would have a right to expect their representatives to be accountable for the subsequent decisions they took – ultimately through the ballot box – but in most cases that opportunity to remove councillors was four years away. Many of the key "austerity" decisions were made by the time such a reckoning with the electorate was at hand.

The accountability process therefore has to be an ongoing process. How could this be achieved? The key to this question revolves around information. Electors need to be told what their representatives are deciding so they can make an "informed" choice. If the tools for such information being disseminated are either removed or dramatically reduced, the electors are less "informed" and, in many cases, less interested.

The tools in question are a well-resourced local media holding councils to account and a responsibility – backed up by resources – on the councils in question to inform the public of the decisions taken and the outcomes achieved.

Back to Northamptonshire Council which– in common parlance – went bust by 2018, when the damning inquiry published its findings and the council halted all but essential statutory expenditure. One comment from a Conservative backbencher sums up the accountability deficit in this case:

> The backbench Tory county councillor Jonathan Ekins refuses to accept that underfunding was entirely responsible. Similar councils are in the same boat and they have not gone bust, he points out. He blames what he calls the council's secretive and dysfunctional leadership.
>
> *(Butler, 2018)*

A councillor from the party in charge blamed the council's failings on a secretive and dysfunctional leadership, raising the obvious question – were the electors and wider public kept fully informed of the council's plight?

Lessons from three case studies

The three case studies highlighted in Chapter 8 raise three very different aspects of the themes of accountability within a developed democracy. The child sex abuse scandal is perhaps the most serious. We see a conspiracy of inaction from those across a range of publicly funded agencies, in turning a blind eye to, and failing to act effectively to tackle the most horrific acts of abuse on vulnerable young people and children. Fearful of being labelled racist in identifying the role of specific minority groups, public bodies dithered whilst abuse continued. In Rotherham's case, child protection agencies were forced, reluctantly, by the sheer weight of media exposure, to call a public enquiry. Without that skilled forensic investigative journalism, what might otherwise have been?

Grenfell Tower is a case study in how a community was denied a voice in raising concerns about a safety issue that led to the tragic loss of 71 lives. As this book goes to press, responsibility – and therefore any culpability – for these deaths have yet to be determined but the story is one of a section of the community being ignored. The warnings were there publicly for anyone to read many months prior to the fire. The community predicted that it would take a serious incident before action would be taken to make the tower safe.

In the absence of local media scrutiny, who was asking the questions of the council, tenant organization, fire safety officials and police? Former local Kensington and Chelsea borough journalists say that, ordinarily, if journalists had been covering that specific area, the story would have been picked up. But as journalist Grant Feller said: "today there is no-one there", and the warnings went unheeded (Ponsford, 2017).

After the fire, the UK and world media jockeyed for position and access to survivor insight. They pored over the detail which was there for the picking about sub-standard cladding and previous warnings ignored. And then they wondered why local people felt exploited by the scale of this post-tragedy attention.

Within weeks the Metropolitan Police had issued its first soundings about corporate manslaughter charges against the council and tenant management organisation. We have yet to see what the public enquiry usefully yields.

Finally, the Sheffield trees case study reveals complex layers of governance which have become so confusing that responsibility for both the future of some of the city's trees and the ultimate accountability for the running of the contract seem mired in confusion.

What marries all these case studies together is a very real concern that parts of communities are being ignored by the state – whether that is through the neglect of a local council or through the actions of central government. In the case of the child abuse scandal, the role of the media, and in particular individual journalists such as Andrew Norfolk, must be praised in playing a part in eventually bringing the terrible facts into the public arena. Grenfell Tower highlights the paucity of local media coverage but it is partially a tale of a local press starved of the journalistic resources to provide effective scrutiny. In Sheffield, the local media were slow to take up the protestors' story and it took an unmitigated horror story of arrests in the middle of the night to ignite public and media interest and bring the saga into the public eye.

Each case does emphasise the need for public accountability and each case provides a clear picture of where the gaps exist in any notion of how such accountability is provided.

For Grenfell and Sheffield, information was not shared – whether it was health and safety information about cladding or a contract that included details of tree felling. The question has to be asked – if there were a better resourced local media with the capacity to properly scrutinize these two councils, would the outcome have been different?

For the child abuse scandal, this is a story of multiple failings by many public agencies – not just the local authority. It is because one or two journalists alerted initially by local media reports, were given the time and resources to piece together a complex and controversial jigsaw of events. We can be grateful these events were brought into the public eye and prosecutions pursued.

What is the future for both local councils and local newspapers?

Local councils

Desperate as the events were for those affected in Kensington & Chelsea, Sheffield, Rotherham and Northamptonshire, the profile of local government and the issues councils face have rarely been out of the national headlines. Of course, central government, as it has always done, has been quick to blame local authorities, condemn them and, in the case of both Rotherham and Northamptonshire, install outside control as part of the remedy.

The challenge that has always faced local authorities is, within the complex and multi- layered structures that exist, to provide citizens with a clear and unambiguous picture both of the role of their local council and the importance of engaging with it through the local democratic structures available.

However, turnout figures for local elections indicate that electors are not engaged enough to want to vote. The 2017 General Election saw a turnout of 68.8 per cent of the electorate (House of Commons Library figures (UK Parliament, 2019)). The 2016 local elections achieved an average of around half that figure at between 33 and 34 per cent. So despite local authorities being the most local form of public services and being the most directly relevant to people's lives through services such as refuse collection, local schools, social care and community facilities, two thirds of those eligible to vote fail to do so.

Election turnout is not the only way of measuring the level of engagement between an electorate and those they elect to represent them. But it does tell us that central government is seen as more important, which may well be a reflection of the battle between the two, which history shows has been more recently won by Whitehall rather than the local town hall.

The introduction of elected mayors is one of the remedies promoted by central government to address the democratic deficit but again the turnout figures for these elections are hardly encouraging. The London mayoral elections topped the turnout poll with 45.2 per cent voting in 2016 but Tees Valley recorded a turnout of just 21 per cent in 2017 and none of the mayoral contests in regions outside London have achieved a higher figure than that for local council elections.

So, again, if turnout is a measure of authorisation, the move towards elected mayors does not seem to have boosted any sense of engagement with local democracy. Indeed it can be argued that elected mayors have further confused the public as to who is responsible for what.

What of other forms of testing citizens' views and engagement with local government? The Local Government Association, which represents and lobbies on behalf of all local councils, runs a regular survey. Fieldwork for its latest survey was run in December 2017 and the results present an interesting set of findings:

- 65 per cent are satisfied with the way their council runs things
- 67 per cent trust their council either a "great deal" or "fair amount"
- 59 per cent responded positively when asked if their council acts on the concerns of local residents
- 63 per cent said their council kept them informed of services and benefits
- 50 per cent said their council provided value for money

All findings have fluctuated slightly over the previous surveys but show a fairly consistent view of their local council.

However, a key question about trust paints a more worrying picture. When residents interviewed were asked which form of government they trusted to make local decisions, 71 per cent said their local council while only 15 per cent cited central government.

When this question was posed about individual politicians and whether they were trusted to make local decisions the figures were local councillor 69 per cent, Members of Parliament 13 per cent and government ministers just 7 per cent. It can be concluded that there is a reasonably high degree of trust in local councils that is not matched for national government figures. But ask this question in parts of Kensington & Chelsea, Sheffield, Rotherham and Northamptonshire and you might not get the same answers.

The truth may be nearer to this comment from a leader published in the *Guardian* newspaper (27th February, 2018): "Britain is the most centralised country in the western world. The Treasury hijacked devolution as a way of palming off responsibility to local councils for making cuts, while keeping the power to make policy" (Guardian, 2018).

Local newspapers

A picture of the demise of the local newspaper has been set out in this book – as it has in a number of articles and contributions elsewhere. But there are signs that this demise is not going to happen without some resistance.

There's a niggling irony about the print versus online debate. By the free admission of both media group manager and editor in Chapter 5, the print product still pays for both iterations, The financial margins are narrowing year on year as print circulation, with associated advertising revenue, continues to fall. In turn online audiences' demand for vibrant content increases. Media owners are therefore on borrowed time.

More worrying still is the impact of online content on the very nature of news. In this book, we have taken soundings from the industry and this has yielded some compelling insight. More detailed research needs to be done to develop a more comprehensive picture across media groups and from across a broader trawl of UK newsrooms.

The threat of the online world has been felt keenly in local newspapers and this is not just through the ease and speed of news reporting that social media can provide. With the financial lifeblood of advertising fast diminishing for local papers, the dialogue – and so accountability – provided by the local paper reporting local affairs has been significantly silenced in many areas.

Year on year closures of local print titles have left many areas with either just one or, (in the case of Grenfell), no dedicated local media. Not only does this loss of plurality result in a lack of scrutiny on local decision making, what is also lost is the more nuanced range of perspectives a multiple media focus can provide.

Historically, each local media title would report through its own specific editorial lens, teasing out the fine detail of events, the players, decisions and their impact. When reduced to basic coverage by one media title, more often than not owned and governed by a large media group, such subtleties and insight are lost.

We see from our interviews with just a few of the UK's most accomplished and experienced journalists, quite how vital a training ground local media has been thus far. Each interviewee told proudly of learning their craft, the essential nuts and bolts of journalism, checking spelling and verifying factual information before committing words to page.

Covering local public-sector issues requires a detailed understanding of public affairs structures; of information rights access; of responsibility and regulations and of the importance of scrutiny and questioning the decision makers. Such skills and training are under direct threat as closures continue and the sunset looms for the media training landscape.

More worrying still are the themes emerging from our delve into the newsroom agenda, where our interviewees bear witness to the impact of online and social on the editorial process. Chris Walker formerly of Trinity Mirror (now Reach plc, the UK's largest media group) is candid about the "online first" policy, where reporters are told not to worry about the printed paper but to seek out stories to drive online audiences. The popularity of such stories in turn advise and drive the next day's content. He freely admits that these can squeeze out "the grout stories", which might otherwise have been covered. This might include "worthy" stories which don't necessarily chime with online audiences. (Walker, 2017).

When you drill down to the detail of potential stories likely to perform well online, these might be of the "puppies chasing squirrels" benign-but-amusing video content variety. Then there is the temptation for media managers to feed a public appetite for crime related online content. CCTV footage of criminal activity used first online, can then readily be developed for use in the print iteration.

The risk, as identified by former Liverpool City Council's Chief Executive Ged Fitzgerald, is a resultant negative reporting profile. In the absence of a further conscious editorial tempering, to reflect other less acute community events, this high crime theme by default risks unfairly stigmatising a whole community.

In the chase for stories likely to attract online hits, journalists are being drawn away from the importance of traditional news value. Their nose for news has been effectively downgraded. There's a distinct and vital difference between news of public interest and importance and that of content likely to entertain online audiences.

The two things are not mutually exclusive but neither are they so easily married. The vital work of journalists to watch the decision makers is much lower on the editorial agenda than finding the next most popular piece of viral content.

Our thanks to Matt Chorley of *The Times*' "Red Box" column for his succinct summary of the implications of all of this:

> Every time a paper closes, lazy MPs, corrupt councillors, dodgy police chiefs, rip off businesses, and anyone in the dock can relax a little. This isn't just

nostalgia. The great and good didn't stop behaving badly because we all got Snapchat and iPlayer.

(Chorley, 2017)

The various independent initiatives to rescue or preserve a local news function are also set out in chapter four. The NUJ's Local News Matters campaign and the BBC's commitment – albeit with a gun to its head at its Charter renewal – to provide £8 million annually as funding for local journalism are both welcome initiatives. The Bureau Local is another inventive and creative approach to supporting and encouraging locally focused investigative journalism.

In 2015 media group Archant also set up its own investigative journalism unit. Emma Youle, based at the *Hackney Gazette*, is now the unit's London Investigative Reporter. Testament to the unit's early impact is her "Hidden Homeless" campaign reporting into homelessness in Hackney. Her work won the 2017 *Private Eye* Paul Foot Award for investigative and campaigning journalism. She wrote of the borough's enormous, but hidden, homeless problem – highlighting the plight of the thousands who live in temporary accommodation.

The newspaper proprietors, through the newspaper publishers' organization the National Media Association (NMA), have been a powerful lobby that has impacted both on council publications – negatively – and on resources for local journalism – positively. The proof of this latter statement will only be realized when some assessment can be made of the impact of the annual boost of £8 million.

There are also other initiatives to boost journalism more generally, coming as a result of pressure on some of the digital giants. Google's Digital News Initiative fund of just over £100 million was launched in 2015 with the aim of funding innovative news projects across Europe working in partnership with existing publishers. But one Google-funded project has already attracted some criticism. In July 2017 it announced an automated news project where, as the BBC reported: "Google is funding a robot journalism project in which computers will write 30,000 stories a month for local media. The Press Association (PA) news agency received £622,000 for its Reporters and Data and Robots (Radar) scheme."

Dr Neil Thurman from City, University of London, commented on the project to the BBC, saying: "You can't really cover [local government] through automation because it's a lot about investigation, politics, personal relationships, who has said what to whom and so forth – it's difficult to get that information in data feed form."

The BBC reported the Charter deal with the NMA with these words:

Now, a bit of subsidy for local news would not be the end of the world. The erosion of local news in the US has already led to calls for a 'radical rethinking of the news ecosystem' in the era of post-truth politics. A similar democratic deficit in the British media has created black spots in local news coverage that may have led to the national media's failure to see Brexit coming. The latest research shows that two-thirds of local authority districts in the UK are not effectively served by a dedicated local daily newspaper.

For some further insights on where local news is heading, it is worth looking further afield and asking whether the crisis in local newspapers is unique to the UK.

It is clearly not. The following extract is taken from an organisation called MediaShift in the United States which describes itself as "the premier destination for insight and analysis at the intersection of media and technology" and it raises some serious issues that go beyond the demise of local papers and into the larger question of a democratic deficit.

Writing on the site, Jo Ellen Green Kaiser examined the reasons why the media in the US was so wrong-footed during the election of Donald Trump:

> It's not that journalists in those communities were not doing their job; it's that there are very few journalists left to tell the stories of those communities.
>
> Over the past twenty years, according to the Pew Research Center, the number of journalists employed by newspapers has shrunk by 39%. In the past ten years, 126 newspapers closed down. Over the same period, circulation has fallen 7% at the papers that remain.
>
> Similar numbers can be found for local radio and TV news stations. Viewership for local TV news is slipping, and staffing levels (never high) remain stagnant or are decreasing. Over a third of all local radio news stations are owned by CBS, which is looking to spin them off.
>
> The reason for these falling numbers is fairly clear. In the 1970s and 1980s, the local news business in print, TV and radio consolidated, with most properties owned by a handful of large corporate players. Their business was based on reaping ad dollars from local communities. The advent of internet shopping—and advertising—killed that business. Now Google (and to a lesser extent Yelp et al) owns local advertising and as a result, the local news business has been crippled.
>
> The 20,000 journalism jobs that were lost over the past twenty years were lost from these local news outlets. The journalists cut were mainly local beat journalists—the reporters who worked in and with the communities they knew best. The handful of digital news sites that have flourished in the Google era — Vox, BuzzFeed, WashingtonPost.com — have few if any reporters on the ground between the coasts.
>
> *(MediaShift, 2016)*

As a sign that the UK is not alone in facing this crisis in local democracy, it is reassuring but there is also no indication that the United States has found solutions to addressing this issue.

Accountability and local democracy – where to now?

In Chapter 1, Patricia Day and Rudolph Klein said:

> The main issue in complex societies is whether the linkages between action and explanation are in place and, in if in place, adequate to the task in hand: whether the channels of communication are operating and whether the sanctions are sufficient to compel a justification if needed.
>
> *(Day & Klein, 1987)*

If this statement is examined, it is clear from the research in this book that the "linkages between action and explanation" and the "channels of communication" are fast diminishing as councils struggle to find the resources to communicate their actions and local newspapers dwindle and so remove a vital platform for "explanation".

For those who respond that we are now in a digital age, the arrival of a digital local media with the same reach, value and viability has yet to be heralded to replace the local newspaper.

Day and Klein go on to argue that a secondary question is whether there is openness in the process and "the existence and availability of the information needed to assess actions".

There can be little doubt that the period of austerity – described by critics as an onslaught on local government – has created a "bunker" mentality among many local authorities.

Sheffield City Council's refusal to engage fully with the media over its trees saga is just one example of a council caught in the headlights of a crisis and retreating into its shell rather than recognizing its duty to be accountable for all its actions.

So Day and Klein's question about "openness" is one that is easy to answer for many local authorities – they are finding it difficult to be open when many of the decisions about cutting their budgets they are taking are likely to be met by a howl of public protest.

The UCL report cited in Chapter 2 on the progress – or lack of it – for the Freedom of Information Act (FOI) is an added concern. The UCL report recognized the crucial role of the local media but talked of "a chilling effect can be seen in a few politically sensitive cases" and raised concerns that spending reductions would make the delivery of freedom of information requests that much harder.

When considering the question of the media, Professor John Street makes the important point that the local media is not just about airing the views and decisions of local councils but "informing citizens about their (prospective) representatives' plans and achievements". He adds that "it also means reflecting the range of ideas and views that circulate with society", which raises the separate issue that the demise of the local newspaper is not just depriving the public of a source of information about their local council – it is also depriving them of a source of information about every other civic activity and issue (Street, 2011).

This is supported by Lewis and Wahl-Jorgensen, who say

> Ever since their emergence, newspapers have been important social institutions precisely because they have provided a forum for citizens (albeit sometimes a fairly limited group of people) to discuss the issues that concerned them and thereby articulate a public (rather than individual) opinion and hold government accountable for its actions.
>
> *(Lewis & Wahl-Jorgensen, 2005)*

The reality of local democracy – for all the debate about its health and current condition – is that the triangular relationship, set out in some clarity by Richard Perloff, of the politicians, the media and citizens is a vital component. Each of these triangular partners is beset by challenges and problems.

For councils it is a funding crisis leading to decreasing resources alongside an alarming apathy when it comes to local elections. For the local media, it is the impending death of the local newspaper as its economic model reaches its sell by date. For citizens, if the electorate still views themselves as such, it is an overwhelming lack of trust in politicians, leading to a lack of engagement with the principles of a civic society.

Add to this the shift to digital communications, the increasing polarisation within party politics, and the impending uncertainty of a post Brexit Britain and the augurs for local democracy are difficult to predict.

References

Beetham, David (1996). *Theorising Democracy and Local Government*. Basingstoke, Palgrave Macmillan.

Butler, Patrick (2014). 'Almost like a PLC: Northamptonshire sees the future of local government now', *Guardian*, December 18, 2014, https://www.theguardian.com/society/2014/dec/18/like-plc-northamptonshire-local-government-funding-cuts-council (accessed February 24, 2019).

Butler, Patrick (2018). 'Northamptonshire council faces up to cost of effective bankruptcy', *Guardian* , February 11, 2018, https://www.theguardian.com/uk-news/2018/feb/11/northamptonshire-county-council-effective-bankruptcy-tories-cuts (accessed February 24, 2019).

Chorley, Matt (2017). 'Closing papers is good news for lazy MPs and corrupt councils ', *The Times*, September 9, 2017, https://www.thetimes.co.uk/article/closing-local-papers-is-good-news-for-lazy-mps-and-corrupt-councils-ktvqvt2zx *(accessed* February 24, 2019).

Day, Patricia & Klein, Rudolf (1987). *Accountabilities: Five Public Services*. Abingdon, Routledge.

Department for Communities and Local Government (2010). https://www.gov.uk/government/news/eric-pickles-to-stop-propaganda-on-the-rates-killing-off-local-newspapers

ESSU (European Services Strategy Unit) (2014). https://european-services-strategy.org.uk.archived.website/news/2014/outsourcing-expands/ppp-strategic-partnerships-database-2012-2013.pdf

Dowell, Ben (2008). 'NUJ chief Jeremy Dear "bemused" by papers' attacks on BBC online plans', *Guardian*, February 21, 2008, https://www.theguardian.com/media/2008/oct/21/nationalunionofjournalists-bbc(accessed February 24, 2019).

Guardian (2018). 'The Guardian view on public transport: End austerity, trust the state', Editorial, February 27, 2018, https://www.theguardian.com/commentisfree/2018/feb/27/the-guardian-view-on-public-transport-end-austerity-trust-the-state (accessed February 24, 2019).

Hutton, Alice (2018). 'The death of the local newspaper?' *BBC News*, February 20, 2018, https://www.bbc.co.uk/news/uk-43106436 (accessed February 24, 2019).

Lewis, Justin & Wahl-Jorgensen, Karin (2005). *Journalism & Critical Issues*. Maidenhead, OUP.

MediaShift (2016). http://mediashift.org/2016/11/post-election-time-radical-rethinking-news-ecosystem/

Ponsford, D. (2017). 'Former Kensington reporter says local press would have picked up on Grenfell fire-safety concerns in pre-internet era', *Press Gazette*, June 22, 2017, http://www.pressgazette.co.uk/former-kensington-reporter-says-local-press-would-have-picked-up-on-grenfell-fire-safety-concerns-in-pre-internet-era/ (accessed October 17 2017).

Street, John (2011). *Mass Media, Politics & Democracy*. London, Palgrave.

UK Parliament (2019). 'General Election 2017: Full results and analysis', House of Commons Library, January 29, 2019, https://researchbriefings.parliament.uk/ResearchBriefing/Summary/CBP-7979 (accessed February 24, 2019).

Walker, Chris (2017). *Regional Manager, Reach plc, interview, April 2017*.

Further reading

BBC (2017). https://www.bbc.co.uk/news/technology-40517420

Department for Digital, Culture, Media & Sport and The Rt Hon Matt Hancock MP, 'Tackling the threat to high-quality journalism in the UK', press release, https://www.gov.uk/government/news/tackling-the-threat-to-high-quality-journalism-in-the-uk

Local Government Association https://www.local.gov.uk/our-support/research/research-publications/lga-perceptions-survey

Open Democracy UK (March 2013). https://www.opendemocracy.net/ourbeeb/jonathan-heawood/why-is-bbc-giving-licence-fee-cash-to-companies-who-have-slashed-local-journalism

Worthy, Ben, Amos, Jim, Hazell, Robert & Bourke, Gabrielle (2011). *Town Hall Transparency? The Impact of the Freedom of Information Act on Local Government in England*. London, University College.

INDEX

Locators in *italics* refer to figures

24/7 culture 40, 41–43, 185

accountability: austerity impacts 71–76; availability of information 4–5, 6–7; council-media relations under austerity 52–58; defining 3–4; digital communication 73–74; future of 188–190; historical context 16–19; and local democracy 8–10, 196–197; local government 2–8, 23, 119–120, 188–190; local media 109, 120–121; partnerships 65–66; political and managerial 4, 8; Sheffield City Council tree felling 178–180
advertising revenue 140
Advertising Value Equivalent (AVE) 145
Akhtar, Jahangir 170–171
Alexander, Nick 147
Amey, Sheffield City Council tree felling 172–180, 187
analytics 125, 139, 149
Archant 81, 88, 194
Athenian model of democracy 3–4
austerity: consultation with local communities 58–64; contemporary context 30–31; council publications and regular communication 47–51; council-media relations 52–58; digital communication 40–47; future of 185–186; history of 21; local democracy and local accountability 71–76; overview of impacts 76–77, 183, 184; partnerships and the private sector 64–71; resources and cuts 31–39, 126, 127, 140–141
authorisation 2, 188

Baistow, Tom 9–10
Baker, Geoff 157–158
Barnsley Chronicle 148
Barron, Peter 99
BBC fund for local journalists 89, 96–97, 194
BBC online content 141
Beetham, David 1–3
Bell, Emily 95, 160–161
Bentham, Jeremy 16, 17
Beveridge Report 18
Big Four 80
Bindell, Julie 167
Blaire, Tony 29–30
Blantern, Paul 188
Bolton News 123
Brexit 36
Brooks, Eileen 114–121, *115*
budgets *see* austerity; income generation; public spending
Bulpitt, James 28
The Bureau Local (TBL) 97–99
Butler, Patrick 187–188
Byrne, Tony 28

Cairncross Review 87, 94, 99
Capita 22

Index

Capital Media Newspapers 157
careers in local media 104; Brooks, Eileen 114–121; Minogue, Tim 109–114; Mosley, Andrew 122–135, 147–149; Norfolk, Andrew 104–109, 161–163, 165–172
Carillion 186
Casey, Louise 164
centralism, history of local government 16, 22
Chandler, Jim 6, 8
Chapman, Michael 6–7
Chapman, Richard 6–7
Chartered Institute of Public Relations (CIPR) 145
child protection agencies 164
child sexual exploitation, investigative journalism 104–109, 161–172, 190
Chorley, Matt 95–96
Clegg, Nick 175
CN Group 81
Coalition Government (2010–2015) 21, 30, 76
Cochrane, Allan 13, 18, 27–28
communications from local government: changing face of council communications 184–186; cuts under austerity 32–39; digital forms of communication 40–47; *see also* public relations
community consultation 58–64
community content curators 83, 130, 138
compulsory competitive tendering (CCT) 21, 186
Conboy, Martin 9–10
consultation, local community 58–64
corporate manslaughter, Grenfell fire case 156
councils *see* local government
Craven Herald 123, 129–130
Cryer, Ann 165–166

data journalism 96
Day, Patricia 3–5, 8, 196
DC Thomson 81
Dearne Valley Weekender 123, 129, 147
democracy: defining 1–8; principles of 183; *see also* local democracy
'democratic deficit' 94
devolution, and partnerships 64–65, 66–67, 71
the 'digital cliff' 148–149
digital communication: austerity impacts 40–47; disenfranchisement 71–73; Fielder, Nancy interview 142–147; future of 196; getting in touch with stories 112–113; impact on local media 123–126; Mosley, Andrew interview 147–149; online versions 139, 141, 144, 147, 148; as priority 127; relationship with print media 123–126, 127–128, 192–193; today's world 137–138, 150; Walker, Chris interview 138–142
Doncaster Free Press 129
Donnygate 107
Dooley, Seamus 157
Dore, Julie 176

education 18–19
Education Act 19
Ekins, Jonathan 189
elected accountability 6
election turnout 72–73, 191
elections, decision-making 188–189
Engel, Matthew 112
equality, and democracy 3–4

Facebook: impact on local media 123–124, 147; public relations 46
feature writing 126–127
Feilding-Mellen, Rock 156
Feller, Grant 158–159, 189
Fenney, Ron 13
Fielder, Nancy 142–147
finance *see* austerity; income generation; Private Finance Initiative; public spending
financial crash (2007) 30, 183; *see also* austerity
fire safety *see* Grenfell fire case
Fitzgerald, Ged 139–140, *140*, 193
Fowler, Norman 94
Freedom of Information Act 2000: and accountability 6, 7–8; coverage of local government 142; decline of local media 120–121; local media 132; mobile phones and social media 98
freedom of the press 10
frontline services, austerity impacts 31–32

Goodman, Helen 86–87
Google's Digital News Initiative fund 194
Greenslade, Roy 97–98
Grenfell fire case 114, 117, 120, 147, 151–161, 189–190
The Guardian 160, 177, 180, 185, 192

Hackney Gazette 114, 194
Hall, Robert 156
Harding, James 96
Hill, Dilys 6
historical context, local government 13–21

hits chasing 150
Holgate, Nicholas 156
housing, history of local government 15, 18–19
housing professionals, Grenfell fire case 158–161
hyperlocalism 89–93

Iliffe Media 81
income generation 67–68
independent papers 124, 148
Industrial Revolution 14
information: and accountability 4–5, 6–7; public access to 98; *see also* Freedom of Information Act 2000
investigative journalism: Brooks, Eileen 116, 119; child sexual exploitation 104–109, 161–172, 190; Norfolk, Andrew 104–109

Jay, Alexis 161, 171
job losses, local media 84–85
Johnston Press (JP) 82, 88, 127, 142–143
Jones, George 27
Journalism Foundation 93–94
journalistic skills 120–121, 128, 141
JPI Media 80

Kaiser, Jo Ellen Green 195
Keighley, child grooming 165–166
Kelner, Simon 93–94
Kennedy, Helena 94
Kensington and Chelsea Tenant Management Organisation (KCTMO) 152–161
Kent Messenger 148
Khan, Sadiq 152
Kingdom, John 14–15
Klein, Rudolph 4–5, 8, 196
knowledge, and accountability 6

Labour Government (1945) 27
Labour Government (1997) 3, 28, 29–30
laws: Freedom of Information Act 6, 7–8, 120–121, 132, 142; Local Government Act 16–17, 21; Municipal Corporations Act 16; Poor Law Reform Act 16
Lebedev, Evgeny 93–94
L'Etang, Jacquie 25–26
Lewis, Geoffrey 26
Lewis, Justin 10, 197
Liverpool Echo 139, 141
Liverpool Post 138
local correspondents 83, 89–91, 130

local democracy: and accountability 8–10, 196–197; austerity impacts 71–76; changing face of council communications 184–186; defining 1–8; media's role 8–11
local government: accountability 2–8, 23, 119–120, 188–190; accountability in historical context 16–19; changing nature of 186–188; coverage in media 114, 119–120, 131–135, 141–142; future of 190–192; history and evolution 13–19; post-war trends 18–21; and the private sector 21–22; publications and regular communication 47–51
Local Government Act 16–17, 21
local media: BBC fund for local journalists 89, 96–97; The Bureau Local 97–99; council-media relations under austerity 52–58; coverage of local government 114, 119–120, 131–135, 141–142; decline of 79–80, 95–96, 99–100; democratic deficit 94; digital communication 40–47, 112–113; future of 192–195; hyperlocalism 89–93; importance of in modern world 55–57; Journalism Foundation 93–94; media groups 81–82; National Union of Journalists 86–89, 97; News Media Association 80–81; ownership 10, 80, 82–85, 120, 124, 195; plurality 54, 79, 84–85, 88–89, 120; readership trends 118–119, 130, 142–143, 148–149; role in local democracy 8–11; social media impacts 123–124, 147, 148–149; *see also* careers in local media
Local News Matters campaign 86–89, 194
local writers 83, 89–91, 130
localism: history of local government 16, 22; hyperlocalism 89–93
Lodge, Bryan 177–178
London local authority 18, 19–20, 22, 28

Macpherson Report 180
McQuail, Denis 10
McShane, Dennis 135
Madison, James 9
magazine publications 47–51
Magna Carta 14
managerial accountability 4, 8
Maxwell, Kerry 89
May, Theresa 94
media *see* local media; social media
media groups 81–82
media ownership: Big Four 80; local democracy 10; overview and trends

82–85; plurality 120; *Rotherham Advertiser* 124
MediaShift 195
Mill, John Stuart 16, 17
Minogue, Tim 109–114, *110*
MNA Media 82
mobile phones, Freedom of Information Act 98
Monbiot, George 180
Moore-Bick, Martin 156
Morphet, Janice 29
Mosley, Andrew *122*, 122–135, 147–149
MP expenses 15
Municipal Corporations Act 16

National and Local Government Officers Association (NALGO) 25
National Health Service: and accountability 5; history of 18; partnership model 64
National Media Association (NMA) 194–195
National Union of Journalists (NUJ) 86–89, 97, 157, 194
neoliberalism 18, 20, 27, 183–184
New Labour 3, 28, 29–30
News Media Association 80–81
news value 139, 149, 150, 193
Newsquest 80, 82, 88, 134
newsroom culture 144
newsworthiness 150
non-governmental organisations (NGOs) 7–8
Norfolk, Andrew 104–109, *105*, 161–163, 165–172

Oldham Chronicle 148
online content 139, 141, 144, 147, 148; *see also* digital communication
opening hours 42–43
openness 133, 196
ownership of media 10, 80, 82–85, 120, 124, 195

Paget-Brown, Nicholas 156
partnerships, impact of austerity 64–71
People's Charter 15
Perloff, Richard 9, 23, 197
personal perspectives on local media: Brooks, Eileen 114–121; careers beginning in 104; Minogue, Tim 109–114; Mosley, Andrew 122–135; Norfolk, Andrew 104–109
Philosophical Radicals 16, 17
photographers 130, 140–141
Pickles, Eric 7, 37, 50–51, 184

Pits n Pots 92–93
plurality in local media 54, 79, 84–85, 88–89, 120
police: Grenfell fire case 152–161; partnership model 64, 70; Rotherham child sexual exploitation investigation 164, 168–171
political accountability 4, 8
political correctness, Rotherham child sexual exploitation investigation 164, 166–167
poll tax 18, 28
Ponsford, Dominic 80, 91, 96–97, 157
Poor Law Reform Act 16
power: and accountability 6; history of local government 16; media ownership 80
Pratchett, Lawrence 3
Press Association 82
Press Gazette 80, 99, 157–158
press offices 133
Preston, Peter 95
print media: austerity impacts 47–51; local media decline 84–85, 87–88; ownership 80; relationship with digital content 123–126, 127–128, 192–193; size of 127–128
Private Eye 104, *105*, 110–114, 194
Private Finance Initiative (PFI) 22, 172–173, 180, 186–187
private sector: austerity impacts 64–71; and local government 21–22; Sheffield City Council tree felling 172–180
professionalism, and hyperlocalism 90–91
public opinion, role of media 10
public relations: austerity impacts 52–58; changing face of council communications 184–186; changing the relationship with agencies 145–147; emergence and history 25–30; resources and cuts under austerity 31–38; spending on 7, 45, 51
public spending: and accountability 5; council-media relations under austerity 52–58; decline of local media 81, 91; future of 185–186; history of local government 18–19; local democracy 7; Pickles, Eric, statement regarding 7, 37, 50–51, 184–185; public relations 7, 45, 51; resources and cuts under austerity 31–38; role of local media 119–120; *see also* austerity
publications by local government 47–51, 60–61
punishment, media coverage as 108
purchaser-provider split 21

race, Rotherham child sexual exploitation investigation and 164, 166–167

Rates Act 28
Reach 80, 81, 82, 88, 138–142, 193
readership trends 118–119, 130, 142–143, 148–149
receptionists, public relations 44
Reed, Garvin 116
regional sub-editing hubs 83
religion, history of local government 15
Representation of the Peoples Act 94
reputation 44–45; *see also* public relations
Rochdale, child sexual exploitation 163, 165, 168, 169–170, 172
Rotherham Advertiser 117–118, 122–123, 124–135, 147–149, 163
Rotherham child sexual exploitation investigation 104–109, 161–172, 190
Rotherham Record 123, 147
"Rotten Boroughs" 109–114
Royal Borough of Kensington and Chelsea Council (RBKC), Grenfell fire case 151–161

sales figures, newspapers 118–119, 130, 142–143, 148–149
Sambrook, Richard 90
Scarborough Evening News 105, 106, 108
schools: and accountability 5; partnerships 69
Senior, Jayne 170–171
Sheffield City Council tree felling 172–180, 187, 190
Sheffield Star 118, 129, 130, 142–147, 163
Sheffield Telegraph 144
Sheffield Tree Action Groups (STAG) 176–180
Shelter 164
size of newspapers 127–128, 140–141
skills, journalism 120–121, 128, 141
Snow, Jon 160
social class, and local government 14–15
social media: and austerity 72–73; Freedom of Information Act 98; impact on local media 123–124, 147, 148–149; public relations 41–42, 43, 45, 45–46, 50–51
social services, Rotherham child sexual exploitation investigation 164, 166, 167, 169–170
South Yorkshire Times 129
Southport Visitor 140–141
spending *see* public spending
sport coverage 126, 149

staff culture 128, 141, 144
Stanistreet, Michelle 86
Stewart, John 27
Stoker, Gerry 1, 17
Straw, Jack 168
Street, John 9
Sunday Times 167
surveillance society 6

taxation: poll tax 18, 28; ratecapping 28
template system 129–130, 131
Thatcher, Margaret: history of local government 18, 20, 22; public relations 27–29
Three Girls (BBC) 165, 168
Thurman, Neil 194–195
The Times 104–109, 161–172, 168, 170, 171
Tindle 80, 82, 88, 157
training as a journalist 111, 128, 141; *see also* careers in local media
transparency 133, 196
transport, history of local government 15
Travers, Tony 77
tree felling in Sheffield case 172–180, 187
Trinity Mirror (now Reach) 81, 82, 88, 124, 138–142, 193
Trump, Donald 195
trustworthiness 44, 192
Twitter: and austerity 72–73; impact on local media 123–124, 147; public relations 43, 45–46

United States: election of Trump 195; public relations 27
utilitarianism 16

video news stories 125–126
visual content 141
voting turnouts 72–73, 191

Wahl-Jorgensen, Karin 10, 197
Walker, Chris 138–142, 193
welfare state, history of 18, 20
Whitby Gazette 108–109
World War II 18, 26
worthy stories 150, 193

Yorkshire Post 106–107, 115–116, 118–119, 163
Youle, Emma 114

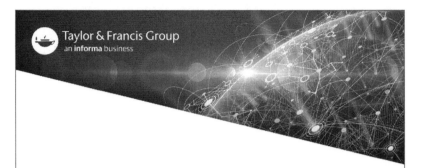